Cooking Plain, Illinois Country Style

COOKING PLAIN,

Illinois Country Style

Helen Walker Linsenmeyer

With a new foreword by
Bruce Kraig

Southern Illinois University Press
Carbondale and Edwardsville

The Library of Congress has cataloged the hardcover edition as follows:
Linsenmeyer, Helen Walker.
    Cooking Plain.
    Includes index.
    1. Cookery, American—Illinois. I. Title.
TX715.L7593   641.5'9773   76-13548
ISBN 0-8093-0782-0 (cloth)

ISBN-13: 978-0-8093-0782-1 (cloth)
ISBN-13: 978-0-8093-3073-7 (pbk. : alk. paper)
ISBN-10: 0-8093-3073-3 (pbk. : alk. paper)
ISBN-13: 978-0-8093-3074-4 (ebook)
ISBN-10: 0-8093-3074-1 (ebook)

To the memory of my parents
Ben and Nora Walker
worthy representatives of the
hardy German and English-Irish-Scotch
stock who settled and peopled early southern
Illinois

Contents

Foreword
Bruce Kraig

SOME years ago, I mentioned to Susan Wilson, then the associate director of Southern Illinois University Press, that I was just beginning to explore the foods of southern Illinois. As a historian of food and foodways who had just moved to the region, I observed the truism that to know a people, start with their food: food is central to a people's culture.

Well, Susan said, years ago we did publish a book on southern Illinois cookery, probably the only one of its kind, and a best seller for a university press back then. The book was and is Helen Walker Linsenmeyer's *Cooking Plain*, originally published in 1976. That this gem of a "good indigenous cookbook," as the author put it, had not been reprinted surprised me. Now, years later, here it is, and what a surprise it will be to new readers who may have forgotten, or never known, the culinary heritage of a unique part of America. And it is eminently usable.

Helen Anna Walker Linsenmeyer Keyser was born on March 3, 1906, in Williamson County, Illinois. The Walkers emigrated from Tennessee in 1834, settling in and around Herrin. As it was for so many others, the Walkers' route was the Ohio River, and that southern origin is really the base of southern Illinois culinary culture: *Cooking Plain* has plenty of recipes for those diagnostic southern dishes, corn cakes, hominy, grits, and biscuits. There are other culinary cultural influences, as well, from northerners, or Yankees, and especially Germans from various regions of their homeland. Helen's book contains examples of each, from English pudding, brought by great-aunts, to cabbage dishes and enough dumplings to fill any German American stomach. In a very American lexical merging, a recipe for spaetzle is called here "German egg dumplings," while elsewhere in southern Illinois noodles appear as "flat dumplings." Later, Italians and East Europeans played some roles in southern Illinois foodways, but none of their recipes appear in what is essentially a family-historical cookbook.

Between the recipes in *Cooking Plain* and others Linsenmeyer composed for *Illinois Magazine* and the *Southern Illinoisan* newspaper, something more comes through, descriptions of the ways that her family, and many other rural families, lived that had all but disappeared during her long lifetime. We hear about the author's early years on a farm, traveling by wagon down to the Big Muddy River to "hog" for catfish that were cooked up on the spot. Wild game was and remains a part of the local larder. Want to cook squirrel, muskrat, raccoon, prairie chicken (rare now), opossum, or venison? Look no further than here. Many of the recipes, or ideas for them, came from Helen's childhood. As she says in a biographical sketch she wrote in 1993,[1] she learned about her family history and country life from her grandfather. Elsewhere she tells us her model for cooking was her mother, as in the incomparable sponge cake that her mother made as the base for strawberry shortcake.[2] Early on, she realized that the food traditions of people (including her large, extended family) tell a lot about who they are.

We also see the author's personality: adventurous and worldly, clearly self-sufficient, humorous but earthbound, as if rooted in her native land. After graduating from high school, Helen moved to St. Louis, where she worked during World War II—having been rejected for military service—and married Robert Linsenmeyer. They had, as she says, "itchy feet," and after stops in Topeka, Kansas, and Chicago (where Robert worked in a publishing house), they joined the great postwar migration to California. There she worked as a book cataloguer for the Xerox Corporation and earned a degree in library science, while Bob always had "agreeable employment." Fascinated by "the state's kaleidoscopic and exciting record," in 1972 she published a history of California through the evolution of its food: *From Fingers to Finger Bowls*.[3] Subtitled *A Lively History of California Cooking*, the characteristics of her later writing are here: recipes (some unusual and not easily reproducible, such as "boiled bear paw") that illustrate social history, many tidbits of information culled from a wide variety of original and secondary sources (a good librarian's training), and a fresh, sprightly writing style. The recipes are not written in standard recipe style, but by the time *Cooking Plain* appeared Helen knew exactly how to compose clearly understood, easy-to-follow, and delicious recipes.

The Linsenmeyers returned to southern Illinois where, after Bob's death in 1976, she lived with her second husband, Joseph Keyser, until his death in 1987. In these years Helen, in her late seventies and eighties, wrote the "Family Recipes" column for *Illinois Magazine* and columns for the *Southern Illinoisan* newspaper. Her first "Family Recipes" piece in the March-April 1983 issue of the magazine begins in an earlier southern Illinois: pokeweed casserole and the ubiquitous wild onion, here, glazed. *Cooking Plain* gives directions for cooking "edible weeds," and one can imagine the young Walker children picking them around their Herrin farm in the teens and twenties of the twentieth century.

Helen had a lifelong interest in local history and genealogy. *Cooking Plain* is an expression of these interests. The recipes, she says, have been collected from her family over many years. Unlike most community cookbooks, where most recipes come from commercial, newspaper, or magazine sources, these are authentically old-time dishes, many made from locally sourced ingredients. And, like many a nineteenth-century cookery book, there are lots of useful household hints and even ways to tell oven temperatures without a thermometer (put your hand in a hot oven and count the seconds before it begins to burn).

Helen Anna Walker Linsenmeyer Keyser died in 2004 at the age of ninety-eight. She had retired to Mountain Home, Arkansas, in 1988 but still wrote for *Illinois Magazine* into the 1990s and in 1998 recollected for the *Southern Illinoisan* her family's small role in the infamous 1922 Herrin Massacre. Reading this wonderful historical book and her other works makes one want to meet her, perhaps at her kitchen table, talking over biscuits and freshly made southern Illinois cider. *Cooking Plain* is testimony to someone who had returned to her roots, looked back over the past, and now gave full compass to her interesting life.

Notes

1. Helen Walker Linsenmeyer Keyser, "Illinois Pioneer, Matthew Moore Walker and His Descendants" (1993), http://dig.lib.niu.edu/ISHS/ishs-1980spring/ishs-1980spring53.pdf.
2. "Family Recipes," *Illinois Magazine* (May-June 1983), p. 31.
3. San Diego: Copley Books, 1972; republished in 1990 by EZ Nature Books, San Luis Obispo, CA.

Preface

WHEN Vernon Sternberg of the Southern Illinois University Press asked me if I would be interested in writing an "indigenous Illinois Country cookbook," I was delighted. Too little has been written about the cooking customs of the pioneers who settled this southern tip of the state from St. Louis to Cairo. The project offered a great opportunity to renew family ties after spending my adult life in cities and supercities across the country, as well as a chance to share some of the old recipes which I have been collecting through the years. I was curious about the outcome of the project. When I did the research for my first book *From Fingers to Finger Bowls,* a history of California cooking, I was an outsider fascinated by the Golden State and the many hands from many lands who stirred the potpourri that came to be called California cuisine.

We also have a rather rich mixture of influences: French, from Canada, Santo Domingo, and France itself; English; German; Polish; Bohemian; Irish; Scotch; the Southerners from Virginia, Tennessee, the Carolinas, and Kentucky, of predominantly English-Scotch-Irish descent; the New Englanders; Pennsylvania Dutch—all of whom contributed their industry, customs, and culture to the southern Illinois amalgam.

The spirit of hospitality was prevalent. The stranger was cordially invited to draw up a chair and share the meal, which more than likely consisted of venison or other wild game, corn dodger, beans or corn in some form, and perhaps a green "sallet." As times got better and the farms prospered with livestock, poultry, field crops, orchards, and large gardens, family gatherings were held on holidays and at intervals through the year, with plenty for everyone and to spare. Friendly rivalry among the womenfolk prompted them to vie with one another for fancier cakes, pies, and other good things to eat, and to remember.

As I have been reminded by the publisher that sentiment cannot prevail over paper and printing costs, I must restrict my expression of appreciation for assistance to a bare minimum. Names of those relatives and friends who have shared their recipes are included in the recipes; sources of others are given, wherever possible. I was not careful to jot down sources of some which were accumulated through the years, I am sorry to say. In some instances where I have been assured that the dish really existed but could find no directions for preparing it as it might have been prepared at the time, I have reconstructed it to the best of my ability. This is largely true in regard to my mother's cookery. She had a habit of jotting recipes down and then discarding the notes after she had memorized them.

Various members of my family do not have the identical recollections as mine in regard to some of these family recipes; since I am the oldest, and hence closer to the "old" way, "I did it my way."

It is my sincere hope that the reader will gain from this book a mental picture of the simplicity of life in the early days of the Illinois Country. It was an era of pride and dignity, self-sufficiency and industry. The homemakers did their best with what they had in the kitchen, as they did in all phases of their lives. In general, the food they offered their families and friends was rather simple; the ingredients therein were *real;* no additives or ersatz material. That was in keeping with their lives, which were also real, sometimes hard, but built on the solid virtues of God, home, and family.

Helen Walker Linsenmeyer

Grand Tower, Illinois
May 1976

Cooking Plain,
Illinois Country Style

Cooking Plain,
Illinois Country Style

With a few exceptions, the early arrivals in southern Illinois brought a bare minimum of cast-iron cookware: a pot for soups, stews, vegetables and puddings; a skillet, and a dutch oven for baking bread, cakes and roasts. Cooking and eating utensils were often carved from wood; the hunting knife doubled for carving. Tin bread pans and other tinware were added as the family's fortunes improved; a 10- or 20-gallon iron kettle for use in butchering hogs, rendering lard, making soap was purchased or bartered for, or used in common with relatives or neighbors; still later, as orchards matured, a treasured copper-lined kettle for apple-butter making and a cider mill were acquired in joint tenancy by several members of the family, to be passed around as needed (this was the case among my own forebears).

The cooking was done in the fireplace, and possibly in an oven built into the wall alongside the fireplace. The fire was kept going the year-round; the careless housewife who permitted it to die out found it necessary to send one of the more responsible younger offspring to the nearest neighbor, often several miles away, to borrow coals for starting the hearth fire anew.

It was several decades before new arrivals brought cookstoves to the settlements. A few experimental models were in use in New England and Pennsylvania, but I find no records of cookstoves being manufactured in the U.S. prior to 1830. Local history records that one Col. James Gill brought a cookstove to Grand Tower in 1806, which was an article of such great curiosity that people for miles around fabricated reasons for calling on him, to look at the wonderful invention. Perhaps he obtained one of the experimental models in his native South Carolina, or imported one from England.

At any rate, the southern Illinois housewife, who had mastered the art of simple, and sometimes not-so-simple cookery with the use of her primitive equipment faced a challenge in adjusting to the cast-iron contraption. She learned to test oven temperature by sticking her hand inside. If a blast of heat hit her in the face, her hand jerked back involuntarily, and she yelped in pain, she had a "brisk" oven and it was

3

time to set the yeast bread, biscuits, and pies inside. By holding back on the wood fuel she allowed the fire to die down slightly and could replace the biscuits with a cake. When the thick juice oozed from slits in the pie's top crust and the bread loaf made a hollow sound when she thumped it, she removed them and set the corn bread in to bake.

With a clock, she devised a timetable for oven-testing by hand. For instance, if she could hold her hand in the oven for twelve seconds (or twelve ticks of the clock without burning it, she had a hot oven (450 degrees), and so on:

Time		Degree of Heat	
12 seconds		*450*	*Hot*
18	*''*	*400*	*Quick*
24	*''*	*350*	*Moderate*
30	*''*	*300*	*Slow*
Over 30''		*−300*	*Warm, or low*

As wheat flour became more plentiful after the 1840s, she developed a less painful oven-testing method—spreading a couple of table-spoons of flour in the tin pie pan and setting it in the oven while she counted. By timing for 3 minutes she could arrive at the heat by observing the color of the flour: black, dark brown, medium brown, golden, and pale tan.

Later in the century as improved stove models came on the market the manufacturers thoughtfully included manuals which not only gave instructions for cooking but included recipes, housekeeping hints, and home remedies.

Unlike the inhabitants of the early French settlements, the first "Americans" lived off the land, with wild game, fish, fruits, nuts, and edible weeds supplementing the cornmeal and hominy.

Hickory nuts, and black walnuts were fairly plentiful in southern Illinois when the first settlers arrived. Pecan trees grew in profusion along the southern and southwestern rim of the state; butternuts in the extreme south. Hazelnut bushes bordered the forest trees. The 22 hickory trees on our homeplace provided us with excellent additions to cakes, cookies, and candy, as well as casual eating throughout the winter. Their flavor is not quite as pronounced as that of the black walnuts. Perhaps because pecans were less accessible, we regarded ourselves as fortunate and did not seek out these two latter varieties.

Recipes calling for all these kinds of nuts will be found herein. When John James Audubon, the famous ornithologist, camped with the Shawnees at the mouth of the Cache River in Alexander County over Christmas 1810, he observed the Indians dining on pecans mixed with bear fat, shaped into flat cakes. He did not describe *his* dinner on that evening.

In discussing the kinds of foods which sustained our hardy forebears, Eb (J. E.) Etherton of Carbondale, a gentleman who represents the best kind of southern Illinoisan, suggested that the chief articles of sustenance were 'taters, 'maters, and 'lasses. The early Californians were enjoying the benefits of vitamin-rich tomatoes long before we timid Easterners were convinced they weren't poisonous; after we accepted them as edible we weren't sure whether they should be treated as fruits or vegetables.

Cookbooks were not published in the United States until around the 1830s, so it is doubtful that many printed recipe collections found their way to southern Illinois before the 1850s. The governing classes and the clergy in the French settlements would have had written recipes; the better-educated New England, English, and Southern housewives certainly brought their precious handwritten "receipts" along; the Germans likewise. Most of their cooking secrets were carried in their heads and passed down to their daughters who worked in the kitchen alongside them. Substitutions were probably numerous, since for the most part these cooks had to use what was at hand.

The cooking tastes of the Southerners and the New Englanders reflected the English influence, with a few favorites of the Scotch and Irish. Having come from a warmer climate they were generally accustomed to greater variety in "garden sass," and fully utilized the wild fruits and vegetables while clearing ground for their own gardens.

The Pennsylvania Dutch and German immigrants were inventive cooks; their sausages and pickles made their neighbors "sit up and take notice" after sampling these delights. The Poles and Bohemians excelled in fancy breads.

Those Were the Days

In the 1850s farmers spent very little money, and that went for staples—salt, soda, matches, and other articles which could not be produced by themselves. A barrel of sorghum served as sugar and syrup (long sweetening). An ad in the November 21, 1859, issue of the *Harrisburg* (Illinois) *Chronicle* quoted prices then current.

Hams	*12 ¢/lb.*
Shoulder	*10 ¢/lb.*
Sides	*11 ¢/lb.*

Beef, fresh	*6 ¢/lb.*
Beef, dry	*12 ¢/lb.*
Chickens	*$1.50/doz.*
Eggs	*8 ¢/doz.*
Salt	*$3.25/bbl.*
Tallow	*10 ¢/lb.*
Wheat	*60 ¢/75 ¢/bu.*
Potatoes	*40 ¢/bu.*

The recipes which appear on the following pages are gleaned from old family receipt collections shared by relatives, from accounts of the foods served at the tables of the rich and poor, from old cookbooks found here and there. Many of them are culled from my own memory, for I was one of those fortunate daughters who learned to cook by watching and then helping my mother in the kitchen. She was a "plain cook" so she maintained, but she would try many dishes. Her mother came from Germany; her father was a third-generation American of German extraction. My mother catered to my father's food preferences also; he was a descendant of those English-Irish-Scotch Southerners and Pennsylvania Dutch who arrived in the 1830s.

Please note that there is no mention of contributions made by Italian cooks to the southern Illinois mix. Their inclusion would have altered the "flavor" of the book. A few Italians, Lithuanians, and Ukrainians had arrived in southern Illinois during the Victorian era to provide labor in the coal mines. The Italians embrace an entirely different philosophy of cooking, which antedates that of the French. It stands alone by virtue of its rich tradition and the different styles in the various provinces. There are many Italian cookbooks on the market which cover Italian cookery far better than I could ever do.

The adventurous diner may find a very interesting menu by choosing recipes for a "typical" southern Illinois dinner: Mead or bourbon (corn "likker" from Kentucky or Tennessee); beer soup (German), sliced sausages, and homemade crackers (German and crackers from Old South); venison, muskrat, or rattlesnake (more on this later); crackling corn bread (Southern); wild greens (native); sweet potato pie, or pudding, or a wide choice of English pudding; any one of several kinds of homemade wine.

There were a few meat items which were rather difficult to find, until I made inquiries right around my own village. I had regarded these as survival foods, not to be used except in dire necessity. For example, rattlesnakes are generally regarded as enemies of man, to be avoided if possible, and killed on sight if encountered. When no other game was available, woodsmen, mountain men, and the like, ate rattlesnake and reported it "good." It was a surprise to find a page in a recent issue of a nationally distributed men's magazine devoted exclusively to instructions for preparing rattlesnake dishes. Curious, I told a new friend about this and she presented me with a rattlesnake to cook.

Muskrat is a small water animal whose skins were collected by the French trappers and many boys in years since. It can be fried and eaten with relish; also opossum and raccoon, in addition to the wild rabbits, squirrels, and birds. The buffalo, once regarded as extinct, is now being bred with beef cattle and soon, it is hoped, the "beefalo" will be marketed, thus releasing millions of tons of corn now required for fattening beef, to help feed the millions of starving people in other less-favored countries. The beefalo is a grass-eating rather than a grain-eating animal.

Mark Twain on Cooking Plain

The story goes that while touring Europe in 1878 Mark Twain, a neighbor of ours, so to speak, grew more and more disdainful of the food in the countries visited. As you will recall this was after his sentimental journey down the Mississippi River in 1875, with stopovers in the river cities and towns along the way, which he had acquainted himself with during his riverboat-piloting days. Twain composed a rather formidable list of satisfying dishes which he planned to dine on when he returned to the United States. Among these were those we have been writing about in these pages, all of which can still be found in southern Illinois homes.

> *American coffee, with real cream*
> *American butter*
> *Fried chicken, Southern style*
> *Hot biscuits, Southern style*
> *Black bass from the Mississippi*
> *American roast beef*
> *Roast wild turkey*
> *Prairie hens, from Illinois*
> *Possum, coon*
> *Hominy*
> *Bacon and greens, Southern style*
> *Butter beans*
> *Pumpkin, squash, asparagus*

Sweet potatoes
Green corn on the ear
Hot light bread, Southern style
Hot corn pone, with chitlings, Southern style
Apple dumplings, with real cream
Apple pie
Peach cobbler, Southern style
Peach pie

We can assume that he was homesick. We may also assume that although he was privileged to eat at the better restaurants, the cookery on the Continent did not suit his taste. We have eaten all of the above except the hot corn pone with chitlings. We agree that any midwesterner would have to travel a long way to top this list.

Mixing and Cooking

The reader will note that all recipes specify only butter, lard or suet; that no ready-mixed foods are included; that there is heavy emphasis on cakes, puddings, pies, and breads; that there is a preponderance of cornmeal dishes; that a section is devoted to home-drying fruits and vegetables. This is the way southern Illinoisans lived during the period covered by this book, during the agricultural phase of our existence. Their lives were vastly different from ours. Strength-giving food was essential to their health and endurance; they worked hard from dawn to long after dusk.

Cooking instructions have been modernized and standardized to give more or less exact proportions, measurements, cooking time and yield, insofar as possible. Directions found in old books and receipts were somewhat sketchy; it was presumed that the experienced cook would know how to proceed.

The old cast-iron cookware has been superseded by modern brightly colored Corning ware and fancy earthenware casseroles. This attractive kitchenware may be used where cast-iron, granite, or enamel cookware are mentioned. As an item of interest, cast-iron cooking pots and pans are again available in department and hardware stores. I cannot guarantee that the finished dish will taste as it did in those olden days. There was some special distinctive flavor to foods cooked in the old cast-iron cookstove or over the fireplace that cannot be duplicated in our modern controlled-temperature stoves. Or perhaps that's nostalgia.

Butter Substitutes

Since this book deals with cookery prior to the early years of the twentieth century, all of the recipes which call for cooking fats specify butter, lard, or in some cases, beef suet. Vegetable oils for cooking, pressed from corn, cottonseed, soybean, sesame, safflower, sunflower seeds, peanuts, or other nuts, were not generally used in southern Illinois until the 1960s.

As the fat content of vegetable oils differs markedly from that of butter, weight for weight and measure for measure, it is not recommended that the cook attempt to substitute oil for butter or lard in any of the recipes which specify these animal fats.

Oil will be satisfactory for frying and general cooking where fat is called for, even though the flavor will be altered.

Margarine may be substituted for butter, weight for weight or measure for measure; however, the texture of the baked dish will be somewhat different in both cooking and baking, and will lack that highly desirable butter flavor.

Lard is softer and oilier than butter. The modern-day hydrogenated, refined, and emulsified lards are better for biscuits and piecrust. The lard sold in bulk or package form is more like that used in Grandmother's day, which was home-processed. If lard is used as a substitute for butter in mixing cakes or cookies, reduce amount by about 20 percent, or 3 tablespoons less per cup. However substitutions are tricky. For most satisfactory results, it is advisable to use the specified ingredients.

An Ounce of Caution

A word of caution to those who would make sausage or jerky, or would smoke fish. The Indians and pioneer families successfully preserved many foods during the growing or hunting season, learning the best methods by trial and error, and passing their knowledge along to their children. There were hazards then, as there are now. Caution is indicated, and readers should be aware that some scattered cases of botulism have been noted in dried or smoked fish, beef jerky, smoked beef, and in sausage products improperly prepared at home. Old recipes for preserved foods are included in this book primarily for their historical interest, and anyone wishing to undertake such ventures should obtain complete and detailed instructions before proceeding.

Beverages

Beverages

Our hardy forebears of southern Illinois did not allow the absence of a corner tavern to deter them from enjoying a hearty draught of the cup that cheers. God knows they needed a little cheering now and then. In fact, it often took a good jolt of the "ole red-eye" to help them forget for a short while the cares and woes of the never-ending battle to keep body and soul together. Distilled corn liquor packed the biggest wallop, and apparently was the favored he-man beverage. The art of distilling was brought along by the arrivals from Tennessee and Kentucky. However, if the supply ran out, or the corn crop was short, just about any fruit or vegetable could be fermented, and with proper handling, yield forth something to wet the lips and fire the stomach.

Applejack, corn whiskey, mead, dandelion, blackberry, grape, gooseberry, currant wine found their way into the kegs and jugs. Weddings, funerals, house and barn raisings, almost any gathering provided a valid reason for partaking of the beverage. A feeling of utter exhaustion at the end of a particularly trying day called for a lift of the jug. Most people worked it off and carried it well. A few found it a trifle too exhilarating. But that's another story.

Mead

According to early accounts, mead, or metheglin, was served to the militiamen of Jackson County and other southern Illinois areas when they reported for duty on Muster Day in the early years of the nineteenth century. After the introduction of corn whiskey made by the Kentuckians and Tennesseans, mead's popularity faded somewhat. During the late 1960s college boys and girls rediscovered mead and it enjoyed a revival. Sellers of spirits offer it to those who enjoy its distinctive flavor. To make mead:

4 gallons water
16 pounds honey
1 ounce hops

Combine honey and water in a large kettle, bring to a boil and cook for about 15 minutes. Set aside to cool and skim off the film which rises to the top. Return to stove and boil again. Add 1 ounce of hops and boil 10 minutes longer. Set aside to cool. Pour into a wooden cask. (This is the ideal procedure. A large glass jug will do, but it won't produce brew quite as fine.) After 3 weeks, bung it closely. After 12 months, pour off into bottles and seal. This produces a pale, strong wine tasting somewhat like dry sherry. *Yield: About 4 to 5 gallons.*

Jeff Russell's Whiskey

Jefferson Russell, son of a Revolutionary war veteran who settled in Williamson County in 1817, favored corn whiskey (his own) and rum from New Orleans. He may have taken both neat, and it is quite likely that when the frost was nipping he treated himself to a whiskey or rum toddy as he sat before his fireplace.

Whiskey Toddy

Place a lump of sugar in a hot toddy glass, add a jigger of hot water to dissolve it. Pour in a generous double jigger of whiskey or rum, and fill glass with hot water. Stir well and decorate with a twist of lemon peel if obtainable. Nutmeg may be grated on top.

Wild Grape Wine

Making your own wine is a tricky process. Purchasers of the wine kits so much in vogue these days have occasional failures. So, proceed at your own risk. This method *should* produce drinkable wine.

1 bushel grapes
4½ gallons water
Sugar

Pick grapes from stems, mash in a large crock (5 gallon capacity) and let stand for 24 hours. Strain through a very fine sieve or cloth. To every gallon of juice add 2 pounds of brown sugar. Pour into a wooden or stone cask, but do not fill container. Let stand open for 14 days, then close bung. Test for drinkability in 2 months. If it tastes good, pour off into bottles, cork and store. *Yield: About 4 to 5 gallons.*

Grape Wine

The following procedure, using cultivated grapes, should produce passable wine, if you're lucky.

½ bushel grapes
12 pounds sugar

Remove grapes from stems, wash with hands, and place in a 5-gallon crock. Add 2½ pounds sugar. Mash slightly. Set in a cool place to ferment for 7 or 8 days. When the juice has ceased fermenting, strain through cloth, return to crock, and add the remaining 9½ pounds of sugar. Cover tightly, set in cool place and allow to ferment 8 to 10 days. When fermentation ceases, pour into bottles and seal. *Yield: About 4 gallons.*

Elderberry Wine

Elderberries can still be found along the roadsides and the borders of fields. A very delicious wine can be made from their juice.

Gather the ripe berries on a sunny day. Wash by immersing heads in a tub of clean water. Strip from stems and place in an earthenware or enameled container. Measure berries, and for 3 gallons, pour in 2 gallons of boiling water. Mash berries slightly, cover tightly, and let stand for one day.

Pour off juice and strain additional juice through a sieve, pressing the berries very lightly. Measure juice again. For each gallon add:

3 pounds sugar
6 whole cloves
1 tablespoon ground ginger

Stir well and boil for 20 minutes, skimming any scum from top. Remove from fire and cool.

Pour into a dry, well-washed cask. (This is the ideal procedure. A large glass jug will do, but it won't produce wine quite as fine.) Be sure to fill the cask, reserving a quart of extra juice to add as the wine evaporates. Pour gently into the filled cask a teaspoon of new yeast which has been well mixed with 4 tablespoons of the juice. Let ripen for 6 months and pour into bottles. Cap tightly. *Yield: About 2 gallons.*

Dandelion Wine

I'd heard of dandelion wine all my life but had had no opportunity to taste it or even see it, since my mother was a strict teetotaler.

On my first automobile trip to the Northwest we stopped over in Montana to visit friends for several days. Our host brought out five bottles of his dandelion wine, with ill-concealed pride, and set glasses on the kitchen table. A good thing. He uncorked the first bottle and it spewed like Old Faithful, spraying the ceiling. Bottle after bottle followed its example. After we mopped the floor, the furniture, and did the best we could with the ceiling, we drained the dregs of the bottles for a small sip of this boasted-of beverage. It was potent all right, clear like vodka, somewhat bitter.

With that introduction you are on your own. Perhaps the southern Illinois dandelions don't grow as wild and free as those Montana weeds.

3 pints dandelion blossoms (stems snipped off)
2 quarts water

Pour water over blossoms in crock and let stand for 6 days. Strain infusion through several thicknesses of cheesecloth. Add:

2 pounds sugar
1 lemon, sliced
2 navel oranges, sliced thick

Blend well with dandelion juice and boil for 30 minutes. Cool, pour into half-gallon-size bottles, and let stand for 6 months. Siphon into smaller bottles and seal. *Yield: About 1 gallon.*

Elderblossom Wine

This pale yellow, delicately flavored wine produced from the elderberry blossoms is a treat for the palate. It is also easy to make, after you find the blossoms, in late June or early July.

1 quart elderberry blossoms only, free of stems
9 pounds sugar
1 yeast cake, dissolved in ¼ cup lukewarm water
3 gallons water
3 pounds raisins, seeded
½ cup lemon juice

Pick blossoms from stems very carefully with fingers or small flower snips, and pack into quart measure until full. Combine sugar and water over heat and stir until sugar is dissolved. Boil 5 minutes without stirring, skim, and add blossoms. As soon as blossoms are stirred in, remove from fire and cool to lukewarm. Add dissolved yeast and lemon juice. Pour into a 5-gallon crock or glass jar, cover tightly, and stir thoroughly three times daily, making sure the blossoms are brought up from the bottom each time. On the seventh day strain liquid through a cloth and add raisins. Pour into sterilized glass jars, seal, and let set until the following January, when the wine can be bottled. Siphon off carefully into bottles, and cap. *Yield: About 3 to 4 gallons.*

Elderflower Wine

This wine is dryer than the foregoing. If you're afraid to risk that much sugar, you might try this version.

1 quart elderberry blossoms
3 gallons water
1 yeast cake, dissolved in ¼ cup lukewarm water
5 pounds sugar
3 pounds raisins

Gather flowers when at the peak of their bloom, in late June or early July. Snip off flowers from stems. Add 3 gallons water, 5 pounds sugar, and yeast. Sir. Cover and let stand 9 days. Strain through several thicknesses of cheesecloth. Add 3 pounds raisins. Mix well. Pour into an oak cask. (This is the ideal procedure. A large glass jug will do, but it won't produce wine quite as fine.) Store in a cool, dark place for at least 6 months. Siphon off into bottles and cap. *Yield: About 3 gallons.*

Barbara's Raspberry Cordial

A smooth, stomach-warming afterdinner drink that will make you feel this old world isn't so bad after all, from Barbara Burr Hubbs.

2 pints red raspberries
2 cups sugar
1 fifth home-distilled corn whiskey (if your still is out of order, a bottle of 86-proof from the local liquor store will serve the purpose)

Pick over raspberries but do not wash. Add sugar and whiskey. Mix well and pour into a glass container or crock. Cover and let stand for a month at room temperature. Stir daily. Strain through several layers of cheesecloth (a clean nylon stocking will do if you can't find cheesecloth). Pour into sterilized bottles and cap. *Yield: About 1 quart.*

Grape Juice

The Bible-reading, God-fearing teetotalers liked liquid refreshment too, but limited themselves strictly to nonalcoholic beverages. This didn't necessarily mean that Grandpa didn't have a bottle of Old Corn stashed away in the barn (mine did). The good wife tried to ignore the whole thing, and served grape juice, lemonade, iced tea, root beer, and the like, punctuated on rare occasions with a tiny glass of blackberry or cherry cordial.

To make grape juice: Immerse grapes in a washtub or other large vessel filled with water and pick the fully ripe, perfect ones from the stems. Pour into pressure cooker or large kettle and cook until soft. Strain. Let juice stand in refrigerator or other cool place overnight. Pour off juice carefully, discarding sediment. Measure. Add ½ cup sugar to each quart of juice and boil 20 minutes. Fill hot, sterilized jars, skim off foam, and seal immediately. It is recommended that the filled jars be laid on their sides in a large kettle of simmering water for 5 minutes. Cool gradually by running cold water into the kettle. *Yield: 1 bushel of grapes will yield about 10 quarts of juice.*

Apple Cider

The pleasant custom of cider-making is being revived in rural areas, under the stimulus of the nostalgia trend. Those collectors who were forethoughted enough to buy a cider press at a country auction in past years are pleased to demonstrate this autumn ritual. Freshly pressed cider is to the Middle West what fresh orange juice is to Florida and California. There's nothing like it.

Almost any kinds of winter apples can be used. They are dumped into the hopper, a few willing hands are pressed into service (no pun intended) and the golden juice comes pouring out of the spout into the jugs.

Our family owned a cider press in years gone by. It has long since disappeared and we indulge our hankering for a draft wherever we can find a goup at work with a press during the apple season. Store-bought cider cannot hold a candle to freshly made country cider. The preservative alters the bottled sunshine flavor.

For those who have access to a cider mill and a crew of willing volunteers: Wash and stem 1 bushel of apples. Feed apples into hopper. Run juice into jugs. *Yield: 1 bushel of apples yields about 3 gallons of juice.*

Hot Spiced Cider

My friend Dot Farnsworth sent some delightful recipes from New England. They are quite similar to those carried across the country to southern Illinois by early arrivals, among whom were the Allyns, Webbs, and Rogerses of Jackson County as well as other New England-born pioneers who were opposed to slavery. This hot spiced cider was a popular holiday beverage in early times, and remains so today.

1 gallon fresh cider
3 bay leaves
1 rounded tablespoon whole cloves
3 sticks cinnamon

Pour cider into an enamelware kettle. Add bay leaves, cloves, and cinnamon. Simmer (do not boil) for 30 minutes. Do not strain. Remove bay leaves and cinnamon sticks and serve piping hot in mugs. *Yield: About 16 servings.*

Cider Eggnog

This is a fine beverage for an autumn party, when the hostess wishes something a bit fancier than plain cider to serve with dainty cookies.

1 quart sweet cider
4 eggs, separated
Sugar

Beat egg yolks until they assume the consistency of thick cream. Beat the whites to a stiff froth. Combine yolks with the cider and sweeten to taste. Fold in half of the beaten whites and add a few dashes of nutmeg. Chill. Serve in punch glasses garnished with a teaspoon of the remaining egg white. *Yield: About 8 servings.*

Red Currant Punch

A nonalcoholic party punch, pretty and refreshing. The currants may still be found in out-of-the-way spots.

1 cup sugar
3 quarts water

2 cups red currant jelly
3 lemons
3 navel oranges

Make a simple syrup by boiling 1 cup sugar with 3 quarts water for 5 minutes. Remove from fire and while still hot add jelly and stir until dissolved. Add 3 lemons and 3 oranges, sliced paper thin and seeds removed. Chill until very cold. Serve in glasses partly filled with crushed ice. *Yield: About 15 servings.*

Sumac Lemonade

The Indians introduced this refreshing beverage to the early Americans. Southern Illinois settlers found an ample supply of sumac trees for use in making this spicy, thirst-quenching drink. Boy Scouts still use it when on hikes. The slightly acid, flavorful drink resembles pink lemonade.

Gather the red heads of the scarlet sumac (vinegar tree) in midsummer. Cut off stems and wash well. Bruise heads in water with a potato masher. Simmer until soft (about an hour), *do not boil.* Strain liquid through several thicknesses of cloth, to remove the tiny hairs, so they don't tickle your throat. Add sugar to taste. Chill. *Yield: 12 to 16 seed heads will yield about 1 quart.*

Root Beer

My brothers made and swigged root beer long before the root beer stands began to dot the landscape. Their pleasure in drinking it was enhanced by their pride in making it themselves. To make:

Dissolve 4 pounds sugar in 5 gallons lukewarm water. Add 1 bottle root beer extract (2-ounce size) and ½ cake yeast dissolved in ¼ cup lukewarm water. Mix thoroughly, and bottle immediately in well-washed bottles or jugs. Cap tightly. Set in a warm place for 35 to 48 hours, then transfer to cellar or other cool place. Drink when thirsty. *Yield: About 20 quarts.*

Maple Drink

Early residents of Randolph and Jackson counties tapped the sugar maple trees in Degognia Township, and boiled the syrup down for sweetening. I am told that the Indians who roamed through southern Illinois introduced those early white arrivals to this sweet source and treated them to a drink made from it. No recipe is available, but those fortunate enough to obtain fresh maple syrup may follow these simple directions:

Combine ½ cup syrup and 6 cups water. Simmer for 15 minutes. Drink hot or cold. *Yield: About 6 cups.*

Coffee

Coffee was purchased in the whole bean until the teen-age of this century, for I recall the neat little coffee mill which I was privileged to brace between my legs while grinding coffee for that day. In earlier times coffee was purchased green, and the pioneer homemaker was obliged to roast it before it could be ground. Families too poor to own a small hand-cranked coffee mill were reduced to pouring the roasted beans into a stout bag and mashing them with the flat side of a hatchet, a rock, or whatever was handy that would break up the beans into small grains. Those families who couldn't afford to buy coffee learned from the Indians to parch corn until it was very dark, pound the grain, and drink the brew concocted from boiling it. Other grains parched and used as coffee substitutes were barley, rye, wheat, dried carrots, dried peas, chicory root, and the Kentucky coffee bean.

The residents of the Old South became so fond of the coffee-chicory mixture during the hard days of the Civil War that to this day shoppers may choose between pure coffee, or a blend composed of part coffee, part chicory.

Although I have no personal experience with the seeds of the Kentucky coffee tree, I have read that the Indians who camped in southern Illinois and some of those hardy souls who lived in these parts before and during the Revolution did use it. The French Canadians who set their traps along the streams which fed into the Ohio and Mississippi rivers called it Chicot (stump). Oliver Perry Medsger says that Stephen H. Long's expedition to the Rocky Mountains in 1820 used these seeds for making coffee, and found the beverage "palatable."

Sassafras Tea

Sassafras tea was introduced to the early colonists by the friendly Indians, and in 1586 Sir Francis Drake took roots to England, with the announcement that they could cure all ailments. The sale of sassafras roots flourished in London, so perhaps some of the early arrivals knew about it before they landed on our shores. Sassafras thickets may be found in fence rows, along roadsides and on the edge of woods throughout southern Illinois. My father heralded the coming of spring by entering the kitchen with 15 or 20 6-inch strips of sassafras roots with the bark peeled off, ready for making sassafras tea. We enjoyed this spicy beverage in spite of our parents' insistence that it was an excellent spring tonic; it "thinned the blood." I have since learned that the tiny new leaves can also be used for the tea, producing a more delicately flavored beverage.

To make the tea, pour boiling water over a 6-inch section of freshly dug and debarked sassafras root, or a couple of tablespoonfuls of new leaves. Steep until it reaches the desired strength and color, about 10 to 15 minutes, and drink very hot, with or without sugar and cream. Be sure to use a china or granite teapot. Do not allow the tea to set too long; it may become bitter.

Soups

Mom's Vegetable Soup

During our mother's most prolific childbearing years, there was always a flock of little ones to be fed at noon. Dad and any of the boys who were old enough to help in the field sometimes took their lunch along, to eat as they sat under the shade of a tree. Mom's clever gambit on such days was her permission to prepare lunch ourselves, and as a couple of us older girls were on hand we soon organized the procedure, to our advantage. Each kid would be sent out to the garden to bring in the vegetable of his or her choice: tomatoes, potatoes, corn, green beans, peas, okra, whatever was available at the time. We peeled, snapped, shelled, cut, and deposited these offerings in the old iron kettle with its beef broth already simmering. After a ½ hour or so of impatient waiting, Mom invariably prepared her "little dumplings." We stood in a half circle as she tilted the bowl over the steaming kettle, and with a knife, cut off the batter as it oozed to the rim of the bowl. The tiny yellow dumplings sank, then rose to the surface, expanding as they cooked. After she scraped the last of the batter from the bowl she covered the kettle tightly; then ensued the longest waiting period of our lives, while all of the dumplings cooked. The 10 minutes finally passed and we were more than ready to be served. A large slab or two of Mom's homemade bread with fresh butter accompanied the soup and filled our stomachs comfortably. If not, there was always more soup. Sometimes there was a watermelon cooling in a bucket down in the well. More often, a second slab of bread, spread liberally with butter and topped with apple butter or jelly or preserves, topped off the meal.

A kettle of rich beef or chicken broth and fresh vegetables from the garden or from your vegetable mixes canned during the growing season will provide ingredients for your soup. I have tried to duplicate my mother's dumpling recipe. Her dumplings were a richer yellow than any I have been able to make. Of course she carried the recipe in her head, as her mother did before her.

2 eggs
1½ cups flour, unsifted

23

½ **cup water**
½ **teaspoon salt**
¼ **teaspoon baking powder**

Beat eggs well and combine with water. Dump in the dry ingredients and beat vigorously. Dough should be fairly stiff. Drop by teaspoonfuls into the simmering broth, cover tightly and cook over low fire for about 10 minutes. Don't peek. The dumplings should be very light and puffy. *Yield: 4 cups dumplings.*

Sorrel Soup

Back-to-nature buffs have revived this colorful soup, which the Kaskaskia French enjoyed as a spring soup, after the dried and preserved winter fare. The sheep sorrel, a member of the oxalis family, grows wild; the so-called French sorrel may be cultivated in your garden.

⅓ **cup shredded sorrel**
3 tablespoons butter
6 cups boiling water
1 teaspoon salt
2 egg yolks
3 tablespoons milk
½ **cup croutons**

Tear the tender green leaves from the midribs of the sorrel. Wash in cold water and chop fine. Melt 1½ tablespoons butter in saucepan and add sorrel. Cook 5 minutes, stirring frequently. Add boiling water and salt and cook 10 minutes. Beat egg yolks, add milk and pour into soup tureen. Add remaining 1½ tablespoons butter. Pour hot cooked sorrel into tureen, stirring constantly, to mix well with egg yolk and milk. Garnish with croutons and serve immediately. *Serves 4.*

Potato Soup

Potato soup is such a simple, unadorned, everyday soup that it was almost decided to omit it altogether. But that would be tantamount to cutting out biscuits for breakfast in Grandmother's day.

3 cups peeled potatoes cut into small cubes
2 tablespoons chopped onion
2 tablespoons flour
2 teaspoons salt

4 cups water
¼ cup chopped parsley

Cook cubed potatoes until fork-tender (about 10 minutes) and set aside. Melt 2 tablespoons butter in heavy skillet and add chopped onion and flour. Cook over medium heat until onion is golden, stirring frequently. Thin mixture by adding several tablespoons of hot water, one at a time, stirring briskly to prevent lumps. Place cubed potatoes in kettle, add 4 cups water and the browned onions, cover and simmer for about 15 minutes. Stir in ¼ cup chopped parsley, season to taste, and serve. *Serves 6.*

Note: 1 medium-sized raw tomato or ¼ cup tomato juice may be added to this soup for a more sophisticated meal-starter.

Beer Soup

There are those who prefer to take their beer au naturel; however, the old-time Germans knew how to make it, so there was plenty on hand for any desired use. If this seems a wanton waste of the foaming brew, try it before passing final judgment. You may be surprised.

2 tablespoons flour
⅛ to ¼ teaspoon cinnamon
Pinch of salt
1 tablespoon sugar
4 eggs, well beaten
Grated rind of 2 lemons
1 quart beer
1 quart water

Blend flour, salt, sugar, and cinnamon, add slowly to beaten eggs, and stir until smooth. Add grated lemon rind. Combine beer and water and cook over high heat until it boils. Remove from heat, stir in egg mixture very slowly, beating constantly. Serve at once, with bread croutons sprinkled over top. *Serves 4 to 6.*

Note: To make croutons—cut stale bread into ½ inch cubes, place in shallow baking dish, and toast 15 to 20 minutes at 325°.

Hominy Soup

A hardy pioneer husband and father was not always overly fussy about what he ate, so long as it was hot and hearty and filling. Here's an example of a quick meal for the hungry male.

2 cups hominy
¼ pound salt pork, cut in ½-inch cubes
1 medium onion, sliced
1 quart buttermilk
½ teaspoon salt
¼ teaspoon pepper

Fry pork cubes in a heavy skillet. Drain off fat, except for 1 tablespoonful. Add sliced onion and fry until golden brown. Mix in hominy and heat for about 5 minutes, stirring gently. Add buttermilk, salt, and pepper. Heat slowly, just to boiling point, and serve. A slab of warm buttered white bread will help satisfy the hunger pangs, or a plateful of Grandmother's homemade crackers. *Serves 6.*

Meats

Meats

Beef Cookery

As this is being written, we consumers are being bombarded by the press with reminders that the average American consumes nearly a ton of grain in a year, and that over 90 percent of it comes not in the form of bread, but as beef, pork, chicken, milk, or eggs.

There is talk of feeding cattle less grain. Grass-fed cattle will produce less-tender beef, hence the steaks, roasts, chops, and other favorite cuts of meat will require different treatment—tenderizing before cooking, or cooking slower and longer.

Every portion of the beef is palatable when properly prepared. Overcooking steaks will not make them more tender. Marinating them in a vinegar or wine marinade for an hour or two before broiling will do so. Possibly more corned beef will be available or can be prepared in the kitchen, if your family has no desire to wear their teeth down to the gums in their attempts to masticate tough beef. This technique was used by good cooks of bygone years, who made their own vinegar or wine. No vinegary taste remains when the meat is cooked.

A favorite tenderizer for tough steaks from the early 1800s may be made as follows:

½ pint red wine
1 large onion, sliced
Few sprigs of parsley
1 stalk celery, or celery tops, minced
Bay leaf
6 peppercorns
1 lemon sliced (if available)

Cover steaks with marinade, let stand for an hour or two. Remove, drain, and wipe dry before broiling. The marinade can be stored in the refrigerator and reused.

Another tenderizer is baking soda, which is less trouble; however, we do not regard it as desirable as the marinade. Rub steaks on both sides with baking soda, using approximately 1 tablespoon for each steak. Wrap loosely and place in refrigerator until next day. When ready to cook, rinse, or wipe well, and proceed with broiling.

Rump, round, or brisket can be corned. Prepare the following for a 5- or 6-pound chunk of beef:

6 cups water
1 cup salt
3 tablespoons sugar
1 bay leaf
6 peppercorns
1 clove garlic, minced
2 teaspoons mixed pickling spices
½ teaspoon saltpeter (optional)
½ cup lukewarm water

Dissolve saltpeter (may be obtained from your pharmacy) in ½ cup warm water and pour into crock or other large earthen, glass, or china container. Add all other above ingredients and stir well. Gently lower meat into marinade. The liquid should cover the meat completely. Cover with a plate and place a heavy weight on the plate. Leave meat in marinade for at least 1½ days. The marinade may be saved for future use if kept in refrigerator.

Steak and Kidney Pie

Straight from England to eastern Illinois this one came, and it is a splendid addition to our cuisine. The English colonists, who were early settlers of southern Illinois, are to be thanked for this contribution.

Suet, chunk about 2 by 2 inches
2 pounds rump steak cut ½ inch thick
1 beef or 2 veal kidneys (about ½ pound)
1 cup mushrooms, sliced
½ cup sliced onions
Beef stock, about 1 to 1½ cups
Salt, to taste
Pepper, to taste
¼ teaspoon nutmeg
½ teaspoon thyme
Pastry for generous 2-crust pie

Trim all fat from kidneys, place in a bowl and cover with boiling water. Let stand for 30 minutes. Meanwhile, cut beef into 2 inch cubes. Drain kidneys, transfer to cutting board and slice very thin. Render suet in heavy skillet until you have at least 2 tablespoons of melted fat. Discard remainder of suet and fat. Roll beef and kidney pieces in flour and place in skillet with ½ cup sliced onion. Fry slowly until meat is browned on all sides. Add enough beef stock to cover, cover skillet, and cook slowly until meat is tender (45 minutes to 1 hour). Meanwhile, mix enough pastry dough to line and cover a 2-quart, fairly deep casserole. When meat has cooled slightly, add sliced mushrooms, season with salt, pepper, nutmeg, and thyme to taste, and turn into the pastry-lined casserole. Add remainder of beef stock. If there is not enough to cover the meat, add water. Top with remaining pastry which has been slit with a sharp knife in a leaf pattern, to permit steam to escape while baking, and crimp edges tightly. Bake 1 hour in moderate oven, 350°, or until crust is golden brown. Let stand 10 or 15 minutes before serving. *Serves 6.*

English Meat Pie

A traditional English dish brought to southern Illinois by the early settlers who came from Virginia, Tennessee, Kentucky, and the Carolinas.

1½ pounds lean beef, cut in 1-inch cubes
2 tablespoons melted suet or bacon drippings
2 cups boiling water
1½ teaspoons salt
4 medium potatoes, peeled, diced
5 carrots, peeled and sliced
1 medium onion, sliced
Salt and pepper to taste

To make pastry:

2 cups all-purpose flour
1 teaspoon salt
½ to ⅔ cup lard
6 tablespoons cold water

Brown beef in fat. Pour boiling water over meat, add salt, cover, and simmer for 40 to 45 minutes, until barely tender. Add potatoes, carrots, and onions to meat and simmer 20 minutes longer. Add more water if needed. Season to taste.

Line sides and bottom of 2-quart casserole with pastry rolled to ¼-inch thickness. Place a teacup upside down in center of casserole. Spoon vegetables into casserole along one side of cup. Place meat on opposite side of cup. (The cup accumulates the gravy and prevents crust from becoming soggy.) Cover top with pastry rolled very thin.

Cut a leaf pattern in top crust to permit steam to escape while baking. Bake for 25 to 30 minutes at 425°, or until golden brown. Serve meat portions, then remove teacup, and serve gravy and vegetables. *Serves 6 to 8.*

Fried Beefsteak

There seems to be a revival of interest in old-fashioned fried beefsteak. Friends and family serve it more often, and it is encountered more frequently in restaurants. When I brought my fiancé home from the city to meet my family years ago, my mother served fried beefsteak for Sunday breakfast, with brown gravy, hot biscuits, eggs, and fruit. He had never heard of eating beefsteak for breakfast, but he did full justice to the meal. Here's how to cook it:

1 pound round steak, ½ to ¾ inch thick

Lay meat on a clean wooden block and pound well with a wooden mallet, being careful not to beat it until it looks ragged. Cut into 4-inch squares, sprinkle with pepper and salt, then dredge with flour. Lay the pieces in a hot skillet which has been greased with 2 or 3 tablespoons bacon drippings. Turn often so that both sides brown well and so the gravy will be nice and brown. If desired, pour 1 tablespoon pepper vinegar over meat, cover frying pan tightly, and lower heat so the meat will simmer for 10 to 15 minutes, depending on tenderness. Sift powdered cracker crumbs over meat and serve hot, with gravy in a serving dish. *Serves 2 or 3.*

Pot Roast

This is what my dad used to call "good old American food." Hearty, filling, sticks to the ribs. With fresh garden vegetables cooked in the same pot, it's hard to beat. It is best cooked in a heavy cast-iron Dutch oven; however, any heavy kitchen kettle with a tight-fitting lid will produce almost the same results.

5-pound beef shoulder, rump, blade bone, etc.
2 or 3 tablespoons fat
¼ cup minced onion
Salt
Pepper
Flour

2 cups water, vegetable stock, tomato juice, etc.
3 slices salt pork (optional)

Rub meat with salt and pepper and dredge with flour. Melt fat in pot and sauté onion lightly. Remove onion and brown meat on all sides. Pour stock over meat, add onions, and cover pot tightly. Simmer slowly until done, about 2 to 3 hours. Add more stock or boiling water if roast becomes dry. Vegetables of your choice may be added for the last half hour of cooking. If you wish, the pot juices may be strained and used for making gravy after removing the roast from the kettle. Mix 2 tablespoons flour with ½ cup water and stir slowly into stock. Simmer for 10 minutes and serve with roast. *Serves 10.*

Note: If preferred, the pot roast may be cooked in the oven at 300° to 325° until tender, about 2 hours.

Roast Beef

While Dad leaned toward pot roasts, our mother varied the cooking of the less choice cuts of meat, with very satisfactory results.

For a 5-pound rump, round, chuck, cross arm, or clod roast, mix marinade according to directions above (see *Beef Cookery*). Place roast in stone crock or deep porcelain or glass dish. Pour marinade over meat, making sure it is completely covered. Set in refrigerator, cover, and let stand at least 24 hours.

When ready to cook, remove from marinade and drain well. Lay on a trivet in roasting pan, rub lightly with salt and pepper and cook at 325° for 3 or 4 hours, or until desired state of doneness has been reached. Baste frequently with marinade.

Cracker crumbs may be sifted over the roast toward the end of the cooking period. Remove roast from oven at least 30 minutes before serving time. Garnish with parsley and serve with grated horseradish. *Serves 10.*

Note: If meat is especially tough, it may be steamed for an hour or so before roasting.

Rib Roast of Beef

A Sunday or special company dinner roast. Attractive, substantial, and gives the host a warm sense of well-being as his guests express their appreciation by asking for a second helping.

The roast may be cooked with the bones in. Roast at 325°, allowing 16 to 18 minutes per pound if you like it rare, or 23 to 28 minutes per pound if you like it well done. Do not baste.

If you wish to roast it without the bones in, have your butcher remove them and roll and skewer the roast. Before roasting, remove skewers, unroll, season well with salt and pepper, add herbs or spices if you wish, and roll again tightly, fastening securely with skewer pins. Place in roasting pan on trivet or rack. Add a pint of water or not, as you choose. With it, the meat may be more tender, but not as brown. Pepper and salt freely, dredge with flour if you choose. Baste frequently. Some persons like ½ cup of pepper vinegar poured over roast just before it is done. Minced onion, thyme, and parsley may be added to the gravy, which should be brown. *A 5-pound roast with bones should serve 8, boneless roast serves 10 to 12.*

Sirloin Beef Roast

One of the choicest cuts for roasting.

Follow roasting directions for Rib Roast of Beef above. Season well with salt and pepper, adding herbs or spices if you wish. Place in roasting pan on trivet or rack. Add a pint of water, if you wish, and dredge lightly with flour. Baste frequently. Some persons like ½ cup of pepper vinegar poured over roast just before it is done. Minced onion, thyme, and parsley may be added to the gravy. *A 5-pound roast with bone in should serve 8. A boneless roast serves 10 to 12.*

Note: If the roast shows signs of toughness, parboil it for 30 minutes or so before roasting. Remove from kettle, cool, and season. Be sure to use the water in which the meat was parboiled for basting.

Yorkshire Pudding

The classic accompaniment for a good beef roast.

3 eggs
2 cups milk
1 cup flour, sifted
1 teaspoon salt

Beat eggs until very light, then add milk. Pour this mixture over flour, add salt, and beat well. Bake in hissing hot baking pan for 45 minutes, basting with drippings from the meat.

Some cooks prefer to bake Yorkshire pudding in the pan with the meat, in which case the roast should be placed on a rack and the pudding batter poured into the pan underneath it. *Serves 6 to 8.*

Sauerbraten

This is another flavorsome way to convert tough beef to tenderness, brought to us by those good German cooks. There's no need to call the menfolk in to dinner more than once when they get a whiff of the tantalizing aroma of sauerbraten in the making.

4-pound sirloin or shoulder beef roast
2 medium onions chopped slightly
3 bay leaves
1 cup cider vinegar
1 cup water
10 peppercorns
6 whole cloves (optional)

Rub meat thoroughly with salt and pepper and lay in a fairly deep earthen bowl. Add onions, bay leaves, and peppercorns to vinegar and water and pour over meat. Marinate for a week to 10 days. Remove meat from marinade and place in roasting pan. Set in oven and brown on both sides at 500°. Reduce heat, pour ½ cup of the marinade over meat, cover pan, and roast at 300° for about 3½ hours, or until tender. Add marinade liquid during cooking time if meat becomes dry. When meat has cooked to the desired tenderness, remove from roasting pan. Let set for at least 30 minutes before slicing. Add 2 tablespoons flour to the pan drippings, set over low flame on stove, and cook until thickened, stirring constantly. Pour into gravy boat and serve with meat. *Serves 8.*

Sweetbreads

A great delicacy for many people but not always available in restaurants. They may be prepared in several ways, but all require these preliminaries:

2 or 3 celery ribs with leaves
2 sprigs parsley
2 tablespoons lemon juice
¼ cup chopped onion
½ teaspoon salt
6 peppercorns

Soak sweetbreads in water for 20 minutes. Drain well and set aside. Place in a fairly deep kettle with sufficient water to cover sweetbreads. Add all of the above ingredients. Bring water to boiling point. Lower sweetbreads into it, reduce heat and simmer for 20 minutes. Drain sweetbreads well and place in a pan of cold water to harden for 12 minutes. Remove skin and membrane. Prepare as directed in following sweetbread recipes, or in your own chosen way. Because of their delicate flavor, sweetbreads should preferably be served with bland vegetables, such as new potatoes and garden peas.

Creamed Sweetbreads

If you have invited your bridge-playing friends for lunch on a late autumn day, and know that they like sweetbreads, this should help them feel at peace with the world.

1 pair sweetbreads
1 cup cream sauce (see below)
2 tablespoons sherry

Prepare sweetbreads as directed above (see Sweetbreads). Heat sauce to boiling point and add sweetbreads. Stir in sherry immediately before serving over toast. *Serves 4.*

Cream Sauce, or White Sauce

A good rule to follow is to use half as much cream sauce as you have meats or vegetables. This gives your dish a nice consistency. Here is a basic recipe.

2 tablespoons butter
1½ to 2 tablespoons flour
1 cup hot milk or cream, or stock
¼ teaspoon salt
⅛ teaspoon paprika

Melt butter in heavy saucepan over low heat. Blend in flour. Stir milk or other liquid in slowly. Season with salt and paprika, or pepper if preferred. Cook until thickened, stirring constantly. From here you may go as far afield as you like. Suggested seasonings are:

Celery salt
1 teaspoon sherry

1 teaspoon onion juice
1 teaspoon lemon juice
½ teaspoon Worcestershire sauce
2 tablespoons chopped parsley
2 tablespoons chopped chives
1 cup grated mild cheese
1 teaspoon curry powder

You get the idea. You can take off in many directions. *Yield: 1 cupful.*

Broiled Sweetbreads

A dainty dish to set before your king.

1 pair sweetbreads
2 tablespoons melted butter
Salt
Paprika
Flour
Bacon strips
1 tablespoon sherry or lemon juice

Prepare sweetbreads as directed above (see Sweetbreads). Break them into large pieces. Season with salt and paprika and roll in flour. Wrap a strip of bacon around each portion and fasten in place with toothpicks. Broil, basting frequently with melted butter and the juices from the bacon. Add the sherry or lemon juice to the juices if desired. *Serves 4.*

Fried Sweetbreads

This is the way our mother served sweetbreads, using the trusty old skillet again.

1 pair sweetbreads
1 egg, beaten
1 cup bread crumbs, seasoned with salt and pepper
1 cup cream sauce (see recipe above)
Butter

Prepare sweetbreads as directed above (see Sweetbreads). Break into 2-inch pieces. Have ready 1 beaten egg to which 2 tablespoons water has been added, and 1 cup fine bread crumbs, seasoned well.

Dip sweetbread pieces into breadcrumbs, then in beaten egg, and again in crumbs. Fry in butter to golden brown. Serve with cream sauce which has been seasoned with sherry or lemon juice. Garnish with fresh parsley. *Serves 4.*

Fried Calf Brains

Like sweetbreads, brains are highly regarded by many people. They combine well with eggs, soufflés, and salads, and need only a dash of sherry or Worcestershire sauce to give them added zing.

Brains
1 teaspoon salt
½ teaspoon pepper
1 tablespoon minced onion (optional)
2 tablespoons butter

Wash brains well and soak in cold water for an hour. Remove membrane and cover with cold water to harden for 15 minutes. Cut in two lengthwise. Season with salt and pepper and roll in flour, or corn-meal if preferred. Place in skillet in which butter has been melted, add onion, and fry until golden brown. Serve immediately with lemon slices, tomato sauce, or Worcestershire sauce. *Serves 2 generously.*

Hog Jowl and Greens

"Hawg" jaw, hominy, and wild greens with corn pone was such common fare for the early settlers that it deserves mention, for historical purposes.

The jowl is the underjaw of the hog. It may be used fresh or smoked. The smoked jowl makes a tasty spring dish when combined with new turnip greens or the wild kind.

2 pounds hog jowl
1 teaspoon salt
4 quarts greens

Wash jowl well, place in a deep kettle, add salt, and cover with cold water. Simmer for about 3 hours, or until tender. Add 4 quarts greens—turnip tops or the wild kind—dandelion, sheep sorrel, poke, wild mustard, etc., which have been well picked over, parboiled, and drained. Simmer for 15 minutes. Do not overcook greens; they will turn yellow and taste rather bitter. Season to taste with salt and pepper. Remove jawbone before serving, by running a sharp knife around the lip. Garnish with poached eggs or sliced boiled eggs. *Serves 4.*

Rocky Mountain Oysters

This is included only as a matter of record. I learned by well-timed eavesdropping during hog-killing time that one of my uncles, now deceased, had a taste for the testicles, cleaned and fried. A bit of research in later years discloses that some other people regard them as gourmet items, and how the name Rocky Mountain Oysters came to be applied is a mystery to me. Never having tried to cook them, and having no inclination to do so, I cannot vouch for their appeal. To each his own.

1 pound "Rocky Mountain Oysters" (or "Lamb's fry")
6 cups water
1 egg, beaten
1 cup bread crumbs, lightly seasoned
1 teaspoon chopped parsley
Salt and pepper to taste

Boil the fry for 15 minutes. Drain, and pat dry. Mix parsley, bread crumbs, pepper, and salt to taste. Dip fry in beaten egg, roll in seasoned bread crumbs and fry for 5 minutes, or until golden brown. Serve very hot, garnished with parsley sprigs. *Serves 4.*

Stuffed Pork Chops

Grandma knew how to set the world right for Grandpa after a winter day's work mending harness in the icy cold barn, by setting a platter of these savory, crusty stuffed chops before him at the supper table.

6 pork chops, ¾ inch thick

If desired, cut bone from meat and trim off all excess fat. Slit a large gash or pocket into the side of each chop. Stuff with the following mixture (you may vary ingredients or proportions to suit your taste):

1 cup bread crumbs
¼ cup chopped celery
¼ cup chopped onion

2 tablespoons chopped parsley
¼ teaspoon salt
⅛ teaspoon paprika
Milk or water to moisten

Fill pockets with stuffing. Sew up with coarse needle and thread. Sear the chops in a heavy skillet and place them in a roasting pan. Moisten with water or milk. Cover pan and bake at 350° until chops are tender (about 45 minutes to 1 hour). Remove from pan and place on heated platter. To make gravy:

1 to 2 tablespoons flour
1 cup stock, or hot water
Salt
Pepper
Pinch of dried marjoram or rosemary

Stir flour into drippings in pan until smooth. Add stock or water while continuing to stir slowly. Season with salt and pepper and marjoram or rosemary. Cook for 10 minutes. If you like a smooth gravy, strain through a sieve. If you prefer it with all the little crusty goodies, pour into gravy boat and set alongside the pork chops. *Serves 6.*

Note: For Old Style German Fruit Stuffing, see section, "Dumplings, Noodles, Stuffings." You may prefer to stuff the pork chops with it.

Red-Eye Gravy

We dubbed this "ham gravy" in our household, to distinguish it from the flour-thickened gravy which Mom served with fried chicken, beefsteak or pork chops. We drenched our hot biscuits with it, and there was seldom enough, no matter how much she made.

After frying the home-cured ham, drain off excess grease so that the ham juices remain in the skillet. Add milk and stir well. One of our sisters-in-law, raised in the same tradition, adds a cup of hot coffee. No matter, you're sure to get a misty-eyed reaction from any born and bred southern Illinoisan far from home when you start talking about "ole" Red-Eye Gravy.

Fried Salt Pork

When hog-killing time came around, a few sides (from whence bacon comes, you city slickers) were reserved for salt-curing rather than being smoked for bacon. This salt pork was boiled with cabbage, or dried beans, and fried for breakfast sometimes.

12 slices salt pork

Place slices in earthenware bowl and pour boiling water over them to cover. After 30 minutes, remove and drain. Roll in flour and fry crisp and golden brown. Drain on paper towels. Pour off drippings, reserving 2 tablespoonfuls. To make gravy:

2 tablespoons drippings in skillet
2 tablespoons flour
1 cup milk
1 teaspoon salt
¼ teaspoon pepper
1 teaspoon chopped parsley (optional)

Stir flour into drippings until smooth. Add milk slowly, stirring constantly to prevent lumps; season with salt and pepper. Simmer gently for 10 minutes and pour into gravy boat for serving. Parsley enhances its appearance. *Serves 4.*

Spare Ribs

A generous slab of spare ribs was always given to relatives and/or friends who helped at hog-killing time, but we kids made sure our dad held back enough for one meal for us. Fresh spare ribs are something to remember with pleasure. Sometimes our mother boiled them; sometimes she baked them. Either way, they were usually served with apple sauce or fried apple slices, sauerkraut, and mashed potatoes. Some of our German neighbors stuffed them.

2 slabs of spare ribs (allow 1 pound per person)
1 tablespoon flour
1 teaspoon salt
½ teaspoon pepper

Do not cut ribs into small pieces.

Lay 1 slab of ribs in bottom of large baking dish or pan. Spread with seasoned sauerkraut or Old Style German Fruit Stuffing (see section, "Dumplings, Noodles, Stuffings"). Cover kraut or stuffing with second slab of ribs. Sprinkle a tablespoon of flour, salt, and pepper over top. Add more if needed. Bake uncovered at 475° for 15 minutes. Lower heat and bake at 325° for 1 hour. Baste frequently with fat in pan. *Serves 8 to 10.*

Note: In earlier times, the woodburning kitchen range heated the kitchen so there was no expense involved in baking foods. In today's energy crisis, cooks may conserve fuel by parboiling ribs until tender before baking. In this case, reduce baking time to 30 or 35 minutes, until nicely browned. Use broth for basting, with pan drippings.

Main Dishes

Main Dishes

Smith and Over Chowder

Contributed by Mrs. Etta Over of Albion, Illinois. As Mr. Over's grandfather came from England I have several of the family's favorites and as they were noted for their chowders and Edwards County is known as the Chowder Capital of the world, here every group, town, and family has a chowder in the fall, so I am including that recipe.

From early summer until late fall, chowder is made and sold by churches, civic and fraternal organizations as well as prepared for family reunions. Many families go together to make chowder at the end of the garden season to can for the coming winter months. The Edwards County Fair is preceded by a community chowder, the kettles of soup being donated by the merchants of the community.

Who knows, you may be cooking for a crowd someday. Family reunions are being revived, I hear. For 54 quarts of chowder:

2 large chickens
4 squirrels
Several soupbones
4 pounds beef, chopped
1 pound suet
¼ pound butter
1½ gallon onions, chopped coarsely
4½ gallons tomatoes, peeled
4 gallons potatoes, cubed
½ gallon butter beans
3 quarts carrots, ground
1 gallon cabbage, ground
1 gallon corn
2 red peppers, chopped
½ pound brown sugar
Salt and pepper to taste.

The chowder is cooked in a large iron kettle over a wood fire and stirred with a long-handled wood paddle. (Chowder may be cooked outdoors over gas burners if wood is scarce and fire-tenders are hard to find.) Once the potatoes have been added, it is necessary to stir

45

continuously until completely cooked because the potatoes will stick and scorch.

If the chowder is to be served at noon, the meat should be started to cook by 7:00 A.M. We begin by bringing two gallons of water to boil and adding the tomatoes. The onions, butter beans, carrots, cabbage, and peppers are added at 9:00 A.M. The seasoning is added about 10:30 A.M. and tasted again about 11:00 A.M. We never put too much salt in the chowder because each person can add more when it is served. The potatoes are added at the time of seasoning.

Stir constantly. Corn is added about 15 minutes before the chowder is finished. The firewood should be removed from beneath the kettle but continue stirring until the chowder has cooled sufficiently to prevent sticking.

Large bones are removed as the chowder is stirred and the meat is cooked until it falls off the bones. Diners remove the small bones remaining in the chowder while eating.

A few cookbooks give scanty instructions for increasing recipes for quantity cooking; fewer still offer help in reducing quantities and producing acceptable results. As Smith and Over Chowder is a variation of the revered and popular Brunswick stew, here is a chowder for serving to six people, offered in a spirit of neighborliness.

1 4 to 5-pound chicken
1 small squirrel
1 small soupbone
½ pound chopped beef
1 tablespoon butter
3 onions, chopped
1 quart tomatoes, peeled
2 cups potatoes, peeled and cubed
1 cup lima beans
1 cup carrots, ground
1 cup cabbage, ground
1 cup corn
1 small red pepper, chopped
2 cups water
½ cup white wine (optional)

Cut chicken and squirrel into pieces and place in large kettle with soupbone, chopped beef, butter, and onions. Simmer until tender. Remove meat from kettle and separate from bones. Discard bones. Return meat to kettle, add tomatoes, lima beans, carrots, cabbage, and simmer for 1 hour. Add potatoes and corn and simmer for about 30 minutes. Season with salt and pepper to taste. Ten minutes before serving, add wine if used. *Serves 6 to 8.*

Company Stew

Our great-grandmothers served it from the old iron pot which hung from the crane over the hearth, using any wild game brought home by her "man." It is equally as satisfying today cooked in any heavy kettle and using meat now available, served with a green salad and a slab of homemade bread.

1 stewing hen, 5–6 pounds
1 squirrel or rabbit, or hunk of beef, veal, or pork weighing about 3
    pounds
5 or 6 large potatoes, peeled and cubed
1 quart lima beans
1 quart whole kernel corn
5 or 6 carrots, peeled and sliced
2 or 3 onions, chopped coarsely
6 or 7 tomatoes, peeled and quartered
Salt
Pepper
Cayenne pepper

Cut chicken into serving-size pieces. Treat squirrel or rabbit likewise. If using other meat, cut into 2-inch cubes. Place in heavy kettle, cover with water, and simmer until very tender, about 1 to 1½ hours. Remove chicken and squirrel or rabbit bones. Return boned meat to broth, add vegetables, season to taste, and simmer until done, about 45 minutes. *Serves 6 generously.*

Note: Variations are in order, to suit your fancy and the garden's offering. Avoid cabbage, turnips, and such; they are a bit strong-flavored for this dish. Use cabbage for slaw, if you wish.

French Canadian Stew

This might be named Woodsman's Stew, for it is a very hearty dish, which will sustain a man on the move.

3 pounds beef, pork, or lamb, cut in 1-inch cubes
1 tablespoon lard or other fat
1 onion, chopped
6 carrots, chopped
2 stalks celery, chopped
1 cup red wine
1 teaspoon sugar
1 cup beef broth

2½ cups baked beans
Salt and pepper to taste

Brown cubed meat in fat, in heavy deep pan. Add vegetables, and just enough water to cover. Season to taste, cover, and cook over low heat for about 2 hours. Add beans and wine 10 minutes before serving. *Serves 8 hearty eaters.*

Irish Stew

Traditionally this dish is built around lamb or mutton. Because of an apparently built-in aversion to these meats on the part of many native southern Illinoisans, beef is widely used instead. Furthermore, this standby has become a sort of ad-lib mainstay which the cook varies according to what she has on hand.

2 pounds beef or lamb cut into 1-inch cubes
2 tablespoons bacon drippings
3 cups water
12 small new potatoes, peeled and whole
24 small white onions, peeled and whole
24 small carrots, whole
1 teaspoon mace
1 large clove garlic, pressed
½ cup chopped chives
½ cup chopped celery leaves
2 tablespoons flour

Heat drippings in deep, heavy kettle and brown meat. Drain off excess fat. Add water, cover kettle, and simmer meat until tender, about 1 hour. Add potatoes, onions, carrots, and mace, and continue simmering for about 30 minutes. Lift meat into a heated tureen. Add garlic, chives, and celery tops to liquid and simmer for another 15 minutes, until onions are tender. Remove from heat. Make a thin paste by stirring flour into ½ cup cold water until all lumps are removed. Add to vegetables, blending in thoroughly, and cook for 5 minutes longer. *Serves 6, with lots of hot biscuits.*

Chicken and Dumplings

Chicken and dumplings are "Good old southern Illinois food"; chicken and dumpling suppers are a favorite fund-raising meal of church groups, ladies' clubs and other small-town and rural organizations. At the drop of a feather, our sister Georgia will treat us to one of these dinners.

5-pound stewing chicken
2 small onions
2 bay leaves
6 peppercorns
1 teaspoon salt

Cut chicken into serving pieces and lay in a deep kettle. Cover with cold water and add onions, bay leaves, peppercorns, and salt. Simmer until tender, about an hour or so, depending on tenderness of chicken. Remove chicken to heated tureen while you make dumplings:

2 cups flour
1 cup hot broth
Salt, about 1 teaspoon

Sift flour and salt into a large mixing bowl. Make a well in the center and pour into it one cup of hot broth, mixing with a fork as you pour. When dough becomes stiff, work with fingers until it is smooth and quite stiff, adding more flour as needed. Knead dough for a few seconds on a floured board and divide into two or three portions for easier handling. Roll out each portion and cut into strips about 1 inch wide. Allow to rest for 10 minutes. With a sharp knife, cut strips into 2-inch lengths and drop into boiling broth. Cover kettle and cook 15 to 20 minutes. *Serves 6 to 10.*

Note: These dumplings are likely to stick together and become slightly gummy after standing for an hour or more; we never had that trouble at our house. If you do not plan to serve them shortly after cooking, try Ma Hale's Dumplings, in section, "Dumplings, Noodles, Stuffings."

Chicken-Rice Pie

This 1870 main dish is as timely today as it was then. It isn't as heavy as chicken and dumplings, and not only serves admirably as a company dish at home but carries well for a potluck supper.

Fat stewing chicken, 5 to 6 pounds
2 cups raw rice (not the quick-cook kind)
6 eggs, well beaten
1 cup milk
1 tablespoon butter
Salt and pepper

Cut chicken into serving pieces, place in deep kettle, add 1 teaspoon salt, and simmer until tender, about an hour. Remove chicken from kettle, separate meat from bones, and set aside. Cook the rice in the chicken broth (about 15 to 20 minutes). Drain off excess broth. Stir eggs into rice, add milk, butter, and season with salt and pepper. Place in a greased 2-quart casserole alternate layers of chicken and rice, with a layer of rice on top, and bake at 350° for 30 minutes, or until golden brown and a knife inserted in center comes out clean. If desired, cracker crumbs may be sprinkled over top before baking, with a few shakes of paprika. *Serves 6 to 8.*

Beef Hash

No matter how carefully the cook plans her meals, there comes a time when there isn't enough of the roast left over for a full meal. By adding a few fresh or leftover vegetables and seasoning it well, it can be set on the dining table without apology.

3 cups cooked beef, cut in ½ inch cubes
1 medium sized onion, minced
2 tablespoons lard
½ teaspoon dry mustard
½ teaspoon pepper
3 cups cooked diced potatoes
½ teaspoon salt
½ cup leftover gravy
½ cup cooked carrots (optional)
½ cup cooked green beans (optional)
2 teaspoons catsup (optional)

Combine all ingredients in mixing bowl. Turn into heavy skillet in which lard has been melted. Cook for 10 minutes over medium flame, or until well browned. Flip over and brown other side. *Serves 6.*

Beef in Grape Leaves

One usually thinks of Greek cookery when reading recipes calling for grape leaves. Actually, the custom of wrapping foods in leaves is older than we are and has become popular again in the past few years. Directions for preserving grape leaves will be found in section, "Pickling, Preserving, Jams and Jellies."

1 pound ground beef, or lamb if preferred
½ cup minced onion
1 cup long-grained raw rice
2 tablespoons olive oil

1 teaspoon fresh dill, chopped
½ cup parsley, chopped
Juice of 1 lemon
Salt and pepper
18 grape leaves, approximately

Fry meat and onion in olive oil until onion is limp and meat has lost its redness. Add herbs, rice, lemon juice, salt, and pepper. Mix well. Place a tablespoon of filling in the center of the underside of a grape leaf, shape with teaspoon into a cylinder, then fold leaf-edges over each end of leaf. Roll leaf into a cigar-shape, beginning at the base and rolling toward the apex. Stack rolls in a heavy iron or aluminum kettle and add cold water to reach top layer of leaves. Simmer for 45 minutes to 1 hour. *Serves 6.*

Pork and Red Cabbage

Red cabbage and apples complement each other very nicely. When pork sausage is added, you have the main dish for a colorful, appetizing meal. This combination wears its German heritage well.

1 pound pork sausage
4 to 6 red apples, unpeeled, cored, and sliced thin
1 head red cabbage
1 teaspoon salt
1 tablespoon flour
3 tablespoons cider vinegar or red wine
3 tablespoons water
2 tablespoons brown sugar

Fry pork sausage until pale brown, about 5 minutes. Drain off all fat. With a fork, break it up into small bits. Remove core from cabbage, cut into sections, and shred coarsely. Mix salt, sugar, and flour, and add water gradually, stirring until smooth. Combine with vinegar and pour over meat mixture. Toss and stir until thoroughly blended. Combine sausage, cabbage, and apples, turn into a 4-quart greased casserole, and bake at 350° for 1 hour. *Serves 4 generously.*

Pork and Kraut

The German and Polish immigrants introduced sauerkraut, a welcome and appetizing addition to winter meals.

4 pork hocks (¾ pound each) or 4 pounds pigtails
2 large onions, sliced thin
4 tablespoons bacon drippings
½ cup celery, sliced thin (optional)
2 cups boiling water
1½ teaspoons salt
¼ teaspoon pepper
1 to 2 pounds sauerkraut
¼ cup brown sugar
½ cup barley (optional)
2 potatoes, cut in ¼ inch cubes

Brown meat and onions in 4 tablespoons bacon drippings. Add celery, water, salt, and pepper. Cover and simmer 3 hours, or until meat is tender. Add sugar, kraut and juices, barley, and potatoes, and about ¼ cup additional water if needed. Mix lightly, cover tightly, and simmer 1 hour longer. *Serves 4.*

Note: Bohemian cooks added 1 clove garlic, 1 tart apple, diced, and a bay leaf to their sauerkraut.

Stuffed Cabbage

The few Poles and Bohemians who came to southern Illinois in the 1800s introduced their own method of cooking cabbage. This simple recipe is only one of many used by Eastern European and Russian homemakers.

1 firm head cabbage
1 pound ground pork shoulder
1 cup cooked rice
1 cup sauerkraut, drained
1 onion, minced
1 teaspoon salt
½ teaspoon pepper
½ cup water

After cutting core out of cabbage, cover with boiling water and let stand for 10 minutes, until the leaves separate easily. Combine pork, rice, onion, and seasonings, and set aside. Separate the cabbage leaves and pat dry. With a sharp knife, cut a V at the tough center end of each large leaf. Arrange a smaller cabbage leaf in the center of each large leaf. Spoon one or two tablespoons of the filling into the center of the small leaf. Spread half of the sauerkraut over bottom of cooking pan or kettle. Roll up stuffed cabbage leaves by folding into flat round balls, and place carefully over the sauerkraut bed. Cover rolls with remaining sauerkraut. Add water and simmer for 45 minutes. This is delicious served with sour cream. *Serves 6.*

Herb Omelet

Being devout Catholics, the French homemakers saw to it that their families observed the fasting days and Lenten regulations to the letter. Eggs, fish, and cheese dishes kept their families well fed and, we hope, happy.

6 eggs
1 teaspoon cold water
Salt and pepper
1 tablespoon chopped parsley
1 tablespoon chives, minced
1 teaspoon fresh tarragon leaves, chopped
1 teaspoon fresh thyme leaves, chopped
1 tablespoon onion, minced
½ small garlic clove, minced very fine

Beat eggs with 1 teaspoon cold water, add salt and pepper, and continue beating until frothy. Mix herbs and chop together with onion and garlic until very fine. Melt butter in heated omelet pan and add herbs. Pour eggs over herbs. Stir several times, and shake pan gently to prevent the eggs from sticking. Gently stir the uncooked eggs on top so they will cook. Try not to pierce the delicate brown cooked surface. Tilt pan and roll omelet out onto heated plate. Fold over, brush top with melted butter, and serve at once. *Serves 4.*

Note: Other fillings which may be spread over the omelet before folding: Grated cheese, sautéed mushrooms, sausages, ½ cup chopped leftover meat, or vegetables.

Hard-Boiled Eggs with Onions

This is as good a summer dish for the family today as it was for a French family of the American Bottoms.

6 large onions
3 tablespoons olive oil
6 hard-boiled eggs

2 tablespoons bread crumbs
2 tablespoons butter
3 tablespoons flour
Salt and pepper
3 tablespoons grated cheese
1 cup milk
½ teaspoon dry mustard
¼ cup cream

Skin onions and cut in thin slices. Cook in olive oil until soft but not browned. Cut the hard-boiled eggs in thin slices. Grease a small, narrow, deep glass or earthenware baking dish and line with 1 tablespoon bread crumbs. Place a layer of onions in the bottom; top with a layer of egg slices. Repeat until all of eggs and onions have been used.

To make sauce: Melt butter in a saucepan. Stir in flour, salt, and pepper. Add milk gradually and stir until the mixture thickens and almost boils. Add 2 tablespoons grated cheese, mustard, and cream. Simmer for 5 minutes. Pour over eggs and onions. Mix remaining cheese with 1 tablespoon bread crumbs. Dot with butter. Brown under broiler for about 6 to 10 minutes and serve immediately. *Serves 6.*

Wild Game and Fish

Wild Game and Fish

Wild Goose

With the several wildlife refuges in southern Illinois being visited by hundreds of thousands of waterfowl each autumn, young cooks are seeking advice from their grandmothers on cooking the wild geese which their husbands bring home, smiling broadly and swaggering a bit.

1 6-pound goose

Dry-pluck goose as much as possible, reserving the down feathers for stuffing pillows. Dunk the bird in a bucket of boiling water to loosen pinfeathers and stubborn outer feathers. Use tweezers if necessary. Soak bird in salt water for several hours to remove the gamy taste which some people find unappetizing. Place goose in deep kettle and cover with cold water. Parboil until fork-tender. Remove from water, cool slightly, rub generously with salt and pepper, and insert a whole onion and apple inside the cavity. Lay bird in roasting pan. Cover breast with buttered butcher's paper or a buttered cloth, to prevent it from becoming hard and browning too soon. Baste bird frequently with melted butter and pan juices. Roast at 325° until quite tender, allowing 25 minutes to the pound. *A 6-pound goose will serve 8.*

Note: The goose may be stuffed with a moist dressing. Place an onion inside the cavity while parboiling and discard before stuffing with chopped celery, chopped onion, mashed potatoes, chopped hard-boiled eggs, well seasoned with salt, pepper, lots of butter, and a dash of sweet marjoram.

Wild Duck

If you have never tried to pluck a wild duck, you would do well to follow the old French method of coating the bird with paraffin, letting it harden, and then peeling it off with the feathers. It can be skinned without using paraffin, but takes longer. By the Gay Nineties, wild

57

duck had advanced from an article of food brought in by the hunter who failed to find a large game animal to a much-desired addition to a fashionable dinner in the smart New York restaurants. The favored way of serving it was very rare, after being roasted for 18 to 20 minutes in a preheated 500° oven, basting every 5 minutes.

If the thought of the red juices turns your stomach, follow the conventional method of roasting domestic fowl: Clean duck and rub with salt. Stuff with chopped onion, diced apple and minced celery, if desired. Place breast side up on rack in roasting pan and rub generously with butter. Roast at 350°, allowing 15 minutes per pound. Baste every 15 minutes with melted butter and with pan juices. Serve with fried hominy. *Serves 2.*

Wild Turkey

Wild turkeys were plentiful when the Indians roamed these prairies and hills. They are shy creatures and fled from the advancing white man. Willis Hughes, Donna's husband, and an otherwise successful hunter, ruefully admits that old Mr. Turkey has outsmarted him to date. If your menfolk are luckier, here are some cooking guidelines.

If the turkey is old, it is likely to be tough. After plucking and eviscerating it, wash inside and outside with cold water to which a tablespoon of baking soda has been added. Rinse well and immerse in a kettle of boiling water for 10 minutes. Drain well and set aside while preparing stuffing.

Clean giblets and parboil. Save broth. Mix:

1 cup chopped celery
2 hard-boiled eggs, chopped
1 medium onion, minced
1 cup bread crumbs
¼ cup butter, melted
Salt and pepper to taste
Pinch of sage (optional)
Pinch of rosemary (optional)
Giblets, chopped fine

Stuff turkey and place on rack in roasting pan, breast side down. Rub well with melted butter and dust with salt and pepper. Pour about a pint of the broth in which giblets were cooked around the turkey. Bake uncovered at 375° for about 20 minutes. Remove from oven and turn breast side up. Lay a sheet of heavy buttered paper over breast to prevent excessive dryness. Continue roasting, basting every ½ hour with pan juices. Add more broth if needed. Test for doneness by gently working drumstick back and forth. If it moves easily, the bird is done. Cooking time: about 3 hours. *Serves 6 to 8.*

Rabbit Deluxe

The hunter's wife became more adventurous in her cooking as the family finances permitted the use of more elaborate ingredients for the preparation of meals. When I watched a two-year-old grand-nephew gobbling stuffed olives at a family dinner recently, I was reminded that I was fourteen years old before I even saw one. A girl friend had an older brother who treated us to a whole jar of these exotic treats when I visited her.

1 rabbit
¼ pound butter
1 to 2 ounces rye whiskey
1 cup chicken broth
20 tiny pickled onions (optional)
20 stuffed olives (optional)
1 clove garlic
2 bay leaves
½ teaspoon thyme
2 slices fried bacon, crumbled, with drippings
½ cup sauterne
Bouquet garni (1 carrot, 1 2-inch strip of celery, 1 sprig of parsley, tied together)

Disjoint rabbit, wash, and dry. Dust all pieces with salt and pepper. Roll in flour and place in heavy skillet in which butter has been melted. Brown all pieces, then remove to a shallow pan. Pour whiskey over the pieces and flame. Place rabbit pieces in a large pot, pour all ingredients except wine over them, and simmer, covered, for about 1½ to 2 hours, until tender. Remove vegetable garni and discard. Thicken gravy with 2 or 3 tablespoons flour rubbed into 1 tablespoon butter. Just before serving, add wine and stir well. *A young rabbit will serve 4.*

Note: Dumplings make a pleasing accompaniment to this dish. For recipes, see section, "Dumplings, Noodles, Stuffings."

Hasenpfeffer

The jugged hare is another of those specialties served up by our German grandmothers. By this time the reader has noted the generous use of vinegar in meat cookery, which stresses the importance of the vinegar barrel in pioneer households.

Clean and cut 1 rabbit into serving pieces. Place in a crock or jar and cover with a marinade of:

¼ cup vinegar
3 bay leaves
2 teaspoons salt
1 large onion, sliced
10 whole cloves
8 peppercorns
1¼ cups water

Add a little more vinegar and water if needed, to completely cover rabbit. Cover container tightly and set in refrigerator or in cold room for at least 2 days. When ready to cook, remove rabbit from marinade, drain, coat with flour, salt lightly, and fry in a heavy skillet in which ⅓ cup of lard has been melted. Turn frequently, and when all pieces are golden brown, add 1 cup of the strained marinade to which 2 tablespoons of brown sugar have been added. Cover and simmer for 1 hour, or until tender. Add 1 cup of sour cream immediately before serving; heat but do not boil. *Serves 6.*

Note: Squirrel may be prepared in the same manner.

Fried Squirrel

Donna Hughes fries squirrel just like her grandmother did. Her husband Willis carries on the hunting tradition and brings the little animals in frequently during the season. He is teaching Shannon to shoot, and Shannon can hardly wait until he grows up and can go hunting too.

1 young squirrel
2 cups lard
Salt
Pepper
Flour

Cut squirrel in serving pieces, wash in cool clean water, and drain. Heat lard in heavy skillet. If a stout paper bag is handy, pour a cup of flour into it, add 1 tablespoon salt and 1 teaspoon pepper. Shake one piece of meat at a time in the bag until well coated. Place in skillet, cover, and fry until well browned and tender, turning each piece so it will brown evenly. *Serves 4.*

Squirrel Stew

Avis McNeill Walker, my father's cousin, remembers squirrel stew which her grandmother made. Her grandfather Blair preferred hunting to farming, so wild game was plentiful in their household.

3 young squirrels
1 green pepper, minced
2 medium onions, chopped
2 medium potatoes, diced
¼ cup celery, chopped fine
Salt and papper to taste
¼ teaspoon dried red pepper seeds
1 cup cooked rice

Cut squirrels into serving pieces and cover with cold water. Add salt to taste and simmer until tender, about 2 hours. Remove meat from bones, chop in 2-inch pieces, and return to broth. Bring to a boil and add all ingredients except rice. Cook about 30 minutes, or until vegetables are done. Add rice, pepper, and more salt if needed, and reheat. Serve with fresh homemade bread and a green salad. *Serves 8.*

Quail

These little birds were still plentiful around here in southern Illinois when I was a child, and my dad, an excellent shot, brought plenty of them home for us to feast on. My mother usually fried the breasts only, as she did chicken. On occasion she baked them, basting them frequently with butter. Quail may also be broiled, and a platter of them will tempt the appetite of almost anyone.

To broil: Pick, draw, and clean birds. Season with salt and pepper and rub liberally with butter. Wrap a strip of bacon around each bird and truss well with string. Place on broiler under a low flame. Cook from 5 to 20 minutes, turning frequently. Remove bacon and string and arrange quail on heated platter. Garnish with sprigs of parsley.

To make gravy: Thicken drippings with 2 tablespoons flour, add milk or hot water for desired consistency, and cook over low heat, stirring constantly, for 10 minutes. Season with salt and pepper. Strain if a smooth gravy is desired, reheat and serve. *Serve 1 bird per person.*

Note: Doves and other small game birds may be cooked as above. These small birds may be split down the back for broiling.

Pheasant

Pheasant and wild rice go together like ham and eggs or chicken and dumplings. And when the mighty hunter gives you the bird, you should know what to do with it. Grandmother did.

1 pheasant, 2½ to 3 pounds

Clean bird well. Stuff cavity with chopped celery leaves and parsley. If you feel like it, add one tart apple, unpeeled, cored, and chopped coarsely. Rub bird with salted butter and roast, uncovered, at 350°, allowing 15 to 20 minutes per pound. Baste frequently with lots of butter, as pheasant is likely to be rather dry. Spoon drippings over bird after removing from oven and serve the juices in a gravy boat. Wild rice is the natural accompaniment. *Serves 4.*

Pheasant in Grape Leaves

The Indians and campfire cooks had a few tricks up their sleeves which are worth preserving. See section, "Pickling, Preserving, Jams and Jellies," for preserving grape leaves, or purchase them from your supermarket's gourmet section.

1 pheasant, 2½ to 3 pounds

In a small saucepan, melt ¼ pound butter. Add ½ teaspoon pepper and 1 teaspoon salt. Rub bird well inside and outside with this butter.

Place a layer of grape leaves on bottom of a heavy earthenware casserole which is equipped with a tight-fitting lid. Pour 2 tablespoons of butter into bird cavity, wrap bird with grape leaves, and place breast-side up in casserole. Pour remainder of butter over bird and cover casserole tightly. Bake at 350° in preheated oven for 45 minutes. Do not remove cover until ready to serve. *Serves 4.*

Note: Prairie chickens, quail, doves etc., may also be cooked in a shroud of grape leaves. Follow directions given above.

Roast Prairie Chicken

Certain areas of southern Illinois are visited each hunting season by sportsmen. The prairie chicken is still found here and there.

Cling to the fervent hope that your mighty hunter will present the fowl cleaned and ready for cooking. Wash well and season the inside with about ½ teaspoon salt. Place over the breast a piece of body fat or a cloth which has been soaked well in melted butter. Roast the chicken uncovered in a moderate oven, 350°, and allow about 1¼ hours cooking time. Baste occasionally with drippings and season with salt when about half done. Remove cloth for the last ½ hour of roasting time, to finish browning.

If the chicken is stuffed, allow 15 to 20 minutes longer for cooking. Wild rice makes a savory stuffing; or you may substitute brown rice or even white rice.

If you plan to include the giblets, clean and chop them and drop into 4 cups cold water. Add ½ teaspoon salt and simmer while preparing other ingredients.

1 cup wild rice (or substitute)
¼ cup butter
2 tablespoons chopped onion
1 tablespoon chopped green pepper
¼ cup chopped celery
3 or 4 sprigs parsley
½ teaspoon rosemary (optional)

Remove giblets from broth with slotted spoon and set aside. Stir wild rice into broth and simmer until almost tender, about 45 minutes. Stir occasionally. Melt butter in skillet. Add onion, green pepper, and celery, and sauté for about 3 minutes. Chop giblets fine, and stir into mixture. Drain rice. Combine with onion-pepper mixture and add parsley, rosemary, salt, and pepper. Stuff loosely into cavity of bird. Spoon remainder around bird in roasting pan, or turn into greased casserole to bake at the same time the chicken is roasting. You should have about 4 cups of stuffing. Roast at 350°. Baste occasionally. *Serves 4.*

Muskrat

This aquatic animal is not generally regarded as food for people, but wives of southern Illinois hunters say they are not unlike squirrels. Donna Hughes of Grand Tower cooks muskrat like this:

After the animal is skinned, cut up as you would a squirrel. Be sure to remove the musky glands. Soak the pieces in salt water for an hour, drain, wipe dry, and rub well with salt and pepper. Coat with flour and fry in lard or oil. After the pieces are well browned, lower heat, cover skillet tightly, and cook for 30 minutes longer, or until quite tender. *Serves 4.*

Baked Raccoon

When I let it be known that I had never eaten baked raccoon, and wondered how it compared with opossum, one was made available to me by Russell Elliott of Grand Tower. It is really delicious. A bit on the fatty side but that assures its tenderness. The meat is dark, very succulent, and its flavor is unlike any other wild game I have sampled, not gamy at all.

1 raccoon, cleaned and skinned

Soak raccoon in salted water for a couple hours. Drain, cover with cold water, add 1 tablespoon salt, and boil gently for 1 hour. It should be tender by then. Place flat on rack in roasting pan (so the flesh will not absorb the fatty drippings); surround with parboiled, halved sweet potatoes; and dust with salt, pepper, and crumbled summer savory. Bake, uncovered, for 45 minutes to 1 hour at 375°. Baste once or twice. Serve on platter, surrounded with sweet potatoes. *Serves 6 to 8.*

Baked Opossum and Sweet Potatoes

'Possum and sweet 'taters is a lusty dish for robust diners, and those who have tried it like it. Skinning the animal is an art your hunter friend or mate has mastered as he will want to save the hide for tanning, so presumably he will hand the carcass to you ready to cook.

Soak opossum in salted water for about 12 hours. Remove from the salty bath, place in a deep kettle, and barely cover with hot water. Boil until tender, about 1 hour, depending on the animal's age. Have ready:

6 sweet potatoes, parboiled and peeled
2 cups stock
Salt and pepper

When ready to bake, lay opossum out flat on rack in roasting pan, so the flesh will not absorb the fatty drippings. Surround with thick slices of sweet potatoes; salt and pepper generously. Add 2 cups stock and bake at 400° until nicely browned, about 45 minutes to 1 hour. Serve on platter, with the sweet potatoes. Garnish with a generous amount of parsley. *Will serve 6.*

Note: Wild greens will go well with this, cooked, or raw as a salad.

Fried Rattlesnake

While I was working on this wild game section, Donna Hughes, who has been mentioned elsewhere in this book as an expert cook of wild game, telephoned me to ask if I would be interested in a gift of rattlesnake meat. I was. Her husband and his hunting companions had killed three of these reptiles that morning, two of them with one shot. It was skinned and cleaned, and she handed it to me in a fancy plastic bag, which I promptly dropped and screamed. When I recovered sufficiently I cut off some of the steaks and fried them as I do chicken. The meat is white, firm, and skimpy on the bony structure.

Assuming you have hunters among your friends, and one hands you a skinned rattler some time, cut it into pieces about 2 inches long, using your kitchen shears instead of a knife, roll in flour which has been seasoned well with salt and pepper, and fry in a skillet in 1 inch of heated lard or other fat.

Once you and your guests enter into the spirit of the occasion, you should enjoy your meal. A glass of homemade mead, dandelion or elderberry wine might help overcome your reluctance to tackle the dish.

Buffalo Roast

The native bison, or buffalo, had left southern Illinois and pushed westward before the white settlers began to arrive in large numbers. The Indian hunting tribes who roamed the area did kill them, and left proof of their doing so. John W. Allen, the late southern Illinois historian, wrote of a picture of a buffalo in Johnson County, known to the early settlers as the Indian Buffalo painting. The Indians and Mountain Men who moved westward ahead of the permanent settlers found the tongue and the hump very tasty, broiled over the campfire; also the ribs.

After the great herds fled this part of the country, to be nearly exterminated by professional white hunters for their hides, the government finally established preserves in a couple of the Plains states, where the animals have increased somewhat under this protection. Buffaloburgers can be found here and there, now and then, and I have been informed that buffalo roasts may be obtained if one knows how to go about it.

The lucky housewife who comes by a buffalo roast would find it more appetizing if marinated in vinegar with onion slices and spices for a day or so before cooking. (See Beef Cookery in section, "Meats.") Roasting in a 350° oven, basting frequently with the marinade, will provide meat to satisfy the craving of a wild-game enthusiast. *A 3-pound buffalo roast will serve 6 people.*

As this is being written, a writer for an organic gardening and farming magazine reports that progress has been made in breeding buffalo with beef cattle. The hybrid, called Beefalo, feeds on grass alone, matures faster and weighs heavier than grain-fed cattle, and produces very tender meat. If this higher-protein, lower fat content beefalo survives, there will undoubtedly be glad cries of joy from American consumers, as the article also predicts lower prices for the new meat because of lower feeding cost.

Venison Roast

Deer meat was a staple enjoyed by the early settlers. The deer population has increased markedly in southern Illinois in recent years, following the establishment of wildlife preserves and control of the slaughter. Several thousand are killed each fall during the hunting season. An assortment of venison roasts and steaks tucked away in freezers is a sort of status symbol nowadays.

6-pound venison roast
6 or 7 strips bacon
Handful of juniper berries (optional)
Salt and pepper
Flour

Press juniper berries into flesh of roast, lard with strips of bacon, and roast uncovered in 450° oven for 30 minutes. Reduce heat and continue to cook at 300°, allowing 20 minutes to the pound. Baste frequently with hot water and later on with the pan juices as they accumulate. When cooked to the desired doneness, remove from roasting pan and make gravy by adding flour (to thicken) to the juices and simmering for 15 minutes. *Serves 10 to 12.*

Note: If the venison seems tough, the roast may be marinated in seasoned vinegar for 12 hours before roasting. The marinade can be used for basting. See Beef Cookery in section, "Meats."

Venison Steaks

6 steaks
Marinade (see Beef Cookery in section, "Meats")

Marinate for 3 to 4 hours in prepared marinade, or in wine vinegar. Drain on paper towels. Broil over hot open fire or under broiler until barely browned—about 3 minutes. The steaks will be tough if overcooked. Serve immediately. *Serves 6.*

Venison Ribs

The Indians and the woodsmen threaded these ribs on green sticks which they held over the open fire. Allow generous servings. They are good, good, good.

3 pounds ribs

Cut ribs in pieces about 3 inches long. Broil quickly. *Do not overcook.* Serve with butter or drippings, well seasoned with salt, pepper, and juniper berries if you can find any. *Serves 3 or 4.*

Deer Meat Sausage

When deer were plentiful and hogs were scarce, cooks mixed venison and pork to produce a very appetizing combination. A breakfast of this sausage with hominy grits, hot biscuits, scrambled eggs, and plenty of coffee made a man feel like going out to look for a wildcat to whip.

3 pounds venison haunch
3 pounds pork shoulder, trimmed of fat
Salt
Pepper
Sage (optional)
Red pepper

Russell Elliott, who runs the Grand Tower Meat Market and has butchered every kind of wild game brought in to the Wild Game Checking Station, headquartered in his establishment during the hunting season, says the sausage should be made this way:

Grind meat, using medium blade. Add salt, pepper, sage, and red pepper to taste. Mix thoroughly and stuff into casings, using sausage stuffer. A small amount of water, not much more than ½ cup, may be added to the ground meat, for greater ease in handling. The sausage is usually frozen nowadays, but our grandmothers packed it in stone crocks and covered it with melted lard. It may also be smoked for winter use. *Yield: About 6 pounds.*

Fish

The rivers and streams of southern Illinois teemed with fish when the first settlers arrived, and for a long time thereafter. Catfish, bass, crappie, and bluegills seemed to be most plentiful. Catfish weighing over 100 pounds have been taken in the Mississippi and there are still a few old-timers around in the river towns who have their own tales to tell of their struggles to land the monsters, which were usually shipped to St. Louis for sale.

When I was a small child I traveled by wagon with my parents and several other families to spend a weekend on the Big Muddy River. The women passed the time by tending the children and cooking. The men entertained themselves by "hogging" for fish. One of the party would wade and dive in the river until he located a submerged hollow log. The others dispersed at a distance of several hundred feet, then swam or waded, or both, toward the log. Usually at least two or three good-sized catfish would flee into the log, and thence into the waiting hands of the reception committee at the other end of the log. It was fun to watch this charade and we usually had catfish for supper that night.

Catfish

Very few recipes will be found in cookbooks for cooking catfish, yet it is regarded with fondest affection by many southern Illinoisans, particularly those who frequent restaurants and fish markets along the Mississippi and Ohio rivers. Much of it served in these restaurants today is grown in ponds under careful supervision. It was not always so.

To prepare catfish for cooking, remove skin by running a knife down the length of the backbone, loosening skin near the head and stripping it off downward toward the tail. Reverse the fish and repeat process. Slit abdomen and remove entrails. Cut off head and tail. Wash well and drain.

Catfish weighing less than 1 pound may be cooked whole. To fry, roll in yellow cornmeal, sprinkle with salt, and lay in heavy skillet in which at least ½ inch of lard has been melted. Lard should be hot enough to brown a bread cube in about 1 minute. Fry until nicely browned, turn carefully with a spatula or tongs, and brown on other side. Test for doneness with a toothpick. Remove from skillet with spatula, drain on paper towel, and serve hot.

Larger catfish may be cut crosswise into steaks after skinning and removing entrails, head, and tail. Roll in yellow cornmeal and fry same as smaller whole fish.

Bass, Crappie, and Bluegills

These fish must be scaled after removing the entrails. This was the fisherman's duty in our family. If you are faced with this task, it should be done outdoors, using a very sharp knife with a handle you can hang onto, as the scales have a way of flying wild as the scaling knife is wielded—more so in the hands of a novice. Heads and tails are left on the small fish. After being scaled and the fins cut off they should be washed well in cold water, wiped dry, and rolled in salted yellow cornmeal. Fry in hot lard until browned on one side. Turn with a spatula or tongs, and fry other side. Cooking time: About 10 minutes. Allow 2 small fish per person, or more.

Bass weighing 1 pound or more may be cut crosswise into two portions and beheaded. The experts in my family fillet the larger fish. Using a very sharp knife they cut out the fleshy portions, discarding the bones, so that the cook has nice meaty fish steaks to cook. This is easy on the eater too.

Side Dishes

Side Dishes

Asparagus

Asparagus, or "sparrowgrass" as it was called by the old-timers, grew in profusion in the fields and byways, free for the cutting. Properly cooked and not oversauced, the fresh, tender early spring cutting of this delicate vegetable is a treat for the stomach. When my dad walked into the kitchen with a bunch of the newly grown spears, one got the feeling that he had just found part of the gold at the end of the rainbow. Mom cooked it simply.

2 pounds fresh asparagus spears
½ teaspoon salt
1 tablespoon lemon juice
¼ cup butter, melted

Break off spears so they are fairly uniform in length. Leave tips intact. Soak in cold water for a few minutes, to remove any trace of loose dirt. Tie bunch with stout string. Stand stalks upright in boiling salted water in a deep kettle, allowing the tips to extend 1 inch above the water. Cook 10–15 minutes. *Do not overcook.* Drain well. Lay gently in oval bowl and pour combined melted butter and lemon juice over them. (When no lemons were on hand, Mom substituted cider vinegar.) Serve immediately. *Serves 6.*

Asparagus Cheese Casserole

This would have been served as a side dish in Grandmother's day; it may be used as the main entree for a ladies' lunch, or family meal.

2 pounds fresh asparagus
4 slices bacon, fried crisp and crumbled into small bits
1 tablespoon flour
½ cup tomato juice
1 cup shredded cheese
1 tablespoon mustard
2 tablespoons minced onion (optional)

Soak asparagus in water for 15 to 20 minutes, to make sure no dirt clings to tips. Cut in 2-inch long pieces. Cook for 10 to 15 minutes, until pieces can be pierced with a fork but are not mushy. Drain, reserving ¼ cup liquid. Fry bacon and pour off all fat except 1 tablespoon. Blend flour into reserved fat. Combine tomato juice and asparagus liquid and stir slowly into flour paste. Continue stirring until it is smooth. Add shredded cheese and mustard and blend in well. Place asparagus in shallow 2-quart casserole. Pour sauce over asparagus and stir lightly with a fork to make sure it is distributed evenly. Crumble bacon and sprinkle over top. Bake at 375° for 20 minutes or until bubbly. *Serves 6 as a side dish; 4 as a main dish.*

Jerusalem Artichokes

This awkwardly ugly, knobby vegetable is coming back into its own, at last, after being ignored for several generations. A few stores offer recipe cards telling how to cook them. Harold E. Driver, in his book *Indians of North America,* says the Indians around here used them rather extensively. My experience with them has been quite satisfactory; they are usually a conversation dish.

Jerusalem artichokes have a delicate, nutty flavor when served raw, as the Indians undoubtedly did on occasion. When cooked, their flavor is faintly reminiscent of globe artichokes. They are an excellent diabetic food as they are high in food value and in the production of levulose sugars (the sweetest sugar known), which diabetics can eat without any risk. They may be cooked in various ways.

Boiled Jerusalem Artichokes

1½ pounds Jerusalem artichokes

Scrub tubers in cold running water, using a very stiff vegetable brush. Cook in boiling, salted water to cover, for 10 to 12 minutes, or until tender-crisp. *Do not overcook.* Drain, peel, or rub the skin off, cut in cubes or slices, season with melted butter, salt, and pepper. *Serves 4.*

Steamed Jerusalem Artichokes

1½ pounds Jerusalem artichokes

Scrub tubers well. Cook in a very small amount of water in a heavy saucepan with a tight-fitting lid. As soon as the water comes to a boil, turn heat down to avoid scorching. Steam for approximately 20 to 25 minutes until tender-crisp. *Do not overcook.* Peel and serve with melted butter, salt, and pepper. *Serves 4.*

Mashed Jerusalem Artichokes

1½ pounds Jerusalem artichokes

Boil or steam Jerusalem artichokes until tender. Rub off skins and mash or put through a food mill. Season with butter, salt, and pepper. The texture will be more moist and not quite as fluffy as mashed potatoes. *Serves 4.*

Jerusalem Artichokes with Meat

6 to 8 Jerusalem artichokes

Scrub 'chokes and place them around roast for the last 30 minutes of cooking time. An excellent substitute for potatoes. Serve with roast gravy or juices. *Serves 4.*

Note: A cup or two of cubed Jerusalem artichokes may be added to beef stew during the last 15 minutes of cooking.

Beets

Beets were regarded as one of the most useful vegetables in this part of the state, and during the early summer a dish of pickled beets was invariably included among the assortment of vegetables on dinner and supper tables.

Pickled Beets

Wash 10 medium-sized beets and trim tops to 2 inches. Place in kettle, cover with cold water, and simmer until beets are easily pierced with a fork (about 45 minutes to an hour). Remove from fire and drain. Cover with cold water. Peel by slipping skins off with hands. Slice beets into glass or earthenware bowl. Cover with cider vinegar and season with pepper and salt. Chill. *Serves 4.*

Whole Buttered Beets

Harvesting tiny beets was regarded as wantonly extravagant years ago among people we knew. Why not wait until they were twice as large? But the tiny ones tasted twice as good, we thought.

25 to 30 tiny beets 1 inch or less in diameter

Cut off tops of beets, leaving about 2 inches of stems. Wash well. Place in heavy kettle, add cold water, and bring to boil. Simmer until tender, about 30 minutes. Drain and cool. Remove skins by rubbing beets in hands. Trim tails and remove tops. Melt 3 to 4 tablespoons butter in saucepan, add beets, ½ teaspoon salt, several shakes of the pepper box, and set over low flame until heated through. Serve hot. *Serves 6.*

Fried Sweet Corn

Those who have not enjoyed this are missing some of the delights of good eating. The secret is to select young, tender sweet corn only recently parted from the stalk.

6 ears sweet corn
6 strips bacon
2 or 3 tablespoons bacon drippings
Salt and pepper

Fry bacon until crisp in a large heavy skillet. Remove from pan and drain. Pour off drippings except for 2 or 3 tablespoonsful. Remove husks and cornsilks from corn. Scrape grains from cob. Heat bacon drippings and when very hot, spoon corn into pan. Season with salt and pepper. Reduce heat a bit and cook until a light crust begins to form on the bottom. With a large spatula, flip corn over and allow to brown well on other side. Slip corn onto a heated platter, crumble bacon over top, and serve. *Serves 6.*

Kale Ring

An Irish and Scottish dish made with kale and potatoes, but frequently made with cabbage. Traditionally served on All Hallows night (November 1). In the Old Country a plain gold ring, a sixpence, a thimble, and a button were often baked in the mixture. The diner who found the ring could expect to be married within a year; the lucky winner of the sixpence would be wealthy; the thimble winner would earn a living by hard work; and the girl or boy who bit the button would remain single.

1 pound kale (or cabbage) cooked until soft
1 pound potatoes, cooked until soft
2 leeks or green onion tops, chopped
1 cup milk or coffee cream
½ cup butter
Salt, pepper and ⅛ teaspoon mace

Chop cooked kale or cabbage fairly fine. While potatoes are cooking, chop leeks or onion tops and simmer in just enough milk or cream to cover, until soft. Drain potatoes until quite dry, and beat until smooth. Add leeks and milk. Drain kale and blend into the potato mixture until it is light green and fluffy. Season with salt, pepper, and mace. Turn into a deep, heated, lightly greased serving dish. Make a well in the center and pour in enough melted butter to fill the cavity. Serve with a spoonful of melted butter over each portion. *Serves 4 to 6.*

Dandelion Greens

Authorities differ as to the origin of this weed. Most gardeners work on its eradication from their lawns with grim determination. Natural food devotees have learned what their great-grandparents did with it and eat it raw or cooked. My grandfather taught me which weeds were edible in our "sallet-picking" outings, and the "tramp with the golden crown" led all the rest.

1 gallon dandelion greens

Cut leaves with a sharp knife. Discard blossoms and outer leaves, which may be slightly bitter. Wash well in cold water, separating leaves. Parboil for 15 minutes. Drain, rinse in cold water, and cook 10 minutes in ham broth if you have any handy; if not, add 1 tablespoon bacon drippings and ½ teaspoon salt to greens in pot. Sufficient water clings to the leaves for cooking in a heavy pan over very low heat. Serve with vinegar. *Serves 4.*

Note: Mustard and turnip greens and beet tops may be cooked the same way.

Mushrooms with Sherry

For many French families mushroom hunting was, and is a pleasant family pastime, for they could look forward to a dish something like this one.

2 cups mushrooms
3 tablespoons butter
Salt and pepper
1 tablespoon sherry
1 tablespoon dill, chopped very fine

Melt butter in skillet. Slice mushrooms, toss into hot butter, and sauté fairly briskly for 2 to 3 minutes. Remove mushrooms from fire, add sherry and dill. Serve as a side dish with chicken. *Serves 4.*

Peas, Scallions, and Lettuce

The French had no monopoly on fresh-picked garden peas, but they cooked them with flair.

1 pound fresh peas, shelled
1 bunch scallions cut into 1-inch pieces
½ head shredded lettuce
2 slices bacon, diced
Salt and pepper
1 cup water
1 teaspoon butter
2 teaspoons flour

Combine peas, scallions, lettuce, bacon, salt, and pepper in saucepan. Work butter into flour and add 1 cup water gradually, stirring until perfectly smooth. Pour over peas, cover, and simmer gently until tender, about 10 minutes. *Serves 4.*

Black-eyed Peas, or Cowpeas

These are traditionally served on New Year's Day in the South, and by Southerners transplanted in far places, for good luck in the coming year. Some southern Illinoisans who do not grow them substitute navy beans. I've attended New Year's Day open houses where black-eyed peas were skewered on cocktail picks stuck into a grapefruit "to assure your good fortune in the New Year."

They are good eating, fresh or dried. In recent years the frozen-food bins in supermarkets as far west as California have featured them, due to the demands of these transplanted Southerners. To cook fresh black-eyed peas:

2 cups shelled peas
2-inch cube of salt pork, or 6 or 8 ham strips
½ teaspoon salt

Cover peas with cold water, add meat and salt and simmer for 30 minutes, or until tender. *Serves 4.*

Black-eyed Peas

Gather the dried peas for winter use and spread out on screens until thoroughly dry. Shell and store in a fairly cool spot. To cook:

2 cups dried peas
¼ pound salt pork or 1 ham hock

Cover peas with water and soak overnight before cooking. Next day drain and cover with fresh cold water. Cut salt pork into thin slices. If using a ham hock, rinse and add. Simmer for 1 hour, or until tender. Add salt to taste. *Serves 4.*

Squashes and Pumpkins

We are deeply indebted to the American Indians for squashes, and the versatility of these vegetables made them invaluable additions to the early settlers' diets, just as they do for us today. In addition to the various ways of cooking squash as a vegetable, the old-time home-maker could offer her family a tasty squash pie for dessert which they devoured with relish. Of course, pumpkin pie is traditionally associated with Thanksgiving all over the country, although its use as a vegetable has declined. One of the most desirable features of the squash family was that they could be dried and stored for winter use by families who lacked storage space.

Summer squashes include crooknecks, zucchini, scallops or pat-typans. These are best used when young and tender. Among the winter squashes are butternuts, hubbards, acorns, and turbans. They are hard-shelled when mature, and store well. I have kept butternuts almost all through the winter, using them as ornaments in a basket in the kitchen, before cooking them.

Summer Squash

2 small, tender squashes

Peel, if necessary. Slice, scoop out seeds if visible, place in a steamer, set over boiling water, cover, and steam until tender, 10 minutes or less. Season with salt and pepper and serve with melted butter. Chopped dill, parsley, or marjoram may be sprinkled over the top. (Or, mash squash slices, season with salt, pepper, and butter, and whip until fluffy. Drain off any extra water.) *Serves 4.*

Winter Squash

2 Hubbard squashes

Cut squashes in two lengthwise. Scoop out seeds and loose fibers. Place 1 teaspoon butter in each hollow and bake. Fill with buttered and creamed vegetables before serving, if desired. *Serves 4.*

Squash Casserole

Any of the squash family may be used for this dish.

4 cups cooked, drained, mashed squash
½ cup mayonnaise
½ cup grated onion
½ cup sweet pepper, chopped
¼ cup pimiento (optional)
1 cup grated sharp cheese
1 teaspoon sugar
1 egg, beaten

In a large mixing bowl blend all ingredients thoroughly and season with salt and pepper. Pour into well-greased 2-quart casserole and bake at 375° for 30 to 40 minutes, or until lightly browned on top. (Bread or cracker crumbs may be sprinkled over top of casserole before baking, if desired.) Serve hot. *Serves 4.*

Spanish Rice

I never knew how my mother came by this recipe. I only know there was never any left over. While living in southern California I learned that it was a "typical" Spanish-Mexican dish and concluded that it must have been one of those introduced to us "Easterners" around the latter decades of the nineteenth century, when any California recipe was regarded as rather exotic and stylish. Being an adventurous cook, Mom adopted it. Of course there are any number of variations, some oven-cooked, others cooked in a skillet on top of the stove. This is the one we liked best at home.

6 slices bacon
1 bell pepper, chopped fine
1 bell pepper, cut into rings
1 medium onion, minced
1 medium onion, cut in thin slices
1 cup raw rice (not the quick-cook kind)
2 cups cooked tomatoes
Salt and pepper

Fry bacon until crisp, crumble, and set aside. Reserve 2 tablespoons drippings. In same skillet, sauté chopped peppers and onions. Remove from skillet and pour rice into it; add more drippings if needed. Reduce heat and brown rice slowly, stirring frequently. Combine with peppers, onions, and tomatoes, add seasonings, stir well, and spoon into a 2-quart bean pot or deep casserole. Arrange pepper and onion slices on top, sprinkle crumbled bacon over peppers and onions. Cover, and bake at 375° for 1 hour. Add 2 or 3 tablespoons boiling water if rice seems dry. *Serves 6.*

Wild Rice

Although I have been unable to prove beyond a shadow of doubt that wild rice was harvested in southern Illinois, Oliver Perry Medsger mentions that it was grown in many marshy places from Manitoba south to Texas, so we may assume that those early settlers along the backwaters of the rivers bordering the southern tip of the state were able to harvest it in small quantities, or buy it from the Indians who habitually gathered it for winter use.

To serve: Wash 1 cup rice and drop into 3 cups boiling salted water. Boil 45 minutes, or until tender and water is almost all absorbed. Set in a warm place, not over direct heat, and let it alone until it is dry and fluffy. Season with butter, salt, and pepper to taste and serve with fowl or game. Or use as stuffing. *Serves 4.*

Sautéed Potatoes

The French home cooks also lifted the lowly potato out of the ordinary by adding fresh herbs when frying them.

2 pounds potatoes (6 to 8)
5 tablespoons butter
1 tablespoon chopped fresh rosemary, thyme, or other fresh herb
Salt and pepper

Peel potatoes and place in a deep saucepan. Cover with cold water and bring to a boil. Cook until barely tender. Drain and dry well in a cloth. Cut in thick slices. Melt butter in heavy frying pan. Add potatoes, salt, and pepper. Shake over fire until they begin to brown. Add half of chopped rosemary, cover, and fry until golden brown, about 20 minutes. Stir gently several times during cooking. Turn into heated serving dish, sprinkle with remainder of rosemary and serve. *Serves 4 to 6.*

Irish Potato Cakes

As one would expect, the Irish have contributed these neat little tasty patties to the list of potato recipes.

4 medium-sized potatoes (russets are best)
2 tablespoons melted butter
½ teaspoon salt
1 cup flour (approximately)
1 egg, if desired

Peel and cook potatoes and mash well. Add butter and salt to taste. Beat egg and stir in. Add flour to form a stiff smooth dough. Roll out on a floured board to a circle about ¼ inch thick. Cut into circles with a cookie cutter, or in triangles with a knife. Sprinkle dough and griddle lightly with corn meal. Bake about 5 to 10 minutes on each side until light brown. Best served immediately. *Serves 4.*

Potato Pancakes

A change from the usual ways of preparing potatoes, introduced by the Germans and Bohemians.

6 medium potatoes (2 cups) grated coarsely
1 small onion, grated fine

6 tablespoons sweet cream
2 eggs, beaten
4 tablespoons flour
½ teaspoon salt
Dash garlic powder or liquid (optional)

Drain grated potatoes on a cloth and transfer to mixing bowl. Add grated onion and remaining ingredients, in order given. Mix well and shape in size desired. Fry in ¼ inch or more hot fat, patting out with spoon to make pancakes as thin as possible without pulling apart. Turn and brown other side. Remove to heated platter and sprinkle with sugar before serving, or serve with applesauce. *Yield: About 12 to 16.*

Note: These are a good accompaniment for fried young squirrel or chicken.

Hominy

Once regarded as a rather plebian dish, hominy seems to have acquired greater status in recent years. Food editors are vying with one another for new and different combinations with hominy as the base.

The name "hominy" comes from the Algonquin Indian word for parched corn. It is made from dried field, or Indian corn, not the sweet corn which graces dinner tables in the summertime. In another part of the book I have included my father's hominy-making process—a fall ritual in our family. (See section, "Pickling, Preserving, Jams and Jellies.") Hominy and grits are staple Southern dishes. Easily obtainable in tin cans today, in past years it could be purchased in bulk in the general stores. The canned hominy bears faint resemblance to the more robust homemade product. My mother frequently prepared hominy like this:

2 cups hominy
½ cup breadcrumbs
4 tablespoons butter, or more
Salt and pepper

Heat hominy and combine with bread crumbs which have been toasted lightly in butter. (Those with gourmet leanings might wish to slice 6 or 8 mushrooms and cook with the bread crumbs.) Season with salt and pepper. Cover skillet and cook over low heat for five minutes. Serve hot. *Serves 4.*

Fried Hominy

In the very early spring when the wintered-over potatoes are beginning to sprout and the new potatoes are not yet large enough to "grabble," this is great with fried ham, or the meat of your choice.

2 cups hominy
4 slices bacon, cut into ¼ inch strips
2 green onions, sliced (including tops)
½ teaspoon salt
⅛ to ¼ teaspoon pepper

Fry bacon until crisp. Drain off all fat except for about 2 table-spoonsful. Add hominy and cook for 5 minutes, stirring occasionally. Add seasonings, mix thoroughly and serve. *Serves 4.*

Baked Hominy

A change from potatoes, which can bake in the oven along with the last hour of cooking the roast.

2 cups hominy
4 eggs, beaten
4 tablespoons butter, melted
1 teaspoon salt
½ teaspoon pepper
½ cup water

Combine ingredients in order given, mix well, and turn into greased casserole. Bake at 350° for 1 hour. *Serves 4.*

Grits

Grits are merely coarsely ground hominy. Those who maintain that white-corn grits are superior to those ground from yellow corn might be compared to people who insist that white-shelled eggs are better than those with brown shells, or vice versa. At any rate, grits have now found their way into the supermarkets. Fortified with a slice of home-cured ham, red-eye gravy, hot biscuits, butter, apple butter, and, of course, a big spoonful of grits, anyone should be able to face whatever the day might bring with equanimity.

1 cup grits
3 cups water

1 teaspoon salt
1 teaspoon butter

Bring water to a rolling boil. Add salt and butter. Drizzle in the grits, while stirring constantly. After mixture has thickened, reduce heat to lowest possible level, and cook for at least an hour. Serve warm with milk, or molasses and cream, or simply a dollop of butter. A housewife of the 1860s wrote that this dish is "very nutritive, wholesome and easily digested. Samp, hominy, and mush made in this way are much more desirable for suppers than meat." *Serves 4.*

Mush

Food of all kinds was plentiful at our house, but for some reason my dad decreed one summer day that once each week our supper would consist of corn bread, mush, and milk. I expressed my objection to this suggested menu in no uncertain terms, and was invited to leave the table, which I did. I found part of an apple pie in the icebox on the back porch and dined on it. The mush-corn bread suppers were discontinued, probably due to a high-level conference between my mother and dad.

1 cup cornmeal
3 cups water
¼ teaspoon salt

Add water to cornmeal and stir until all lumps are removed. Add salt and cook slowly until quite thick. Serve with milk or cream. The judicious application of honey, molasses, or sugar might be in order. A dab of butter does no harm either. Pat any leftover mush into a rectangular baking dish, or make a fresh batch if none is left. Let set overnight. In the morning, cut in ½ inch thick slices and fry in butter until browned. Serve with syrup, jam, or jelly. *Serves 4.*

Aunt Nell's Hush Puppies

Several Southern regions lay claim to the origin of the hush puppy. Since most of the earliest southern Illinois settlers came from the Carolinas, Tennessee, Virginia, and Kentucky, we would like to believe that these delectable fritters came from one of those states. Each cook had her own unwritten version. This one most closely resembles Aunt Nell's own recipe, which she mixes up as an accompaniment to whatever fish may have been caught that day.

1 egg
2½ cups corn meal
1 cup buttermilk
1 teaspoon salt
1 teaspoon soda
1 teaspoon sugar (optional)
1 medium-sized onion, minced

Beat egg, add buttermilk, and stir in dry ingredients. Add onion and mix well. Shape into balls about 2 inches in diameter and fry in fat used for frying fish. Serve while hot. *Yield: 12 to 16.*

Potato Salad

Like the squash, the potato originated in South America, from whence it traveled northward through Central America and Mexico to the North American Indians. They in turn introduced it to the early English explorers. It was introduced to our forefathers across the Atlantic and of course we are all familiar with the fact that it saved the lives of thousands of famine-stricken Irish. It was reintroduced to the then United States and has become known as the Irish potato. Most main farm meals are built around the potato and in preparing our meals at home our mother invariably began with detailing one of us girls to "peel the potatoes." This potato salad holds its own most admirably for any kind of meal, indoors or outdoors.

3 quarts cooked, sliced potatoes (they may be cubed)
¼ cup sugar
1 cup vinegar
1 or 2 tablespoons cornstarch
1 cup water
1 tablespoon dry mustard
2 tablespoons ham drippings
1 tablespoon celery seeds
2 tablespoons minced onion
½ cup diced celery
½ cup chopped bell pepper (optional)
2 or 3 hard-boiled eggs, chopped (optional)

Scrub potatoes and place in large kettle. Simmer until fork-tender. Remove from fire, drain, and set aside until cold. Peel and slice or cut in cubes. The eggs may be boiled with the potatoes. Combine sugar and vinegar. Stir cornstarch and mustard into water and mix until all lumps are removed. Add sugar-vinegar mixture and ham drippings and cook over low flame until thickened. Blend in celery seeds, onion, celery, and pepper. Pour over potatoes while hot and toss until all potato pieces are coated. Garnish with egg slices. *Serves 10 to 12.*

German Potato Salad

A traditional standby for a cold supper or a picnic. A survey of German senior citizens brought out the fact that they preferred this to potato salad with mayonnaise.

15 tiny boiled potatoes, peeled
1 medium onion, chopped fine
¼ pound bacon, fried until crisp and well drained
½ cup chopped celery
¼ cup potato water
1 tablespoon flour
½ cup vinegar
¼ cup sugar
Salt and pepper

Cook potatoes until barely tender and drain, reserving ¼ cup liquid. Place them in a large mixing bowl. Fry onions and celery in 2 tablespoons bacon drippings until limp but not brown. Add reserved potato water. Blend flour and vinegar to a smooth paste, add salt, sugar, pepper, and stir into mixture in skillet. Crumble bacon over potatoes. Pour dressing from skillet into bowl over potatoes, lifting and turning until all potatoes are coated. Serve warm. *Serves 6 to 8.*

Note: A couple of hard-boiled chopped eggs may be added for color, if desired.

Old-Fashioned Wilted Lettuce

In the early days, it was a constant struggle to keep rabbits and deer out of the lettuce patch, and when wild greens were plentiful some housewives simply didn't bother with it. As the wild game retreated before the oncoming settlers, and tastes became more refined, the lettuce patch became a fixture in the vegetable garden. Wilted leaf lettuce was a part of most supper tables, and is still enjoyed during the spring and early summer growing season.

1 quart leaf lettuce (Simpson, oak leaf, red leaf, romaine, or your own choice)

2 slices bacon, fried crisp and crumbled
1 tiny green onion, chopped
2 tablespoons bacon drippings
¼ cup cider or tarragon vinegar
1 tablespoon sugar
½ teaspoon salt
Pepper
1 hard-boiled egg, chopped (optional)

Wash lettuce and tear into bits (*do not cut*). Pat dry and place in a large mixing bowl. Combine crumbled bacon with chopped onion and sprinkle over lettuce. Add sugar, salt, and pepper and toss lightly. Heat bacon drippings and stir in vinegar. Remove from fire and pour over lettuce. Toss. Garnish with hard-boiled egg and serve immediately. *Serves 4.*

Note: Some old-timers covered the bowl with a serving plate, to really wilt the lettuce.

Day Lily Buds

Roadsides, abandoned farmsteads, and old-fashioned gardens in this part of the state are highlighted with orange-colored patches each June. There was a large patch of these common day lilies on our old home place, not quite hidden by several hundred madonna lily plants cultivated by my brother Ben Allen. Neighbors would come asking for day lily blossoms for weddings, funerals, and other occasions, and my mother never refused them. One time a neighbor asked for several bakets of them to be used as church decorations for her daughter's wedding. Mom told her to help herself, but warned her that the blossoms folded up tightly as the sun set. Mom was invited to the wedding, of course, and ever afterward told us in the family with some amusement that she sat during the twilight ceremony watching the baskets full of blossoms lose their color as the flowers closed.

It never occurred to us that the day lilies were edible until research was started for this book. I am sure we would have tried them had we known. Here's a recipe, for those willing to try. They taste quite like tender young asparagus, and fresh summer savory is better than dried.

1 quart of not quite-opened day lily buds
¼ teaspoon dried summer savory, or 1 teaspoon chopped fresh summer savory

¼ **teaspoon salt**
1 teaspoon butter

Remove buds from stems, wash, and drain. Place in a saucepan, add salt, barely cover with hot water, and boil for 4 to 5 minutes, until barely tender. Crush savory, or chop it if fresh, and sprinkle over buds. Add butter and stir gently until melted. Serve at once. *Serves 4.*

French-Fried Elderberry Blossoms

The Poles and Bohemians grow lyrical over fried squash blossoms, which led me to do some research on the versatile elderberry blossoms. Sure enough, this treatment is quite old, and as elderberries grow throughout this end of the state I tried this dish.

Two large blossom heads will yield about 2 dozen clusters of frying size. Handle very carefully to prevent the tiny blossoms from falling. Dunk gently in clean water and lay on paper towels to drain. Snip off clusters about the size of a walnut. Prepare a thin batter:

1½ cups bread flour
1 teaspoon salt
2½ teaspoons baking powder
2 eggs
1 tablespoon melted butter
1¼ cups milk

Sift flour before measuring and resift with salt and baking powder. Beat eggs lightly and add butter and milk. Make a well in the center of the dry ingredients. Pour in the liquid ingredients and stir lightly. Heat 1 cup cooking oil or lard in deep skillet. Test by dropping a bread cube into the fat. If it sizzles you are ready for action. Dip each cluster into the batter, coating well, and drop into the cooking fat. As soon as they turn golden brown, remove with a slotted spoon, and place on folded paper towels to drain. Serve with elderberry syrup, your favorite not-too-strongly-flavored syrup, or powdered sugar. *Serves 6.*

Dumplings, Noodles, Stuffings,

Dumplings, Noodles, Stuffings,

Ma Hale's Dumplings

There is a small restaurant in a little town on the Mississippi—Grand Tower—where the tradition of bountiful southern Illinois meals is being continued. Although Hale's Restaurant is distinctly a twentieth-century institution and came into being later than the turn-of-the-century deadline set for this book, it seems worthy of mention because it typifies the meals served by our grandparents when times improved after the first hard years. Thousands of visitors from all over the country and students from foreign lands who attend Southern Illinois University in Carbondale flock to this restaurant to meet the challenge of the laden tables.

"Ma" (Melissa) Hale cooked in true Southern style. She has passed on to that special place in Heaven reserved for superb cooks, but her recipes are still in use. This one was reduced to family proportions by Mildred Hale, Tom's wife, who learned firsthand from "Ma" Hale exactly how to make these delectable egg dumplings:

6 eggs
1 cup water
4 cups flour (approximately)

Beat eggs and water together until foamy. Stir in flour until dough is fairly stiff. Turn out on floured board and work with hands, until dough is no longer sticky. Roll out on lightly floured board to ⅛ inch thickness. Cut into long strips approximately 1 inch wide and slash strips crosswise into 1½ inch lengths. Lay 1 or 2 at a time in well-seasoned, rich chicken broth. Cook, uncovered for 10 minutes. The absence of salt in the dumplings is not an oversight. They absorb enough seasoning from the broth. They are addictive, fattening, but oh so delicious. *Serves 10 to 12.*

German Egg Dumplings

These dainty little dumplings are well worth the time spent in making them, but too many will transform a dainty little fraulein into a grossly fat hausfrau.

3 eggs, beaten
3 cups sifted flour
1¼ cups milk
1 teaspoon salt
¼ teaspoon nutmeg (optional)
½ teaspoon baking powder
2 tablespoons melted butter
2 tablespoons bread crumbs

Combine all ingredients, except butter and bread crumbs, in order given in a large mixing bowl and beat hard until smooth. Force batter through a large-holed colander into boiling salted water, scraping excess batter from botton of colander with a knife which has been dipped in boiling water. Cover tightly and cook for about 10 minutes, or until done. They should be very light and delicate. Remove with a slotted spoon, drizzle 2 tablespoons of melted butter over dish, and add a sprinkling of crumbs if desired. Excellent with sauerbraten. *Serves 4 to 6.*

Raised Bread Dumplings

Both the Germans and Bohemians lay claim to these light-as-a-feather puffy dumplings. Regardless of their origin they are very good. Perfect with pork and sauerkraut.

1 cake yeast
½ teaspoon sugar
¼ cup lukewarm water
1 cup lukewarm milk
2 eggs, lightly beaten
1 tablespoon salt
4½ cups flour, or more
3 toasted bread slices, diced

Dissolve yeast and sugar in ¼ cup lukewarm water and set aside to cool for about 30 minutes, or until doubled in bulk. Add 1 cup luke-warm milk, eggs, and salt and beat well. Add flour a little at a time, beating well after each addition. Stir in toasted bread cubes. If dough clings to side of bowl, work in more flour. On floured board, divide dough into 3 portions and shape into loaves. Set aside to rise until light (about 45 minutes). Place gently in a large kettle of salted boiling water. Cook for 10 minutes. Turn and cook 10 minutes longer. Remove from kettle and immediately cut both ends with a thread to remove steam and prevent sogginess. Cool slightly, slice, and serve with gravy. *Serves 8.*

Potato Dumplings

German cooks do very interesting things with potatoes too. These are good with fried or roasted chicken.

10 medium-sized potatoes, cooked in skins
4 tablespoons flour
1 teaspoon salt
1 egg, beaten
Croutons

Peel potatoes when slightly cooled and force through ricer, or mash. Add flour, salt, and egg and beat until thoroughly mixed. Cut squares about ½ inch in size from slices of bread and brown lightly in butter. Form potato mixture into 2 to 3-inch balls, pressing one or two croutons into each ball. Drop dumplings one by one into a large kettle of boiling water. Cook for 2 to 3 minutes. Remove with slotted spoon and serve on a platter, garnished with melted butter and chopped parsley. *Serves 8 to 10.*

Egg Noodles

I watched my elderly German cousin Nellie Louden as she mixed her noodle dough, rolled it out deftly and evenly, cut it into neat strips, and draped them over the rack to dry before they were snipped into short, 2-inch lengths to cook with stewed chicken. They had body and real taste.

3 whole eggs
1 teaspoon salt
3 tablespoons melted butter
2½ cups all-purpose flour

Beat eggs slightly and add salt and butter. Stir in flour gradually. This will make a very stiff dough. Divide into three parts for easier handling. Roll each portion out on floured board until about ⅛ inch thick and spread on cloths to dry slightly. Before they are too dry to handle without breaking, roll into cylinders and cut into strips about ½ inch wide. Separate strips and spread apart over rack to dry thoroughly.

This takes several hours. Cut or break into 2-inch lengths and store in glass jars until needed. When ready to cook, drop by handfuls into boiling broth. Cover kettle and simmer for about 20 minutes. *Serves 6 to 8.*

Corn Bread Stuffing

A distinctly Southern dressing which some of my cousins make. Corn bread stuffing gained status when Lady Bird Johnson's favorite variation was published during Lyndon Johnson's presidency.

2 cups corn bread, well crumbled
3 cups dry bread, cut into ½ inch cubes
3 cups broth from cooked giblets
3 eggs, beaten slightly
Turkey or chicken giblets, cooked until tender and chopped fine
1 cup celery, chopped fine
1 cup onion, minced
1 cup light cream
¼ cup melted butter
1 teaspoon (or more) poultry seasoning

Pour broth over bread in large mixing bowl and stir until well moistened. Add eggs and all other ingredients in order given, beating until thoroughly blended. Add more seasoning if needed. Pour into 2-quart casserole or shallow baking pan and bake 1 to 1½ hours at 350° until a nice crust is formed. *Serves 8.*

Note: Of course, this may be used for stuffing the fowl's cavities if desired.

Old Style German Fruit Stuffing

A fruity stuffing, ideal for ducks, geese, pork chops, or spare ribs.

1 loaf stale rye bread
10 dried, pitted prunes, cooked and chopped
6 to 8 tart apples, cored, quartered, and partly cooked
½ to 1 teaspoon cinnamon
¼ cup sugar

Cut or tear bread into ½ inch pieces, discarding heavy crusts. Mix with remaining ingredients and stuff cavities loosely. Fasten openings with skewers, or sew loosely, using heavy string. *Serves 6.*

Grits Dressing

A fairly bland but highly satisfying stuffing for a 5-pound chicken. The grits can be purchased at the grocer's nowadays.

1 cup grits
4 cups water
¼ teaspoon salt
¼ pound butter, melted
1 cup diced celery
12 soda crackers, crushed
1 cup pecans, chopped fine
1 medium-sized onion, minced
Salt and pepper
Rosemary

Combine grits, water, and salt in top of a double boiler set over boiling water and cook until thick, about 45 minutes. Remove from fire and stir in melted butter, celery, soda crackers, pecans, and onions. Add pepper, ½ teaspoon rosemary, and more salt if desired. Mix well and stuff chicken cavities, or turn into greased casserole and bake for 1 hour. *Serves 6.*

Breads, Biscuits, and Pancakes

Breads, Biscuits, and Pancakes

Wheat Bread

Making bread is far more than the dull, drab, routine task of supplying sustenance to one's family. It is the homemaker's sacrifice to those under her care. It is an Experience. Young brides with culinary ambitions and husbands who ask them to entertain a lot yearn to produce the perfect loaf of yeast bread. Many men strive for perfection in breadmaking, as evidenced by Bob Farnsworth's detailed directions below. Whether made from rice, corn, wheat, rye, or any other flour, bread is regarded as the staff of life and is used as the yardstick of a nation's economy and status. This section first deals with the wheat breads made by the people who settled this southern tip of Illinois, and their descendants of whom I am one.

Wheat flour was a great luxury among these southern- and European-born settlers in the early days. The French in the "American Bottoms" grew wheat for their own use, and probably sent small shipments to New Orleans to trade for goods from France. The Saline County history contains an account of one man who recalled that he was eleven years old before he saw wheat growing, and did not taste a wheat-flour biscuit until 1846. Although it was flat, hard, and heavy, it tasted "delicious" to him.

Bob Farnsworth's Bread

Bob isn't strictly a native southern Illinoisan, but he was raised in Missouri just across the river and up a little way, and his sentiments are akin to those of us "Egyptians." His bread is really a treat for his many friends. He is a professional engineer who manufactures doll furniture and cooks as well as his wife Dot, a home economics major, expert homemaker-designer, and full-time partner in their business. Note Bob's directions:

You need a large earthenware bowl, 12 inches in diameter or larger; a small saucepan or kettle; a measuring cup and a mixing spoon; 4 8-inch aluminum baking pans, the one-piece extruded kind, not the ones with folds. Five hours are required for a batch of bread.

Pour 2 cups of milk into saucepan. Heat over a low flame until lukewarm. Test with a fingertip. Pour ½ cup warm water, not tepid—not hot—into the mixing bowl. Sprinkle in 4 envelopes dry yeast and rub with spoon until dissolved. Add 3 tablespoons of sugar and 2 of salt and dissolve. Pour in the warm milk and add 3½ cups flour, unsifted. Stir until flour is mixed with milk mixture, then add 3 tablespoons softened butter and 3 more cups flour. Mix and turn with a big spoon until flour is absorbed and dough becomes too thick to stir. Turn out on a floured counter or table top. Allow 2 to 3 feet of working space, each way.

Knead for at least 10 minutes. If batter is sticky at start, rub hands together so batter falls back into bowl. Turn dough every few strokes; keep hands and bowl well floured. Dough is kneaded sufficiently when it is a smooth and shiny ball and does not stick to hands. Plop ball of dough into mixing bowl which has been washed and buttered. Turn over so that it is completely covered with a film of butter. Cover with damp cloth and set in a warm, draft-free place to rise. Let stand until doubled in bulk—about 1½ hours. Punch dough down with fist to release air, reknead lightly in bowl, re-cover, and let rise again for same length of time—or until it looks big and billowy. Tilt bowl and turn dough out gently onto floured board and cut into 4 equal pieces with a sharp knife, pulling apart as you cut. Shape into rough balls, cover with cloth, and let stand 10 minutes or so. Shape into loaves and place in buttered pans. Cover and let stand for 10 or 15 minutes for final rising. Brush tops with a mixture of equal parts of egg white and water, about a teaspoonful of each, beaten together with a fork. To prevent wasting a whole egg, poke a hole in one end of the shell, let a bit of the white ooze out and return egg to rack. (Glaze gives the bread a shiny brown crust.) Pop loaves into preheated oven (400°) for about 40 minutes. Turn out on wire rack to cool. *Yield: 4 loaves.*

Egg Bread

Easy to make, richly colored, sure to add distinction to an otherwise ordinary meal.

2⅔ cups whole milk
¼ pound butter, softened
1½ tablespoons sugar
1½ teaspoons salt
2 eggs, beaten

2 cakes yeast, or 2 packages dry yeast, dissolved in ½ cup lukewarm water
8 cups flour

Scald milk (*do not boil*). Pour into a large mixing bowl and stir in butter, sugar, and salt. Set aside until cooled to lukewarm. Add eggs and yeast and blend well. Add flour gradually, beating constantly. This will require about 10 minutes. Cover bowl with a clean cloth and set in a warm, draft-free place to rise until doubled in bulk (about an hour). Grease 2 10-by-4-inch loaf pans. Punch dough down and divide into halves. Lift one half, shape into a loaf, and place in one of the pans. It will seem rather misshapen, but don't worry. Repeat process for second loaf. Cover pans, set in warm place, and let rise again until doubled in bulk. Bake in preheated 375° oven for 50 minutes, or until bread has shrunk away from sides of pan. Remove and turn onto wire rack. Brush tops with soft butter. Cool before slicing if you can stand the suspense. *Yield: 2 loaves.*

Salt-Rising Bread

There are so many ways to make salt-rising bread that it is a bit confusing to read the recipes which appear in many old cookbooks. Some use potato starter; others do not. Proportions vary rather widely. Since salt-rising bread looms rather large in pioneer cookery, it was felt that at least one recipe should be included in this collection, and here it is. Ronald Reed and his wife Ann were kind enough to share their old recipe, which they have used successfully many times, and we are grateful for their sharing spirit. A word of caution: Salt-rising bread is not as foolproof as yeast bread, so if you succeed in turning out excellent loaves on your first attempt, it will be quite a feather in your cap. To make yeast:

2½ cups potatoes, pared and cut into thin slices
2 tablespoons cornmeal
1 tablespoon salt
4 cups boiling water

Place sliced potatoes in deep bowl and sprinkle salt and cornmeal over them. Stir until salt is dissolved. Pour boiling water over them. Cover bowl with a cloth and set in a warm, draft-free place for 18 hours. This is no problem in warm weather. Those who have gas stoves can set the bowl in warm water over the pilot light. One old cookbook suggests that the cook set the bowl in a nest of straw! A more practical suggestion is that the water be kept warm by pouring off part of the cooled water and adding warm water. At the end of the 18 hours, squeeze out the potatoes and discard them. Drain the liquid into a bowl and add the following:

1 teaspoon soda
1½ teaspoons salt
5 cups flour

Stir until blended, then beat and beat "until your arm rebels," Ann says. Set the sponge in a warm, draft-free place to rise. This should take about 1½ hours. As a signal "bubbles should rise to the surface, the sponge should increase its volume by about ⅓ and smell simply awful."

Scald 1 cup milk, to which has been added 1 teaspoon sugar, and set aside to cool to lukewarm.

When lukewarm, add 1½ tablespoons butter. Stir this mixture into the sponge and add 6 cups flour. Beat as hard as possible, turn onto floured board and knead for about 10 minutes until dough is elastic. Divide dough into 3 equal portions, shape into loaves and place in well-greased pans. Cover, set in warm, draft-free place and permit to rise until light and not quite double in bulk. Bake in moderate oven, 350°, for about 1 hour. *Yield: 3 loaves.*

Oatmeal Bread

We usually think of the Scotch when we think of oatmeal, and so we will give credit for this bread to the many fine Scottish settlers who came to southern Illinois from the South during the first half of the nineteenth century. Regardless of its ancestry, the updated version of the old recipe is so popular in our household that it almost literally melts away.

½ cup rolled oats (not the quick-cook kind)
2 cups boiling water
1 yeast cake or 1 package powdered yeast
½ cup lukewarm water
½ cup molasses
½ tablespoon salt
1 tablespoon softened butter
6 cups flour (approximately)

Pour boiling water over oatmeal in a large earthenware bowl and let stand until lukewarm, about an hour. Dissolve yeast in ½ cup lukewarm water and set aside to cool. Combine oatmeal and yeast and add molasses, salt, and butter. Stir in 2 cups flour, beat hard for 1 minute and set in warm, draft-free place to rise. Cover bowl with clean cloth. Check in 1 hour. If there are large broken bubbles on the surface and the batter has risen, add 2 or more cups of flour to produce a dough stiff enough to handle. Turn dough onto well-floured board and knead until it is smooth and elastic and no longer sticks to hands. By this time you will have used all or most of the 6 cups of flour. Divide dough into halves, shape into loaves and place in two well-greased loaf pans. Cover pans and set in warm place (85°) to rise until doubled in bulk. Bake at 375° for 50 minutes. Turn out on rack to cool. Brush tops with melted butter if you desire a softer crust. *Yield: 2 loaves.*

Hickory Nut Bread

A rich, nutty bread that should win a prize at any fair.

1 cup graham flour
1 cup white flour
1 cup milk
½ cake yeast
¼ cup lukewarm water
2 tablespoons brown sugar
1 teaspoon salt
½ cup hickory-nut meats, chopped coarsely

Sift graham and white flour together. Scald milk and when cooled to lukewarm, add yeast which has been dissolved in ¼ cup lukewarm water, sugar, and salt. Beat in the white flour and set in a warm place free from drafts (85°) to rise (about 1 hour). When doubled in bulk, beat in graham flour and hickory-nut meats. The dough should be quite stiff. Shape into a loaf, place in a greased baking pan and set in a warm place to rise. When doubled in bulk and very light (this takes about 1 hour) bake in moderate oven, 350°, for 1 hour. Turn out on rack to cool before cutting. Brush top of loaf with melted butter if a soft crust is desired. *Yield: 1 loaf.*

Irish Raisin Bread

Note the slightly different method of combining ingredients, in this traditional Irish bread.

4½ to 5½ cups flour, unsifted
½ cup sugar
1½ teaspoons salt
1 teaspoon grated lemon peel
3 packages dry yeast or 3 cakes yeast
¾ cup water
½ cup milk
¼ cup butter or margarine
2 eggs
1¼ cups raisins
⅓ cup chopped mixed candied fruits

Combine 1½ cups flour, sugar, salt, lemon peel, and yeast. Heat water, milk, and butter in saucepan over low heat until barely warm. Add to dry ingredients and beat hard for at least 3 minutes. Add eggs and ¾ cup flour, or enough to form a thick batter. Continue beating for at least 3 minutes. Stir in more flour to form a soft dough. Turn out onto a lightly floured board and knead until smooth and elastic, about 8 to 10 minutes. Place in a greased bowl, lift and turn bottom side up, so both sides will be greased. Cover and let rise in warm place free from drafts, until doubled in bulk. Check after 40 minutes. Punch dough down, turn out on lightly floured board, and knead in raisins and candied fruits. Divide into halves. Shape into loaves and place in two greased 8½-by-4½-inch loaf pans. Cover and let rise in a warm place free from drafts (about 85°) until doubled in bulk, about an hour. Bake in preheated (400°) oven about 40 minutes, or until well browned. Turn out on wire racks to cool and brush tops lightly with melted butter if desired. *Yield: 2 loaves.*

Welsh Raisin Bread

This is quite similar to Irish raisin bread; a bit spicier, richer, fruitier.

5½ cups flour, unsifted
¾ cup sugar
½ teaspoon salt
¼ teaspoon cinnamon
¼ teaspoon nutmeg
1½ packages dry yeast
1½ cups milk
6 tablespoons water
6 tablespoons butter
1 egg

1 cup raisins
1 cup currants
¼ cup chopped candied peel

Combine 1¼ cups flour, sugar, salt, cinnamon, nutmeg, and yeast. Heat combined milk, water, and butter in a large saucepan over low heat until lukewarm. Gradually add dry ingredients and beat hard for about 3 minutes. Add egg and ¾ cup flour, or more if needed to make a thick batter. Beat for about 3 minutes longer. Stir in raisins, currants, candied peel, and sufficient additional flour to form a soft dough. Turn onto lightly floured surface and knead until smooth and elastic. Return to bowl which has been washed and greased. Turn over so both sides will be greased, cover, and set aside in a warm, draft-free place (85°) until doubled in bulk (about an hour). Punch down, knead lightly, and divide into halves. Shape into loaves and place in two greased loaf pans. Let rise until doubled in bulk. Bake at 375° in preheated oven for 45 minutes, or until loaves sound hollow when tapped lightly with finger. Turn out on wire racks to cool. Brush tops with melted butter if desired, to provide a softer crust. *Yield: 2 loaves.*

Fruit Bread

This bread is as good as any panetone I have ever sampled; a substantial loaf which cuts well. Spread liberally with butter and home-made apple butter or peach preserves, it is something to make the world look like a brighter place. Raisins, citron, dates, figs, prunes, currants, mixed fruits—take your pick of this assortment. I tried citron and prunes; the citron because I had it on hand and it looked pretty, and the prunes because I wanted an accent for the citron. A loaf or two as a hostess gift or for that bake sale should establish your reputation quite solidly. This recipe is adapted from an old nineteenth-century-cookbook listing. The directions therein were rather sketchy. I have amplified them a bit.

2 cups sweet milk
2 cakes yeast or 2 packages dry yeast
½ teaspoon salt
4 cups flour (or more)
5 tablespoons butter or lard
4 tablespoons sugar
1½ cups dried fruit, cut fine

Scald milk and cool to lukewarm. Dissolve yeast in ¼ cup luke-warm water and let stand until cool. Sift flour with salt. Combine milk and yeast in a large bowl, add 3 cups flour and beat vigorously until all lumps disappear. Cover bowl with a cloth and set in a warm, draft-free place (85°) to rise until it doubles in bulk (about 1 to 1½ hours). Cream butter and sugar until fluffy. Dredge chopped fruit lightly with flour and combine with butter-sugar mixture. Stir into the risen sponge. Add remainder of flour to make a rather soft but firm dough. Turn onto a well-floured board and knead until smooth and elastic, using more flour if needed to keep board and hands from becoming sticky. Return dough to bowl which has been washed and greased well, turning so that all sides are greased. Cover and allow to rise until doubled in bulk. Punch down, knead a little bit more and divide into 2 large portions, or 3 smaller ones. Shape into loaves, place in well-greased pans, cover, and allow to rise again until doubled in bulk. Bake in preheated oven at 375° for about 1 hour, or until loaves are nicely browned and sound hollow when thumped. Turn out on rack to cool and brush tops with melted lard or butter to obtain a glossy sur-face. *Yield: 3 loaves.*

German Fruit Bread

Makes 5 or 6 loaves of beautiful gift-breads, or for the church bazaar.

1 pound dried prunes
1 pound dried apricots
1 pound dried peaches
1½ cups sugar
3 cups water

Add ½ cup sugar and 1 cup water to each of the above fruits and cook until soft. Set aside to cool.

2 cakes yeast, or 2 packages dry yeast
½ cup lukewarm water
1 teaspoon sugar
3 cups raisins, chopped coarsely
½ cup maraschino cherries, cut in halves or fourths
1 cup chopped nuts
1 cups mixed candied fruits, chopped
⅓ teaspoon allspice
1 teaspoon cinnamon
½ teaspoon anise oil

½ teaspoon nutmeg
2 teaspoons salt
2 ounces sherry, whiskey, or brandy
Juice of ½ lemon
2 tablespoons butter or lard
6 cups flour

Dissolve yeast in ½ cup lukewarm water with 1 teaspoon sugar and set aside to cool. Mix fruits, nuts, salt, wine, and spices, using only ½ cup of juice from the cooked dried fruits. Pour dissolved yeast into a large mixing bowl, add sufficient flour to make a soft sponge, and let set for about 30 minutes, or until it rises. Dump remainder of the 6 cups of flour into another large bowl and combine all of the ingredients including the yeast mixture. Add more flour if necessary for handling dough. The dough should be fairly stiff. Form into a flat ball, place in a large bowl which has been lightly greased and set in a warm draft-free place, about 85°, and let rise for 2 hours, or until doubled in bulk. Check after an hour, as dough rises faster in warm weather. Shape into 5 or 6 loaves, lift into greased baking pans, cover, set in warm place and let rise for about an hour, or until doubled in bulk. Bake in preheated oven at 375° for 45 to 50 minutes. Turn out on racks, brush tops lightly with melted butter. *Yield: 5 to 6 loaves.*

Bohemian Christmas Twist

We should not overlook the good Bohemians who settled on farms here and there. They also excelled in making fancy breads.

1 cake yeast or 1 package dried yeast
¼ cup lukewarm water
3 cups flour
½ pound butter
2 whole eggs or 4 egg yolks
1 cup sugar
Grated rind of one lemon
1 teaspoon salt
½ teaspoon mace
1½ cups cream or milk
1 cup seeded raisins
½ cup chopped blanched almonds

Dissolve yeast in ¼ cup lukewarm water and set aside to cool. Sift flour into deep bowl, cut in butter with 2 knives or pastry blender to pea size. Add eggs or egg yolks, after reserving 2 tablespoons of egg yolks for brushing top of twist before baking. Beat well. Dissolve sugar in cream, add salt, lemon rind, and mace and beat into flour mixture. Continue beating until dough no longer sticks to sides of bowl. Cover with a cloth and set in a warm place (about 85°) to rise until doubled in bulk. Punch down, stir in raisins and almonds, turn onto a floured board and knead until dough is shiny. Add more flour if needed. Divide dough into 4 large portions and 5 smaller ones. Roll each portion into a long roll, let rise, then braid the 4 larger pieces together to form a loaf. Place on buttered baking sheet. Braid 3 of the smaller pieces together and place on top of large loaf. Shape remaining 2 pieces attractively on top of loaf. Let rise again. Brush with reserved beaten egg yolk and bake in preheated oven at 350° for an hour, or until loaf is golden brown. Cool, and sprinkle with powdered sugar. *Yield: 1 large loaf.*

Holiday Stollen

Any day will be a holiday when this is served. It fairly bulges with goodies and points up the "good life" of the thrifty German newcomers to southern Illinois.

4 cups milk
3 cups sugar
4 cakes yeast, or 4 packages dry yeast
5 cups flour
5 eggs, beaten
1 teaspoon salt
1 pound butter, melted
1½ pounds raisins, chopped
½ pound candied cherries, or
  1¼ pounds mixed fruit, chopped coarsely
¾ pound citron, chopped
2 teaspoons almond extract
Grated rind of 2 lemons

Scald milk and cool to lukewarm. Add sugar and stir until dissolved. Pour out ½ cup, partially dissolve yeast in it, then stir into milk until completely dissolved. Add flour, 1 cup at a time, add salt, and beat for 5 minutes. Cover bowl, set in a warm, draft-free place, about 85°, and let rise for about 1 hour, or until doubled in bulk. Punch down. Stir in beaten eggs, fruit, lemon rind, almond extract, and melted butter. Add more flour if necessary, to make a stiff dough. Cover, set in warm, draft-free place, and allow to rise for 3 hours. Turn onto floured board and divide into 8 portions. Shape into loaves, place in baking pans and allow to rise for an hour. Bake at 375° for about 1 hour. Turn onto wire racks to cool. *Yield: 8 loaves.*

Note: This can be frozen, for use during the holiday season, or given as "little gifts."

Kolacky

A traditional Polish delight, contributed by the few Poles who settled here and there in Illinois in the nineteenth century.

1 cake yeast
2 tablespoons lukewarm milk
½ teaspoon sugar
4 cups flour
4 tablespoons sugar
½ teaspoon salt
1 lemon rind, grated
1 cup butter (do not substitute)
4 egg yolks
1 cup sweet cream, scalded and cooled
Prune or apricot jam
½ cup chopped nuts

Dissolve yeast in lukewarm milk, add ½ teaspoon sugar and set aside to cool. Scald cream, and set aside to cool. Sift flour, 4 tablespoons sugar, and salt into large bowl, add grated lemon peel, and cut butter into the mixture with 2 knives or a pastry blender, until it reaches the consistency of pie dough. Beat egg yolks, combine with cream and yeast. Stir into flour and beat lightly but thoroughly. Cover and set in refrigerator overnight. Divide into 4 portions. Roll out to ¼ inch thickness. Using a small glass about 2 inches in diameter, cut rounds and place on cookie sheet. Let rise about 10 minutes. Press a hollow in center about 1 inch in diameter with thumb and fill with 1 teaspoon prune or apricot jam. Let rise again for 10 minutes. Sprinkle chopped nuts over filling and bake at 400° for 10 to 15 minutes. *Yield: About 6 dozen.*

Sweet Potato Bread

This is another nineteenth-century "find," which will impress friends when used for small sandwiches spread with your choice of fillings. Its orange color is quite attractive. It is extremely easy to make.

Baking the sweet potatoes rather than boiling them seems to enhance their flavor and color. Can be frozen, and will remain moist for a couple months. Makes delicious toast.

1 cup mashed sweet potatoes which have been roasted
1 package dry yeast
¼ cup lukewarm water
1 cup scalded milk
1 tablespoon salt
½ cup sugar
3 tablespoons melted butter
Flour (4 cups more or less)

Dissolve yeast in lukewarm water. Add milk which has been cooled to lukewarm, salt, sugar, and sweet potatoes which have been mixed thoroughly with the melted butter. Set aside until almost cold. Beat until light. Stir in with a wooden spoon enough flour to make a soft but fairly firm dough. Cover bowl with a cloth and set in a warm, draft-free place (about 85°) to rise until doubled in bulk (about 1 hour). Punch down and knead on a well-floured board until board and hands are no longer sticky. Add more flour if needed. Shape into 2 loaves and place carefully in well-greased loaf pans. (If preferred, the dough may be divided into 3 smaller loaves.) Cover and let rise until doubled in bulk (about 1 hour). Bake in preheated 350° oven for about 40 minutes, or until nicely browned. *Yield: 2 to 3 loaves.*

Turk's Cap

The German housewife who created this must have had a good sense of humor. Which merely proves that there can be fun in cooking.

½ cup milk
½ cup sugar
¼ teaspoon salt
¼ cup butter
1 package dry yeast or 1 yeast cake
¼ cup lukewarm water
2 eggs, well beaten
4 egg yolks
2½ cups sifted flour (or more if needed)
½ cup golden raisins, coarsely chopped
2 tablespoons citron peel, grated or chopped fine
1 cup almonds coarsely chopped
2 tablespoons fine bread crumbs

Combine milk, sugar, and salt in a saucepan and scald. Add butter and set aside to cool. Dissolve yeast in ¼ cup lukewarm water and stir until dissolved. When both liquids are quite cool, combine and beat in eggs, egg yolks, and flour. Beat hard for 6 minutes, cover, and set in a warm, draft-free place to rise until doubled in bulk (about 1 to 1½ hours). Punch down and beat with a wooden spoon. Stir in raisins which have been lightly floured, citron peel, and almonds. Butter a Turk's cap mold or round baking dish and line with fine bread crumbs. Turn dough into mold, set in a warm, draft-free place and let rise for 1 to 1½ hours or until doubled in bulk. Set in preheated oven and bake at 375° for 35 to 40 minutes. Unmold on rack to cool. *Serves 8 to 10.*

Note: Mix ½ cup powdered sugar with 1 tablespoon melted butter and enough orange juice to pouring consistency. After Turk's Cap has cooled slightly, pour this icing over the top.

Pumpkin Spice Bread

The origin of pumpkin bread goes back to the early 1800s in southern Illinois, but the manner in which we were introduced to this fabulous Pumpkin Spice Bread may have something to do with our fondness for it. On a windy California Sunday afternoon we drove a hundred miles to visit the daughter of an old friend of mine. Our beloved dog Domino went along. After we had talked ourselves out and played with our hostess's two adorable youngsters, meanwhile greeting her dog Peaches, who had been banished to the back yard to allow our spoiled Domino full run of the house, we stood up to take our leave. Our young hostess had set out a plateful of goodies, including slices of this bread. While we were engrossed with our good-byes, Domino busied herself at the coffee table, leaving the plate licked clean. We hastened on our way, quite embarrassed.

Some weeks later the little family returned the visit and as she entered the door our friend handed me a beautifully wrapped package "For Domino," with the recipe attached. Needless to say, Domino was given only one very small slice. Every time I make this bread, the memory of that visit and our dear, departed Domino returns.

1¾ cups flour
1½ cups sugar
1 teaspoon soda
1 teaspoon cinnamon
½ teaspoon salt
½ teaspoon nutmeg
⅛ teaspoon ground cloves

½ cup butter, melted
1 cup cooked pumpkin
1 egg, beaten
⅓ cup water

Sift dry ingredients together into a large bowl and make a well in the center. Combine pumpkin, beaten egg, water, and melted butter. Pour into flour mixture and blend until batter is moistened. Turn into greased and floured 9-by-5-inch loaf pan and bake at 350° 1 hour and 10 minutes, or until done. Restrain yourself until it cools before slicing. *Yield: 1 loaf.*

English Lemon Tea Bread

A tasty sweet bread that's nice for afternoon parties. It's easy to make and will maintain your reputation as a good cook.

½ cup butter
1 cup sugar
2 eggs, slightly beaten
1¼ cups flour, sifted
½ teaspoon salt
1 teaspoon baking powder
½ cup milk
½ cup pecans or other nuts, chopped
Grated rind of 1 lemon

Cream butter and sugar until fluffy. Beat in eggs. Sift flour, salt, and baking powder together and add to butter mixture in thirds, alternately with milk, beating well after each addition. Fold in nuts and lemon peel. Pour into greased loaf pan and bake at 350° for 1 hour, or until done. While bread is baking, prepare topping:

¼ cup sugar
Juice of 1 lemon.

While cake is still warm, poke a few holes in top with a fork and pour topping slowly over the surface, allowing it to penetrate the cake. *Yield: 1 loaf.*

Irish Soda Bread

A traditional St. Patrick's Day bread which is easy to make. Goes well with a cup of Irish coffee.

4 cups flour
½ teaspoon salt
1 teaspoon baking soda
1⅓ cups buttermilk

Sift together dry ingredients into a mixing bowl and make a well in the center. Add buttermilk and mix quickly with a wooden spoon. Add a little more milk if dough seems too stiff, but it should not be wet and soggy. Turn out onto a floured board and knead until dough becomes smooth on both sides. Flatten into a circle about 1½ inches thick with the palm of your hand. Cut a deep cross in the center with a knife that has been dipped in flour. Place loaf carefully on a floured baking sheet and bake in a hot oven, 425° for 30 to 35 minutes. Cool slightly and serve with butter and a mound of whipped cream. *Yield: 1 loaf.*

French Coffee Cake

Contributed by Dot Farnsworth, who turns out simply elegant dishes. I followed her example in making these for bake sales. They hold up well and are always in demand.

¼ pound butter
1 cup sugar
2 eggs
1 teaspoon vanilla
2 cups flour
1 teaspoon soda
1 teaspoon baking powder
½ pint sour cream

Cream butter and sugar thoroughly. Add eggs, one at a time, and vanilla. Beat well. Sift dry ingredients together and add to egg mixture in thirds, alternately with sour cream, beating after each addition. Pour half of the batter into a greased 9-inch bundt pan and sprinkle with well-mixed blend of:

½ cup brown sugar
⅓ cup chopped nuts
1 teaspoon cinnamon

Pour remaining batter into pan and top with remainder of nut mixture. Bake at 350° for 1 hour, or until done. For special occasions Dot spreads half of the nut mixture around the bottom of a bundt pan instead of sprinkling it on the top. This makes a very attractive topping when unmolded. I tried this, and she's so right. *Yield: 1 generous coffee cake.*

Pecan Rolls

A traditional Bohemian quick bread for morning coffee, or when you invite friends to drop in on a wintry evening.

1 cup butter
¼ cup powdered sugar
1 tablespoon water
2 teaspoons vanilla
2 cups flour, sifted
1 cup chopped pecans
Powdered sugar

Cream butter and sugar and work in water and vanilla. Blend in the sifted flour thoroughly. Fold in pecans. Form dough into small crescent-shaped rolls 1 inch long. Bake on ungreased cookie sheet for 20 minutes at 300°, or until delicately browned. While hot, roll in powdered sugar. *Yield: About 18 rolls.*

Potato Doughnuts

This is the kind of doughnuts served to the threshing crew when they paused in their arduous labors in midmorning and midafternoon for refreshments. For those who don't remember, combines had not yet come into their own, and the old-fashioned steam-powered threshing machine moved from farm to farm until the wheat crop in the area was all readied for the market. Sometimes the doughnuts were accompanied by fresh, cold buttermilk, cider, or more rarely, hard cider. I can recall frying 5 gallons of these doughnuts one blistering July day, for the threshers who harvested our wheat crop.

1 cup hot mashed potatoes
1 cup sugar
2 teaspoons lard or butter, melted
1½ cups milk
2 eggs, beaten
1 cup bread flour (approximately)
2½ teaspoons baking powder
1¼ teaspoons salt
¼ teaspoon nutmeg

Blend potatoes with sugar, lard, and eggs. Stir in milk. Sift flour with salt, baking powder, and nutmeg, beat into potato mixture, and continue beating until well mixed. Add more flour if needed, to make a soft dough. Roll out on lightly floured board, cut with doughnut cutter, and fry in hot lard. May be served plain or dusted with powdered sugar. *Yield: About 36 doughnuts.*

Corn

Archeologists generally agree that corn originated in Mexico. It found its way to North America and the Indians called it maize. It kept the Pilgrims alive during that first hard, cold winter in New England. It is responsible for our end of the state being nicknamed "Egypt." During a time of corn crop failure in northern Illinois, merchants came to southern Illinois to buy corn, reminding the residents of the incident of biblical times.

Corn's versatility as a food—in the young and tender stage, dried and cooked into hominy and grits, ground into meal for use in cooking into mush and making breads and puddings—earned for it the status of the staff of life for those Europeans who settled this country.

There is a wide variety of corn breads, and they fall generally into three categories: those raised by air beaten into them; those raised by baking powder and/or soda, and those raised by yeast. Yeast-raised corn breads do not dry out as quickly as the other types, and they are more palatable, whether eaten hot or cold. If eggs are not used, a certain amount of flour should be included, to make the bread more light and porous. The simpler breads, such as ashcake and hoecake, are the very old types most closely resembling the bread of primitive people.

In the Old South the colonists learned from the Indians how to make their first corn bread, which the Indians called "appone," later shortened to "pone" by the whites. The New England housewives attempted to use the cornmeal as they had used wheat, barley, or rye flour back in England, without success. By 1828 Mrs. Eliza Leslie of Philadelphia had included recipes calling for cornmeal in her *Directions for Cookery,* which spread the good word about better results.

By 1861 a recipe for corn bread had found its way into the cookbook of Mrs. Isabella Beeton of London. She listed it as Indian Corn Flour Bread, and offered a recipe calling for a mixture of cornmeal and flour with yeast. She described this bread as "the principal daily food of a large portion of the population [in America] especially of the colonists . . . and when partaken in moderation, suitable food for almost anybody.''

Those good homemakers of the South and New England eventually learned how to combine cornmeal with wheat flour to concoct numerous kinds of corn bread, corn muffins, sweet breads, hush puppies, puddings, etc. Southern Illinois homemakers who came here from both the South and from New England, as well as Europe, had the best of all worlds, as will be evidenced by the variety of recipes calling for cornmeal which appear on the following pages.

Cornmeal is ground from both yellow and white corn. The white meal is a bit finer, and there are those who prefer it for all recipes including cornmeal. The eye appeal of yellow cornmeal has its own merits, and should be considered in preparing dishes where cornmeal is to be used, and where the finest texture is not essential.

Corn Pone or Ashcake

Pioneers from the Southern states had already learned many cooking tricks from the Indians, or devised them for themselves, to compensate for the lack of pots and pans. Basic cornbread was mixed in a wooden bowl, shaped into a flat cake with the hands, and baked in the hot ashes of an open fire, well covered with more hot ashes.

4 cups yellow cornmeal
2 teaspoons salt
1 tablespoon lard or other fat
2 cups boiling water.

Scald meal, add salt and shortening. Set aside to cool. When cold, form batter into rectangular cakes, adding more water, if necessary, to make a stiff batter. Wrap cakes, or ''pones,'' in cabbage leaves, or place one cabbage leaf under cakes and one over them. Cover with hot ashes and bake. *Yield: 16 pones.*

Corn Pone

A more refined version, combining wheat flour with white cornmeal.

2 cups white cornmeal
⅓ cup water
⅓ cup sour milk or buttermilk
¼ teaspoon soda

¼ **cup wheat flour**
1 **teaspoon salt**
1 **tablespoon sugar**
2 **teaspoons baking powder**

Pour water and milk over cornmeal in a double boiler and cook for about 5 minutes. Or, boil the water and pour it over the cornmeal, then add buttermilk. Set aside to cool. Sift together flour, salt, sugar, baking powder, and soda, and add to cooled meal-milk mixture. Shape into cakes, or pones. If mixture seems too stiff, add a little more water. Place cakes in a hot, well-greased pan and bake in a hot oven, about 425°, until browned. Handle cakes lightly. *Yield: 12 pones.*

Hoecake

So-called because the frontiersman or woman working in the field could still have hot food for the midday meal, merely by making a very small fire, mixing cornmeal with a little water from the nearest stream, and baking the cake on the flat metal part of a hoe held over the fire. No less a person than Henry David Thoreau wrote of doing this during his stay at Walden Pond. No messy pans to wash!

1 **cup yellow or white cornmeal (water ground if available)**
½ **teaspoon salt**
1 **tablespoon soft lard**
Water (boiling water if available)

Combine cornmeal and salt, add lard and just enough water to make a stiff dough that will hold its shape. Pat into 2 oblong shapes and place in a heavy, heated well-greased pan. Bake at 375° for about 25 minutes. Serve hot. *Yield: 2 large cakes.*

Corn Dodger

When the luxury of a cookstove was attained, a bit of sugar was added to the basic batter and the daily bread acquired more "class."

1 **cup yellow cornmeal**
1 **teaspoon salt**
1½ **teaspoons sugar**
1 **tablespoon butter or bacon drippings**
1 **cup boiling water**

Mix dry ingredients with butter and pour boiling water over mixture until it is thoroughly blended and no lumps remain. Cool slightly, and shape into cakes with hands dipped in cold water, or with a large spoon, and place on a greased cookie sheet or griddle. Bake in a hot oven, 400°, for about 8 to 10 minutes. *Yield: 4 cakes.*

Johnny Cake or Journey Cake 1

The origin of this name is in dispute. One version has it that it was called "Journey Cake" because it was easily made before campfires by westward-bound pioneers. They mixed the batter like this:

1 cup boiling water
1 heaping teaspoon lard
¼ teaspoon salt
1 cup yellow cornmeal

Melt lard in boiling water. Stir into cornmeal and beat until smooth. Add salt. Batter should be quite thick—not runny. Pat onto a pan or board and set in a slanting position close to the fire to bake. Baking time, about 45 minutes. *Yield: 4 servings.*

Johnny Cake or Journey Cake 2

The name survived long after the travelers had settled down in southern Illinois. The simple old recipe was fancied up for baking in an oven. The molasses transformed it into a dessert.

3 cups yellow cornmeal
1 cup wheat flour
⅓ cup molasses
¼ teaspoon salt
½ cup buttermilk (or more, to make a stiff batter)
1 teaspoon soda

Combine cornmeal, flour, and salt. Stir soda into molasses. Beat buttermilk into dry mixture until smooth. Add molasses and stir until well blended. Pour into a greased pan and bake at 350° for about 35 minutes. *Yield: 6 to 8 servings.*

Skillet Corn Bread

After the early hardship-times had eased a bit and mills were grinding wheat flour, white cornmeal gained preference over the yellow variety. A status symbol, as it were.

2 cups boiling water
1 cup white cornmeal
1 cup milk
1 teaspoon salt
3 teaspoons baking powder
2 tablespoons melted butter
4 eggs, beaten

Pour boiling water over cornmeal. Cool. Beat in milk, salt, baking powder, butter, and eggs. Pour into 2-quart skillet. Bake at 400° for 25 to 30 minutes. Serve hot. *Yield: 6 servings.*

Spoon Corn Bread

One might consider this the ultimate refinement in corn bread. It would be a welcome addition to a winter lunch or dinner. It's especially good with ham.

4 cups milk
1 tablespoon butter
2 cups white cornmeal
1 teaspoon salt
1 tablespoon sugar
2 eggs, separated

Heat milk to boiling point in a double boiler. Add butter and stir until it is melted. Pour milk over cornmeal to which salt has been added. Stir this for 15 minutes. Or if you wish to cheat, pour it in your mixer bowl and flip on "On" switch. Beat egg yolks until pale yellow and blend into cornmeal batter. Fold in stiffly beaten egg whites. Pour into a warmed earthenware dish which has been lightly greased and bake at 400° for 30 minutes. *Yield: 6 to 8 servings.*

Southern Corn Bread

I can personally recommend this to those who prefer a richer sour milk corn bread.

2 cups white cornmeal
1 teaspoon salt
1 teaspoon soda
2 cups buttermilk or sour milk
2 eggs, well beaten
¼ cup butter, melted

Sift dry ingredients. Add to beaten eggs in three parts, alternating with milk and butter. Beat well and pour into a well-greased and heated iron or other heavy baking pan. Bake at 375° for 30 minutes. Cut in squares to serve. *Yield: 6 to 8 servings.*

Aunt Ett's Corn Bread

Although this recipe, a favorite of my dear little great-aunt Etta, originated in southern Illinois, it did not come into my hands until I moved to California to live for ten years. A cousin shared it with me, and since Aunt Ett is long gone, this is dedicated to her memory.

2 cups white cornmeal
1 cup flour
½ cup sugar
1 teaspoon salt
3 teaspoons baking powder
1 tablespoon butter, melted
1 egg
2 cups sweet milk

Sift cornmeal, flour, sugar, salt, and baking powder together and set aside. Melt butter in pan. Beat egg and add butter. Beat dry ingredients into beaten egg alternately with milk and continue beating until batter is smooth. Pour into heated, well-greased baking pan. Bake at 350° for 30 minutes, or until golden brown. Cut into squares for serving. *Yield: 8 to 10 servings.*

Crackling Corn Bread 1

In predominantly rural areas, where families still butcher their own pigs, cracklings are tasty by-products of the process. City-bred readers may find it a bit difficult to obtain them. Cracklings are the crisp, brown bits left after the lard has been "rendered." At butchering time, when the hogs are being cut up into hams, shoulders, bacon, ribs, and other portions, the skin and fat trimmings are tossed into an iron kettle. A fire is built beneath this kettle and these trimmings are cooked for several hours, until the kettle is filled with grease and the browned bits of tissue float on the top. They are removed and the grease poured into containers of various sizes. This is lard, which is used throughout the winter for cooking purposes. The crisp brown bits are the cracklings. They are usually shared with neighbors and relatives. If you hanker for crackling corn bread and have no friends or relatives who butcher their own hogs, convey your wishes to your butcher. He may be able to obtain a supply for you.

A word of caution to those who have bought cracklings and are making crackling corn bread for the first time. Because of the large amount of fat remaining in them, it is best to warm them and then squeeze them in a thin cloth to remove excess fat. This fatty corn bread is not recommended in quantity for diners with high cholesterol.

4 cups yellow cornmeal
2 cups cracklings
3 teaspoons salt
Boiling water (1 cup more or less)

Mix cornmeal and salt and pour over enough boiling water to moisten, but not enough to make a mush. When this meal has cooled, work the cracklings into it with the fingers. Form the batter into cakes about 4 inches long, 2 inches wide, and 1 inch thick. Bake on a greased pan for 30 minutes at 350°. Serve very hot. No butter or other shortening needed because of fat in the cracklings. *Yield: 12 cakes.*

Crackling Corn Bread 2

A less rich bread than the foregoing recipe.

4 cups yellow cornmeal, sifted
1 cup cracklings
1 teaspoon salt
1 cup warm water (more or less)

With a wooden spoon rub the cracklings into the cornmeal as fine as you can. This may take a little time. Add salt and as much warm water as needed to make a stiff batter. Shape into pones (round cakes) place in a pan which has been greased and sprinkled lightly with cornmeal and bake at 350° for about 20 minutes, or until lightly browned. If preferred, spread in a baking pan which has been well greased with bacon drippings and heated in oven until quite hot. Bake at 350° for about 25 minutes. Serve hot. *Yield: 20 servings.*

Crackling Corn Bread 3

A more refined, modern version of the old Southern standby which may appeal more strongly to those whose palates have become accustomed to fancy cookery. A word of caution: don't use those dried-out cracklings which are found in some supermarkets in tin containers. They won't give you the true taste of cracklin' bread.

2 cups yellow cornmeal
½ cup flour
¾ cup buttermilk
2 eggs
1 cup cracklings
¼ teaspoon salt
¼ teaspoon baking soda

Sift together all dry ingredients. Beat eggs lightly, stir in buttermilk, and add slowly to dry ingredients in thirds, beating well after each addition. Blend in cracklings. Pour into greased shallow pan and bake at 400° for about 30 minutes, or until golden brown. *Yield: 16 servings.*

South Carolina Yeast Corn Bread

This is the result of experiments of a well-to-do Southern-born lady who yearned for something a bit more fancy than the usual everyday fare.

6 cups fine white cornmeal
10 cups wheat flour

Or reverse proportions and use:

10 cups fine white cornmeal
6 cups wheat flour
2 cups warm water (more or less)
2 teaspoons salt
2 cups mashed sweet potatoes
1 cake yeast, or 1 package dry yeast, dissolved in ¼ cup lukewarm
water

Mix 2 cups each of the cornmeal and flour and add sufficient water to form a stiff batter. Stir in the dissolved yeast. Blend thoroughly. Turn into a greased bowl, cover, and set in a warm, draft-free place until it doubles in bulk (about an hour). Scald remainder of cornmeal with just enough boiling water to allow you to stir the mixture. Stir until all lumps are removed and set aside to cool. When cooled to lukewarm, combine with yeast mixture, remainder of flour, sweet potatoes, and salt. The dough should be stiff enough to knead without sticking to the board. If not, add a bit more meal. Knead until smooth and return to bowl, which has been washed and well greased. Cover, set in warm, draft-free place to rise. When doubled in bulk, punch down by poking your fist into the center of the dough and divide into 4 portions. Form into loaves and place in greased loaf pans. Cover and let rise again until doubled in bulk. Bake at 350° for about 50 minutes, or until the loaves sound hollow when thumped and are golden brown. Turn out on wire rack to cool. *Yield: 4 loaves.*

Apple Corn Bread

Inevitably, an inventive cook, tired of baking the same old corn bread in the same old way, added sliced apples. Her innovation is worth preserving.

2 cups white cornmeal
2 tablespoons sugar
¾ teaspoon salt
1 teaspoon soda
1 teaspoon cream of tartar
1⅔ cups milk
3 tart apples, peeled, cored, and sliced thin

Mix the dry ingredients, add milk, and beat hard until perfectly smooth. Stir in apples, pour into a well-greased baking pan, and bake at 350° for 30 minutes, or until golden brown. Cut in squares and serve hot. *Yield: 6 to 8 servings.*

Note: Dried apricots, cooked to the soft stage, may be used instead of apples. Drain apricots well before adding to batter, and serve the slightly thickened juice as sauce.

Hominy Bread

The humble hominy is accepted in the best circles nowadays. This old Virginia recipe found its way to southern Illinois several generations ago.

2 cups hot cooked hominy
1 tablespoon butter
2 eggs beaten until very light
2 cups milk
1 cup cornmeal
Salt and pepper

Melt butter in hot hominy and stir in beaten eggs. Add milk and when well mixed, add cornmeal gradually. The batter should be of the consistency of custard. If it seems too thick, add a little more milk. Season to taste with salt and pepper and pour into a deep greased baking dish. Bake at 350° on center oven grill until golden brown, about 40 minutes. *Yield: 6 to 8 servings.*

Beaten Biscuits

It is doubtful whether these were served to the typical frontier family, due to the strength and endurance required for obtaining most satisfactory results. They saved their energy for other endeavors. Those early arrivals who brought slaves served them, and descendants of old Southern families still serve them on special occasions. When baking powder became available after 1850, the popularity of these beaten biscuits waned.

3 cups sifted flour
1 teaspoon salt
¼ cup cold lard or other shortening
½ cup cold milk

Sift flour and salt together and cut in shortening with a pastry blender or fork. Add milk and mix to a very stiff dough. Place on well-floured board and beat with rolling pin or wooden potato masher for 30 minutes, folding in edges after each stroke, until dough is elastic. Roll ⅓ inch thick and cut with biscuit cutter. Place on greased baking sheet and prick with the tines of a fork. Bake in 400° oven for 20 minutes. *Yield: 24 biscuits.*

Fried Biscuits

When the old wood-burning stove was balky on a windy day and the oven refused to heat properly so our mother could bake biscuits for breakfast, she was not at all fazed; she fried the biscuits in the trusty old black iron skillet. We treated them like extra-thick pancakes, drenching them in butter and syrup or molasses.

1¾ cups bread flour (sifted before measuring)
1 teaspoon salt
3 teaspoons tartrate or phosphate baking powder, or 1 teaspoon combination type
1 teaspoon sugar

½ teaspoon baking soda
4 tablespoons butter or lard
⅔ to ¾ cup buttermilk or sour milk

Sift dry ingredients together. Add butter and cut in with two knives or a pastry blender until it resembles coarse cornmeal. Add buttermilk and stir until barely mixed, about ½ minute. Turn onto a lightly floured board and knead quickly, for about ½ minute. Roll or pat out to ¼ inch thickness. Cut with 1½-inch biscuit cutter. With a spatula, lower biscuits into a skillet containing melted hot lard 1 inch deep and fry for about 3 minutes. Flip over and fry 3 minutes longer. Drain on paper towels. *Yield: 24 biscuits.*

Company Biscuits

Fine for lunch with chicken salad. Very light and dainty.

2 cups flour (sift before measuring)
4 teaspoons baking powder
½ teaspoon salt
½ teaspoon cream of tartar
2 tablespoons sugar
½ cup lard or butter
⅔ cup milk
1 egg, beaten

Sift dry ingredients together into a large bowl. Add shortening and blend with fork or wire blender until of cornmeal consistency. Stir in milk and egg and continue stirring until dough is stiff. Turn onto lightly floured board and knead just a little bit, about 5 turns. Roll to ½ inch thickness. Cut with 1½-inch biscuit cutter, place on cookie sheet and bake at 450° for 10 to 15 minutes. *Yield: 24 biscuits.*

Note: Biscuits will brown more evenly if a cookie sheet is used rather than a baking pan with sides.

Buttermilk Biscuits

Devotees of buttermilk biscuits hold out for their conviction that these are superior to biscuits made with sweet milk. Biscuit mixes are inexpensive and "easy," true, and those dedicated cooks who prefer to work "from scratch" suffer condescending glances of friends. But there is a difference between those "bought" biscuits and these home-made ones.

2 cups sifted all-purpose flour
2 teaspoons baking powder
½ teaspoon baking soda
1 teaspoon salt
½ teaspoon sugar (optional)
¼ cup shortening
1 cup buttermilk or sour milk

Sift flour, baking powder, soda, salt, and sugar together into a mixing bowl. Add shortening and cut in with 2 knives or a pastry blender until mixture looks mealy. Stir in the buttermilk with a fork until dough holds together in a soft ball. Turn onto a floured board and knead lightly for about one minute. Roll out to ⅓ inch thickness and cut with biscuit cutter. Bake on ungreased cookie sheet 15 to 20 minutes at 400°. Serve immediately. *Yield: About 24 medium-sized biscuits.*

Homemade Crackers

No need to worry if there's homemade soup and the cracker jar is empty. Make your own.

4 cups flour
2 tablespoons sugar
1 teaspoon salt
¼ cup butter
1 cup milk (more or less)

Sift dry ingredients together. Blend butter into flour mixture with 2 knives until mixture looks mealy. Stir in sufficient milk to form a stiff dough. Roll out about ¼ inch thick on a lightly floured board and cut into squares with a sharp knife. Prick holes about ¼ inch apart with the tines of a fork and brush surface with milk. Place on an ungreased baking sheet and bake at 425° for 15 to 18 minutes, or until lightly browned. Remove with spatula and store in an airtight container. (Extra-good when served hot from the oven.) *Yield: About 5 dozen.*

Apple Pancake

A favorite of German families and all others who appreciate good foods. Tested for me by my friend Dot Farnsworth, who recommends it most highly.

1 large tart apple
1 or 2 tablespoons butter
½ cup milk
3 eggs beaten very lightly
½ cup flour
1 teaspoon sugar
⅛ teaspoon salt

Peel, core, and slice apple and fry in butter in a large pan, swirling butter around all sides so batter won't stick. Mix milk and beaten eggs with flour, sugar, and salt which have been sifted together. Pour batter over apples, tilting pan so all slices are covered, and set pan in 500° oven; bake for 30 minutes. When pancake has raised and is almost done, powder with:

1 tablespoon sugar
½ teaspoon cinnamon

Dot with butter, and return to oven until golden brown. If desired, sprinkle with lemon juice before serving. *Serves 2.*

Buttermilk Pancakes

Pancakes were a very special treat at our house because there were so many of us that it required at least four hands to cook them fast enough to supply the demands. When Mom was fresh and rested on occasional Sunday mornings she tackled the task, with one of us older girls assisting.

4 eggs, beaten
2½ cups buttermilk
1½ teaspoons salt
2 teaspoons sugar
1 tablespoon baking powder
1½ teaspoons soda
3 cups flour, sifted
¼ cup melted butter

Mix eggs and buttermilk. Sift dry ingredients together and blend with egg mixture, beating only until well mixed, ignoring a few lumps. Add melted butter. Grease griddle lightly and heat until a drop of cold water will dance about on cooking surface. Spoon batter carefully onto three locations on griddle and cook until edges are dry and some of the bubbles break. Flip over with spatula and cook about half as long. The cakes may be stacked in a warm oven if you get ahead of the demands, which is not likely to happen. Serve with butter and the usual syrup, jelly, or powdered sugar. *Serves 8.*

Note: These pancakes may also be served flat or rolled up with creamed chicken spooned over top.

Cattail Pollen Pancakes

Gather the pollen in late May or early June when the staminate, upper parts of the cattail heads are beginning to shed their golden pollen. Shake pollen into a bowl or onto a clean cloth and use with equal portion of flour in mixing pancake batter.

¾ cup sifted all-purpose flour
¾ teaspoon salt
2½ teaspoons baking powder
2 tablespoons sugar
¾ cup cattail pollen
1 egg
¼ cup milk
3 tablespoons melted butter

Sift flour, baking powder, sugar, and salt together. Break egg into bowl and beat well. Add milk and butter. Slowly add to flour mixture, mixing only until dry ingredients are moistened. Blend in pollen. Bake on heated griddle until each cake is full of bubbles. Turn and brown other side. Serve immediately with melted butter and your favorite syrup, jam, or jelly. *Serves 4.*

German Pancake Marbles

Ever try eating pancakes with a spoon? Here's how.

2 cups milk
2 or 3 eggs, well beaten
3 cups flour
1 teaspoon baking powder
1 teaspoon salt
¼ cup lard

Combine milk and eggs and mix well. Sift flour, baking powder, and salt and add to egg mixture, beating until smooth. Melt ¼ cup lard in a 9-inch iron or other heavy skillet and heat to medium high temperature. Pour batter into hot lard and stir with a knife. As batter cooks, break it up into small lumps the size of marbles, using a spatula. Remove when nicely browned and serve immediately with your favorite syrup. *Yield: 6 to 8 servings.*

Pancake Swirls

A German forerunner of the fancy funnel cakes of today.

1 cup flour
1 teaspoon baking powder
Pinch of salt
1 egg
Milk (about ¾ cup)

Sift dry ingredients together. Beat egg and combine with flour mixture, adding sufficient milk to make a thin batter. Pour into heavy skillet in which 1 teaspoon of lard has been melted, and cook, stirring lightly until browned on underside. Flip over and brown on other side. Serve with syrup or powdered sugar. *Yield: 4 servings.*

Pies

Pies

Egg Pastry

Every homemaker worth her keep has her own favorite piecrust recipe which she can depend on. Here is one, however, which can be held in reserve for very special occasions when a little extra cooking skill seems called for—sort of a kitchen status symbol, as it were. The egg yolks assure a robust yellow tint to the piecrust—a note of opulent authority.

5 cups flour, sifted
½ teaspoon salt
4 teaspoons sugar
½ teaspoon baking powder
1½ cups lard
2 egg yolks
Ice water

Combine dry ingredients. Cut in lard with two knives or a pastry blender. Dump egg yolks into a measuring cup and stir with a fork or whisk until smooth. Add water to fill the cup. Drizzle over the dry ingredients, tossing with a fork, to form a soft dough. Shape into a ball, and divide into 3 portions. *Each portion is sufficient for 3 9-inch, 2-crust pies.*

Soda Cracker Pie

Homemade crackers were pressed into service for pies in bleak times when no fruits or vegetables were available. Remember, there were no supermarkets or automobiles, and the nearest neighbor's cupboard was probably also bare.

8 crackers, pounded fine (large homemade 3-inch squares)
¼ cup boiling water (slightly more if needed)
8 tablespoons vinegar
8 tablespoons sugar
Juice and grated rind of 1 lemon (optional)
1 unbaked 7-inch pie shell

Pour boiling water over crackers to soften. Stir in vinegar, sugar, and lemon juice. If mixture is too stiff, add a little more water. Beat until crackers are well dissolved and turn into unbaked pie shell. Bake at 350° until set and lightly browned, about 35 to 40 minutes. Best served hot. *Makes a 7-inch pie.*

Vinegar Pie

Lemons being scarce and the larder also being reduced in late winter, the pioneer housewife turned to the vinegar jug. Vinegar was usually plentiful in thrifty households. There was little market for apples, so after canning and drying, making cider, and "hilling up" several bushels, the peelings were converted to vinegar.

1 cup sugar (½ brown, ½ white)
½ cup flour
1 teaspoon cinnamon
1 cup vinegar
2 cups water
2 tablespoons butter
1 9-inch unbaked pie shell

Mix sugar, flour, and cinnamon and dissolve in vinegar. Combine with water and cook over low heat until thickened, stirring constantly to prevent lumps from forming. Remove from fire and add butter. Cool slightly. Pour into pie shell and bake at 425° for 15 minutes. Reduce heat to 350° and bake 30 minutes longer, or until filling has set and is lightly browned. Test for doneness by inserting knife into center of filling. If it comes out clean, pie is done. *Makes a 9-inch pie.*

Buttermilk Pie

My ninety-five-year-old cousin Merta McNeill Sonner generously shared some of her favorite recipes handed down by our mutual forebears who came to southern Illinois in the same party in the early 1830s. Here is her version of buttermilk pie: "This receipt goes as far back as I know. The buttermilk pie is as old as the Hills, I guess. I think it either came through the Tranbargers from Germany or the Campbells from Scotland. My mother was a Tranbarger and she made it by this receipt, and her mother, a Campbell, also made it."

½ cup sugar
½ cup butter, melted and cooled slightly

1 cup buttermilk
3 eggs, beaten
2 teaspoons flour, sifted
1 teaspoon vanilla
½ teaspoon nutmeg
1 9-inch unbaked pie shell

Add sugar to melted butter and stir until sugar is well dissolved. Set aside. Beat eggs until frothy. Add vanilla. Blend flour and nutmeg. Add 2 tablespoons of the beaten eggs to flour and stir to a smooth paste, then add slowly to the remainder of the egg mixture and stir until well mixed. Add buttermilk and stir until thoroughly blended, then beat this mixture into sugar-butter mixture. Let set for a few minutes to "marry." Pour into pie shell and bake at 425° for 10 minutes. Reduce heat to 350° and bake 35 minutes longer, or until a knife inserted in center comes out clean. *Makes a 9-inch pie.*

Fresh Coconut Pie

A well-made coconut cream pie is as tempting today as it was back in the mid-1800s when coconuts were scarce and expensive in southern Illinois.

½ cup sugar
1 scant ¼ teaspoon salt
2 heaping tablespoons flour
4 egg yolks
2 cups rich milk
1 teaspoon vanilla
½ cup fresh-grated coconut
1 scant tablespoon butter
4 egg whites
2 tablespoons sugar
Dash cream of tartar
1 9-inch pie shell, baked

Sift sugar, salt, and flour together and combine with slightly beaten egg yolks. Add milk and stir until smooth. Cook in top of double boiler until thick, stirring constantly. Add butter, vanilla, and coconut and set aside until cold.

For the meringue, beat egg whites until stiff and dry, adding cream of tartar and 2 tablespoons sugar a little at a time. Pour filling into baked pie shell. Spread meringue over top, extending well into edges to make sure filling is sealed in, and brown in 300° oven (about 10 minutes). *Makes a 9-inch pie.*

Pecan Pie

Pecan trees grow along the riverbanks in southern Illinois, so pecan pies are no great rarity. We could always count on one of these delightful desserts made by my sister-in-law Carmen as a special added attraction for holiday dinners.

3 eggs
⅔ cup sugar
½ teaspoon salt
⅓ cup melted butter
1 cup light or dark corn syrup
1 teaspoon vanilla
1 cup pecan halves
1 unbaked 8-inch pie shell.

Heat oven to 375°. Beat eggs, sugar, salt, butter, and syrup together with rotary beater. Add vanilla. Mix in pecan halves. Pour into pastry-lined pie pan. Bake 40 to 50 minutes, or until filling is firm and crust is nicely browned. *Makes an 8-inch pie.*

Hickory Nut Pie

A real oldie, contributed by Mrs. Etta Over of Albion, Illinois. Hickory nuts are becoming more scarce in our neck of the woods, and there is really no other nut which tastes like them. The patient hiker who roams the woods and out-of-the-way places may still find a bushel or two during the autumn, if the squirrels don't beat him to them.

1 cup bread crumbs
1 cup sugar
1 cup hickory-nut meats
1 cup sweet milk
1 teaspoon vanilla
1 unbaked 7-inch pie shell

Mix bread crumbs, sugar, and nutmeats thoroughly and place evenly in pie shell. Mix milk and vanilla and pour over nuts very slowly, so as not to disturb arrangement. Bake at 450° for 10 minutes. Reduce heat to 350° and continue baking for 25 to 30 minutes until golden brown, or until a knife inserted in center comes out clean. Cool before cutting. *Makes a 7-inch pie.*

Note: Those who wish may add a beaten egg to this filling.

Blackberry Pie

Wild blackberries grew in unhindered profusion throughout southern Illinois. The Indians used them for stews, dried and pounded into pemmican, and for eating out of hand. Although they are not as plentiful as they were once, they can be found by those who know where to look, and of all things, are being cultivated by a few growers.

We picked them by the bucketfuls when I was young, going out at least three days each week during their ripening season. Our mother made blackberry jelly, blackberry jam, canned hundreds of quarts, and we feasted on fresh blackberries with cream for breakfast and blackberry pie or cobbler whenever Mom had time to make it.

4 cups blackberries, washed and hulled
¾ to 1 cup sugar (more if needed)
1 tablespoon butter
¼ teaspoon nutmeg
Pastry for 9-inch, 2-crust pie

Discard any unripe or overripe berries. Line pie pan with pastry and pour berries into pan. Sprinkle sugar over the top. Dot with butter and sprinkle with nutmeg, if desired. Cover with top crust, slit in a leaf pattern to permit steam to escape while baking. Bake at 400° for 10 minutes. Reduce heat and bake at 350° about 35 minutes longer, or until nicely browned. *Makes a 9-inch pie.*

Note: To make blackberry cobbler, follow instructions for Dewberry Cobbler, on page 149.

Ground Cherry Pie

While reminiscing with old-timers about their diet "in the good old days," Harry Killion, ninety-five-year-old resident of Ava, recalled that he was fond of picking ground cherries in the field and eating them on the spot. Frankly, I wasn't too sure his memory was 100 percent accurate, but I tucked away his story in the back corner of my mind. Later on, while checking out something else during the second typing of this manuscript I ran across a recipe for ground cherry pie in a not-too-old cookbook, with the introduction, "the ground cherry is a luscious golden little fruit that grows wild on a low bushy plant in the Mississippi Valley. It is first cousin to the Japanese Lantern." I am happy to bow to Harry's excellent memory.

4 cups husked ground cherries, washed and drained
2 eggs
⅛ teaspoon salt
⅔ cup sugar
1 tablespoon flour
1 cup milk
1 teaspoon vanilla
1 unbaked 7-inch pie shell

Place ground cherries in pie shell. Beat eggs with salt and add sugar and flour. Stir in milk and vanilla. Blend well. Pour carefully over cherries. Bake at 425° for 10 minutes. Reduce heat to 350° and bake 25 to 30 minutes longer, or until a knife inserted in center comes out clean. Serve plain or with whipped cream. *Makes a 7-inch pie.*

Imitation Apple Pie

Apple orchards were scarce in southern Illinois before the Civil War, but pumpkins were plentiful. An anonymous cook of the 1860s voiced her assurance that this green pumpkin pie "takes longer baking than apple pie, but when done is in no respects inferior."

4 cups raw green pumpkin, peeled and sliced thin
¾ cup sugar, or more if needed
½ teaspoon salt
¼ cup vinegar
3 tablespoons flour
¼ cup water
Dash of nutmeg (about ⅛ teaspoon)
Pastry for 2-crust, 9-inch pie

Mix pumpkin with sugar and set aside. Dissolve salt in vinegar. Mix flour and water until smooth and combine with vinegar. Pour over pumpkin, add nutmeg, and set aside while mixing pie dough. Line pie pan with pastry. Turn pumpkin into pie shell and cover with top crust, which has been slit in a leaf pattern to permit steam to escape while baking. Bake at 400° for 15 minutes. Lower heat to 350° and bake for 45 minutes longer, or until well browned. *Makes a 9-inch pie.*

Mulberry Pie

The native mulberries were and still are highly esteemed by birds, children, pigs, and some grown-ups, just as they were by the early Indians and settlers. The fruit is somewhat insipid in taste, but was used for pies when no other fruit was available and the family sweet tooth needed to be appeased. Old-time farmyards often had a tree tucked away in a far corner, in the hope that the birds would choose its fruit rather than the more valuable cherries, peaches, apricots, apples, and plums.

4 cups ripe mulberries
⅔ cup sugar
1 tablespoon lemon juice
1 tablespoon grated lemon rind
1 tablespoon butter
1 teaspoon cinnamon
Pastry for 2-crust, 9-inch pie

Wash mulberries, discarding imperfect ones. The flavor will be improved if a few red but not quite ripe ones are included. Turn fruit into prepared pie shell, mounding slightly in the center, and sprinkle with sugar. Sprinkle a tablespoon of lemon juice and another of grated lemon rind over the berries and dot with butter. Cover with top crust, slit in a leaf pattern to permit steam to escape while baking. Bake at 425° for 10 minutes, reduce heat to 350°, and bake 25 to 35 minutes longer, until crust is nicely browned and the juice begins to ooze out through the slits in the top crust. *Makes a 9-inch pie.*

Gooseberry Pie

The Indians harvested and ate wild gooseberries. They had no problems in introducing English colonists to this fruit, as there are about a thousand varieties grown in Great Britain. Mrs. Isabella Beeton's authoritative cookbooks of the mid-1800s contain recipes for gooseberry jams, jellies, puddings, tarts, vinegar, and wine. English colonists imported plants from their homeland which were acclimated or grafted onto the native plants. My family grew them as a matter of course, and I loathed picking them. The thorns seemed bent on piercing my hands no matter which way I turned. However, a gooseberry pie was, and still is most welcome during the drab days of winter, and the tang of gooseberry jam is equaled by few other jams.

4 cups gooseberries
1 cup sugar (or more)
2 tablespoons flour
1 tablespoon butter
Pastry for 9-inch, 2-crust pie

Snip or pinch off the blossoms and stems of berries and wash well. Place in a deep bowl and sweeten with 1 cup or more of sugar, depending on acidity of fruit and desired degree of sweetness. Sprinkle flour over bottom crust of pie in pan and heap sugared berries on crust, mounding slightly in center. Cover with top crust which has been slit in a leaf pattern to permit steam to escape. Bake in hot oven, 425° for 10 minutes. Lower heat and continue baking for about 35 minutes at 350°, or until crust is nicely browned. Serve hot or cold. *Makes a 9-inch pie.*

Cherry Pie

No account of the foods enjoyed by my forebears should omit cherry pie. My extreme fondness for this pie probably dates back to my early childhood, when my grandfather Walker sang "Can she bake a cherry pie, Billy Boy?" The fact that he sang off-key did not dim his obvious enjoyment of the sentiment inherent in the song. This weakness was shared by my brothers and sisters. We watched the sour cherry trees anxiously as they began to turn red and were more than willing to obey our mother's bidding to "pick enough for a pie." Only the threat of cholera morbus if we ate too many deterred us from stripping the tree. Pitting them was something else. Sometimes the old cherry pitter missed a pit or two, and there were wails of anguish by the victim who bit down on one.

Once an uncle and aunt visiting from Alabama came while the cherries were at their ripest. Our mother baked dozens of cherry pies for them, as the uncle could not seem to satisfy his craving for "Nora's cherry pie."

4 cups fresh sour cherries, pitted
1⅓ to 1½ cups sugar
4 tablespoons flour
Pastry for 9-inch, 2-crust pie

Fit bottom crust into pie pan. Dump cherries into pan, mounding slightly in center. Combine sugar and flour and sprinkle over fruit. Cover with top crust, which has been slit in a leaf pattern to permit steam to escape. Bake in preheated oven at 425° for 10 minutes. Lower heat to 350° and continue baking until crust is golden brown and juice begins to ooze out of openings, about 35 minutes. Cool before cutting. *Makes a 9-inch pie.*

Lemon Pie

One of my great-uncles on my father's side married a great-aunt from another line, both families having arrived in Williamson County in the 1830s. Uncle Hen had itchy feet so his family was privileged to live in a number of places before finally settling down in southern California early in this century. Aunt Em carried her favorite family recipes along, and one of her daughters, Avis McNeill Walker, has generously shared them. I have eaten this melt-in-the-mouth pie several times when visiting Avis.

1 cup sugar
2 tablespoons flour
3 egg yolks and 1 egg white
1 cup boiling water
½ teaspoon salt
Juice of 1 lemon
2 egg whites
2 tablespoons sugar
Pinch of salt
1 baked 9-inch pie shell

Sift sugar and flour together. Beat egg yolks and 2 egg whites until frothy and blend with flour-sugar mixture until smooth. Add salt. Pour boiling water slowly into mixture, stirring constantly to prevent lumps. Set pan over low flame and cook until thick and smooth, stirring constantly. Remove from fire, add lemon juice, and cool slightly. For the meringue, beat 2 reserved egg whites until stiff, gradually adding 2 tablespoons sugar and pinch of salt. Pour filling into baked pie shell, spread meringue over top, making sure entire surface is covered, and brown in slow oven, 300°, 15 to 20 minutes, until lightly browned. *Makes a 9-inch pie.*

Note: Since living in California, Avis has added the juice of an orange, which was not in the original recipe.

Carrot Pie

Modern nutritionists urge everyone to include a yellow vegetable in the daily diet. This sneaky way of feeding carrots to carrot-haters is as rewarding today as it probably was a couple generations ago.

1 cup hot, cooked, mashed, and sieved carrots
2 cups milk, scalded

2 eggs, beaten
1 tablespoon melted butter
1 tablespoon lemon juice
½ cup molasses or red syrup
1 9-inch unbaked pie shell

Combine carrots and scalded milk and set aside to cool slightly. Beat eggs until frothy and stir into carrot mixture. Add butter, lemon juice, and molasses and stir until thoroughly blended. Pour carefully into pie shell. Bake at 400° for 10 minutes. Reduce heat to 350° and bake for 35 minutes longer, or until lightly browned and filling is firm. *Makes a 9-inch pie.*

Green Tomato Pie

A distinctively flavored pie: sort of a cross between green grapes and apple, but with its own special appeal.

8 medium-sized green tomatoes, washed well, peeled, and sliced thin
1 tablespoon lemon juice
¾ cup sugar
½ teaspoon salt
½ teaspoon cinnamon
2 teaspoons tapioca
1 9-inch pie shell, unbaked

Mix ingredients well, in order given. Let stand for 10 minutes. Turn into pie shell and bake in preheated oven at 425° for 10 minutes. Reduce heat to 350° and continue baking until delicately browned, about 35 minutes. A top crust may be added if desired. *Makes a 9-inch pie.*

Note: Some old-style cooks recommend the following mixing procedure: Sift dry ingredients, except tapioca. Blend in tapioca and sprinkle half of mixture over bottom crust. Place sliced tomatoes in pan and cover with remaining dry ingredients. Dot top with 2 tablespoons butter. Bake 15 minutes at 425°. Reduce heat to 375° and continue baking for 30 minutes, or until browned.

Ripe Tomato Pie

It's different, all right, and not at all bad. Some of your guests will ask what they are eating, and when you tell them, they will look at you strangely.

6 large ripe tomatoes
1 cup brown sugar
1 teaspoon cinnamon
1 tablespoon flour
1 teaspoon lemon extract
Juice of ½ lemon
Pastry for 2-crust, 9-inch pie

Line pie pan with crust. Peel tomatoes and remove seeds. Slice very thin and lay on crust. Combine sugar, cinnamon, and flour and sprinkle over tomatoes. Combine juice and lemon extract and pour over filling. Roll out remainder of dough, cut into strips with pastry wheel, and weave lattice-fashion across top of pie. Bake at 450° for 10 minutes. Reduce heat to 350° and bake 25 to 30 minutes longer, or until crust is lightly browned. *Makes a 9-inch pie.*

Sweet Potato Pie 1

This is another treasured McNeill family recipe carried from Williamson County to California, and returned through the generosity of cousin Avis McNeill Walker, who wrote "This is really called Sweet Potato Custard, and may be served without the crust."

1 large or 3 small sweet potatoes, cooked and mashed, about 2 cups
1 cup sugar
1 egg, beaten
⅔ cup milk
1 teaspoon lemon juice or orange juice
1 unbaked 7-inch pie shell

Mix warm sweet potatoes and sugar, stirring until sugar is dissolved. Beat egg into mixture and stir in milk. Add lemon juice. Pour into unbaked pie shell and bake at 350° until firm, about 30 minutes. *Makes a 7-inch pie.*

Sweet Potato Pie 2

This filling is richer than Aunt Em's, and it too could be baked as a pudding without the crust, by those weight watchers who are fighting the battle of the bulge.

2 cups hot, boiled, mashed sweet potato
6 eggs, well beaten
¼ cup plus 2 tablespoons butter

¼ teaspoon salt
2 cups sugar
1 teaspoon grated lemon rind
1 tablespoon brandy (optional)
1 unbaked 9-inch pie shell

Press sweet potato pulp through sieve. Add beaten eggs, butter, sugar, salt, and lemon rind and beat hard, until butter is melted. Stir in brandy. Turn into unbaked pie shell and bake at 400° for 10 minutes. Lower heat and continue baking for about 30 minutes at 350°, or until top is puffy and lightly browned. Serve hot or cold with freshly whipped cream. *Makes a 9-inch pie.*

Sweet Potato Pie 3

Here's still another sweet potato pie from an old-time cook. This one calls for fewer eggs and more spice.

2 cups hot, boiled, mashed sweet potatoes
2 tablespoons butter
2 tablespoons lemon juice
1 cup sugar
Grated rind ½ lemon
1 teaspoon ginger
1 teaspoon cinnamon
½ grated nutmeg or ½ teaspoon powdered nutmeg
1 teaspoon salt
2 cups milk
3 egg yolks, well beaten
3 egg whites, beaten stiff
1 unbaked 9-inch pie shell

Press sweet potatoes through sieve, add butter, lemon juice, sugar which has been well mixed with lemon rind, spices, and salt. Beat egg yolks and combine with milk. Blend into sweet potato mixture and stir until thoroughly mixed. Fold in stiffly beaten egg whites. Turn into pie shell and bake at 400° for 10 minutes. Reduce heat to 350° and bake about 30 to 35 minutes longer, or until filling has set and is lightly browned. *Makes a 9-inch pie.*

Sorrel Pie

When friends and family learned I was working on a book of old-time recipes of southern Illinois, I was assailed on all sides with the query, "Are you going to include sorrel pie?" Everyone remembered it as being "old" but few knew how to put it together. Sorrel isn't as easy to find as it once was. But here's a recipe, for auld lang syne.

1 gallon sheep sorrel (or garden French sorrel)
¾ cup sugar, or to taste
⅛ teaspoon salt
1 tablespoon lemon juice
⅛ teaspoon nutmeg
1 unbaked 7-inch pie shell and dough for top crust

Wash sorrel well and pinch off heavier stems. Drain thoroughly and pat dry. Cut or tear each cluster into smaller pieces. Blend sugar, salt, and nutmeg. Pour over sorrel in bowl and toss lightly with a fork. Turn into pie shell. Sprinkle lemon juice over top. Weave pastry strips lattice-fashion over pie. Bake at 425° for 15 minutes. Reduce heat to 350° and bake 30 minutes longer. Best served hot. *Makes a 7-inch pie.*

Fried Pies

I'm not sure of the origin of these calory-laden goodies. One finds them in old German and New England cookbooks and the recipe below gives evidence of their popularity in southern Illinois for the past century or more. Merta McNeill Sonner wrote, "This is an old Southern receipt, and is delicious."

2 cups fruit puree (apple, apricot, peach, etc.)
Lemon juice
Sugar to taste
Dash of nutmeg
Pastry for 2-crust pie

If using dried fruit, cook until mushy. Cool. Mash until soft and free of lumps and sweeten to taste. If using fresh fruit, remove seeds and peel, wash, and simmer in very little water until very soft. Puree by mashing, or forcing through food mill. Add sugar to taste and mix well. Drain off any excess juice, as the pulp should not be watery. If desired, add ½ teaspoon lemon juice. Apples and peaches will benefit by the addition of ⅛ teaspoon nutmeg.

Mix your favorite pie dough. Pinch off portions about 2 inches in diameter and roll out to ⅛ inch thickness on floured board. You should have circles approximately 5 to 6 inches in diameter. Place two table-spoons of the pureed fruit on the dough, a little off-center, and spread to within ½ inch of the edge. Moisten border with cold water and flip the unadorned side of the dough over, to form a semicircle. With a fork, crimp the edges tightly so the filling will not ooze out while frying. Prick top of pie with tines of a fork in several places.

Melt lard in a deep kettle to a depth of at least 2 inches. Test by dropping a tiny scrap of the pastry dough into the fat. If it browns almost immediately lower pies gently into the hot fat, using a wide spatula. It is advisable to fry no more than 2 at a time. When they rise to the surface, turn them and fry to golden brown on other side. This frying operation should not require more than 10 minutes, so don't wander away from your stove. When the pies rise to the surface again, they are done. Remove very gently with a slotted spoon or a spatula and set on several thicknesses of paper towels to drain. Serve hot or cold; they taste great either way. *Makes 6 pies.*

Strawberry Tart

The tiny, sweet wild strawberries once grew in profusion in southern Illinois. Those who have visited the Pierre Menard home, overlooking the Mississippi near Chester, and have read something about the early French in Illinois can visualize these tarts being served by that distinguished official to visiting dignitaries from France. For 8 individual 3-to-4-inch tart shells mix:

6 tablespoons butter
2 tablespoons lard
1½ cups flour
¼ teaspoon salt
3 to 5 tablespoons ice water

Combine the above ingredients in a large mixing bowl. Working quickly with fingertips, rub the flour and fat together until the mixture resembles coarse meal. Pour 3 tablespoons of water over the mixture all at once, toss together lightly, and gather dough into a ball. If the dough seems crumbly, add up to 2 tablespoons more ice water, a little at a time. Dust a little flour on the dough ball, and wrap it in waxed paper. Refrigerate for at least 3 hours. Remove dough from refrigerator 5 minutes before using it. Divide it into 6 portions. Place portions on lightly floured board and, using the heel of the hand, press it into a flat 1-inch circle. Dust a tiny bit of flour over it and roll it from center to within an inch of the far edge. Lift dough and turn clockwise, rolling toward far edge, until the circle is ⅛ inch thick and 3 or 4 inches in diameter. Fit into tart shells. Preheat oven to 400°. Prick bottom of pastry with tines of a fork to prevent it from puffing up. Bake for 10 minutes, or until it is pale golden colored and shrinks from the sides of the pan. Unmold shells and slip onto wire rack to cool. To make filling:

1 egg plus 1 extra egg yolk
¼ cup sugar
3 tablespoons flour
Pinch of salt
1 envelope unflavored gelatin
1 teaspoon vanilla
1 cup hot milk
1 cup heavy cream, chilled

Break egg into heavy 2-to-3-quart saucepan, add extra egg yolk and beat with a wire whisk or rotary beater until the mixture thickens and turns pale yellow. Add sugar, flour, and salt and blend thoroughly. Beat in powdered gelatin and vanilla. Pour the hot milk in a thin stream over the egg mixture, beating constantly. Set over low heat and cook until smooth and thick, stirring constantly with a whisk. *Do not allow custard to boil.* If lumps form, beat vigorously until smooth. Pour custard into a large mixing bowl and set in refrigerator to cool. When it is cold and seems to be starting to become firm, whip cream until it forms soft peaks. Fold into custard with a rubber spatula and beat gently if any lumps form. Pour or spoon custard into the pastry shells, and cover with glaze. To make glaze:

1 cup red currant jelly
1 tablespoon hot water
1 tablespoon kirsch
1 to 1½ quarts ripe strawberries, cleaned and stemmed
Confectioners' sugar

In a small saucepan warm currant jelly and hot water over low heat, stirring occasionally, until they begin to froth and thicken. Remove saucepan from heat, stir in kirsch, and let glaze cool. Meanwhile, arrange the strawberries on the custard, stem side down, until the top of each tart is completely covered with berries. Spoon the warm glaze over the berries. Chill tarts for at least 2 hours or until custard is firm. Sprinkle lightly with confectioners' sugar before serving. *Makes 8 tarts.*

Dewberry Cobbler

Dewberry cobbler was a much-appreciated dessert at our family table. Perhaps because we kids picked the berries ourselves, a back-breaking task, for it involved stooping double, lifting the extremely thorny runners, and often picking each berry separately. They are much softer than wild blackberries, hence more easily mashed. One day we children had found an especially well-berried patch in an open field on a relative's farm nearby. As I was encouraging my younger brothers and sisters to pick more and faster, so we could return home sooner with full pails, I happened to glance more closely at the vine I was stripping of its luscious fruit. A snake had entwined itself around the heart of the vine and appeared to be resentful of my intrusion. I tarried not in my departure, pausing only to caution my siblings to inspect each vine carefully before picking. We filled our pails that day, but the real joy had fled, so far as I was concerned.

5 cups ripe dewberries, hulled and gently washed
Rich pie pastry to line 12-by-8-by-2-inch oblong baking pan

Combine:

1¼ cups sugar, more if needed
4 tablespoons flour
2 tablespoons butter
½ teaspoon cinnamon

Pour berries into crust. Sprinkle dry ingredients over berries. Dot surface with 2 tablespoons butter. Let stand for 15 minutes. Cover with a top crust which has been slit in a leaf pattern to permit steam to escape while baking. Bake in preheated oven, 425° for 10 minutes. Reduce heat to 350° and bake for about 45 minutes longer, or until crust is golden brown. *Serves 8 to 10.*

Note: Cobblers are made with a rich biscuit dough, or pastry dough. We preferred the latter. In our family, the only difference between a fruit pie and a fruit cobbler was the size.

Cakes

Cakes

Then and Now

In these times with food prices spiraling from day to day, it was interesting to find among a sheaf of old-time recipes the penciled notes of some long-ago thrifty housewife who was probably struggling with her budget even then. The heading reads "White Fruit Cake." Exact date unknown; around the 1800s.

1 cup shortening	9¢
Sugar (probably 1 cup)	5¢
2 lbs. flour	10¢
Raisins (probably 1 cup)	19¢
½ citron	15¢
½ cherries (½ cup?)	25¢
½ orange peel	17¢
½ lemon peel	18¢
¼ pineapple	15¢
1 lb. almonds	40¢
8 egg whites	24¢
1 cup water	no cost
½ (tsp.?) salt	no cost
2 tsp. baking powder	no cost

Total cost of these ingredients: $1.97. At today's prices it would cost three or four times that amount to create a 2½-to-3-pound fruit cake. The itemization included no directions for putting the cake together; however, an experienced cook would have no difficulty in doing so.

Butter Cake

Our sizable family had made away with several tons of cake before I realized that not every family was served cake still warm from the oven. My complacent acceptance of this table luxury was viewed in new perspective after the comment of a spinster schoolteacher friend of our mother's who stopped off now and then on weekends enroute to her home from her rented room in town. Elsie mentioned casually that she really liked Mom's warm cake. I made a few inquiries among my friends and learned that we were indeed the only family in my rather limited circle who were privileged to eat *warm* cake, so fresh from the oven that the icing sometimes ran a bit. This icing was invariably the simplest kind, made by reserving the whites and beating them until they were very stiff, after the sugar and vanilla were added, so that it remained firm when spread over the cake. I'm sorry I never did compliment Mom on this culinary treat, as it finally dawned on me with a great light that the reason we were treated to this delightful dessert was obvious: if she had baked it in the morning it might not be around at supper time. With nine of us kids hanging around the kitchen when the oven was going, chances of the survival of anything sweet and edible were practically nil. Mom learned early.

1¾ cups cake flour, or 1½ cups all-purpose flour sifted 3 times before measuring
2 teaspoons baking powder
½ teaspoon salt
⅓ cup butter
1 cup sugar
2 egg yolks, beaten slightly
½ cup milk
½ teaspoon vanilla

Sift flour with baking powder and salt and set aside. Cream butter thoroughly, add sugar gradually, and beat until fluffy. Stir in egg yolks and add flour mixture alternately with milk and vanilla, beating well after each addition. Pour into greased 10-by-10-by-2-inch pan and bake 30 to 45 minutes at 350° or until top of cake springs back when touched with fingertip. Turn out on wire rack to cool.

For the icing, beat reserved egg whites until frothy. Add 2 tablespoons sugar, a little at a time, and continue beating until very stiff. Spread over cooled cake. *Serves 10 to 12.*

Note: If preferred, egg whites may be beaten stiff and folded into the cake before baking. In that case, the cake may be iced with Butter Icing (see page 172), or your favorite icing.

Scripture Cake

"Behold, there was a cake baker," I Kings 9:16
This well-loved traditional recipe is generally featured in women's

club cookbooks, particularly those published by church groups. Each group has its special preference: there is more than one reference to many of the ingredients.

¾ cup Judges 5:25 (butter)
1 cup Jeremiah 6:20 (sugar)
3 whole Jeremiah 17:11 (eggs)
2½ cups 1 Kings 4:22 (all-purpose flour)
2 teaspoons Amos 4:5 (baking powder)
½ teaspoon Leviticus 2:13 (salt)
1 teaspoon Exodus 30:23 (cinnamon)
¼ teaspoon each 2 Chronicles 9:9 (cloves, allspice, nutmeg, saffron)
¼ cup Judges 4:19 (milk)
2 teaspoons 1 Samuel 14:25 (honey)
1 tablespoon Genesis 24:20 (water)
1 cup 1 Samuel 30:12 (raisins) chopped
1 cup Naham 3:12 (figs) chopped
½ cup Numbers 17:8 (almonds) chopped

A brief interpretation of the above directions: Cream butter with sugar until smooth and fluffy. Add eggs one at a time, beating after each addition. Sift dry ingredients together and blend into creamed mixture alternately with milk. Blend honey and water and fold into batter. Add raisins, chopped figs, and almonds to batter and fold in thoroughly. Turn into a 10-inch tube pan which has been generously greased and dusted with flour and bake for 1 hour and 10 minutes in moderate oven, 325°. Test for doneness by inserting toothpick into top of cake. If it comes out clean, cake is done. Cool 10 minutes. Remove from pan and cool completely. Top with burnt sugar syrup:

1½ cups Jeremiah 6:20 (sugar)
½ cup Genesis 24:25 (water)
¼ cup Genesis 18:8 (butter)
¼ cup whole Numbers 17:8 (almonds) blanched

Melt sugar in heavy skillet over low heat. Continue cooking until syrup is deep amber. Add water slowly and cook until syrup is smooth. Remove from heat, add butter and stir until melted. Cool slightly. Pour slowly over cake and decorate with whole almonds. *Makes a 10-inch cake.*

Pork Cake

Notice of the imminent arrival of the traveling "preacher" for dinner, or a group of relatives from afar seldom caught Grandmother unprepared. If she found herself short on some staples, there were always others, and she put them to good use. For instance:

1 pound salt pork
2 cups boiling water
1 pound raisins, coarsely chopped
¼ pound citron, shaved fine
1 pound chopped dates (optional)
2 cups dark-brown sugar, firmly packed
1 cup molasses
1 teaspoon baking soda
4 cups all-purpose flour (or more if necessary)
1 teaspoon cinnamon
1 teaspoon ground cloves
1 teaspoon allspice
1 teaspoon nutmeg
1 teaspoon salt

Chop pork very fine, or put through grinder, using medium blade. Pour boiling water over it. Add raisins, citron, dates, and brown sugar, stirring well to soften fruit. Stir soda into molasses and blend with pork mixture. Sift flour with spices and salt and beat into liquid mixture, adding more flour, if needed, for a stiff batter. Turn into a large 9-by-5-by-4-inch loaf pan or 10-inch bundt pan which has been well greased and floured, then lined with greased paper. Bake at 350° for 1 hour or more. Test for doneness by inserting a toothpick in center of cake. If it comes out clean, cake is done. This cake will keep well if wrapped in foil or placed in a tin container. Powdered sugar may be dusted lightly over the top if desired. *Serves 10 to 12.*

Buttermilk Cake

Buttermilk was plentiful when all farm families had their own cows and all that sour cream to be churned. This is an out-of-the-ordinary white cake.

1 cup butter
2 cups sugar
3 cups cake flour
1 teaspoon soda
½ teaspoon salt
1 teaspoon cream of tartar
1 cup buttermilk
6 egg whites
1 teaspoon vanilla
1 teaspoon lemon extract

Cream butter and sugar until fluffy. Sift flour, salt, soda, and cream of tartar together and add to creamed mixture in thirds, alternately with buttermilk. Beat egg whites until stiff and add vanilla and lemon extract. Fold into batter. Turn into ungreased 10-inch tube pan and bake at 350° for 45 minutes. Test for doneness by inserting a toothpick into cake. If it comes out clean, cake is done. Loosen cake by running a knife around sides. Invert pan over wire rack to cool. Remove from pan. Frost with orange-flavored Butter Icing (*see* page 172). *Serves 10.*

Jane's Lane Cake

This famous cake originated in the Old South. Proud cooks who were fortunate to have a recipe brought it to southern Illinois and made it for very special occasions. It survives despite the time involved in putting it together. Its lofty four layers, assembled with bourbon-spiked filling, are hard to resist. Jane Cole of Grand Tower creates one for bake sales when she's in the mood, and it lends an air of distinction to the laden table.

3¼ cups sifted cake flour
3½ teaspoons double-acting baking powder
¾ teaspoon salt
1 cup butter, at room temperature
2 cups sugar, sifted
1 cup milk
1 teaspoon vanilla
8 egg whites, stiffly beaten

Sift together flour, baking powder, and salt. Cream butter and sugar until light and fluffy. Fold in flour mixture alternately with milk, beginning and ending with dry ingredients. Add vanilla. Fold in stiffly beaten egg whites. Turn into four 9-inch round layer cake pans which have been greased and lined with greased waxed paper. Bake at 375° for about 20 minutes, or until outer edges shrink slightly from sides of pans and tops spring back when gently pressed with forefinger. Cool in pans set on wire rack for about 5 minutes. Turn out of pans onto racks, remove waxed paper, turn right side up and cool completely. Put layers together with Lane Cake filling:

8 egg yolks
1¼ cups sugar
¼ teaspoon salt
½ cup butter, at room temperature
1 cup seedless raisins, finely chopped

1½ cups freshly grated coconut
1 cup chopped pecans
1 cup candied cherries finely chopped
⅓ cup bourbon or brandy
1 teaspoon vanilla

In a 2-quart saucepan beat egg yolks until lemon colored. Beat in sugar, salt, and butter. Cook over moderate heat until thick and transparent, stirring constantly. Remove from heat, stir in raisins, coconut, pecans, cherries, bourbon, and vanilla. Cool slightly. Spread filling between layers. If you think it necessary to gild the lily, you may cover top and sides with Boiled White Frosting (see page 173). *This 4-layer, 9-inch cake serves 16 to 20.*

Red Devil's Chocolate Cake

The name of this old-fashioned cake intrigued me so much that I coaxed the recipe out of a friend of my childhood. Don't let the evil connotation mislead you. It's a very good cake.

2 cups cake flour
1¼ teaspoons baking soda
¼ teaspoon salt
½ cup butter
1 cup sugar
2 eggs, beaten well
2 squares (2 ounces) unsweetened chocolate, melted and cooled
¾ cup buttermilk or sour milk
1 teaspoon vanilla
⅓ cup boiling water

Sift, then measure flour. Sift three times with soda and salt. Cream shortening until fluffy. Add sugar gradually, beating well after each addition. Beat eggs until they are almost as stiff as whipped cream and add slowly to sugar mixture. Stir in melted chocolate. Combine milk and vanilla. Add to batter alternately with dry ingredients, beating after each addition until smooth. Pour in boiling water and continue beating until thoroughly blended. Turn into 10-by-5-inch greased loaf pan. Bake in moderate oven, 350° about 45 minutes, or until top springs back when touched with forefinger. Let cool in pan for 10 minutes. Turn onto rack. Let stand 2 hours before cutting, to allow the red coloring to fully develop. Ice with Boiled White Frosting (see page 173) or serve with whipped cream. *Serves 10.*

Angel Cake

Dieters love this cake, which is easy to make if your arm holds out. Very simple, and inexpensive in the spring when eggs are plentiful and cheap. For those cooks who are too lazy to beat the eggs by hand and prefer to cheat and use their electric mixer, the cake will be smaller and more firm, as less air is beaten into the eggs.

1¼ cups granulated sugar
1 cup cake flour
⅛ teaspoon salt
9 egg whites
1 level teaspoon cream of tartar
1 teaspoon vanilla
½ teaspoon almond extract

Separate egg whites from yolks at least ½ hour before needed. They beat better at room temperature. Sift sugar twice and set aside. Sift flour 3 times with salt, and combine with ½ cup sifted sugar. Whip egg whites until foamy. Add cream of tartar and continue beating until they are stiff but not dry. Gradually whip in ¾ cup of sifted sugar, 1 tablespoonful at a time. Add vanilla and almond extract. Fold in sifted flour mixture very gradually, 1 tablespoonful at a time. Turn batter into an ungreased 9-inch tube pan. Bake in a slow to moderate oven, 325°, 50 to 60 minutes. Cake is done when it shrinks from sides of pan and is pale golden-colored. Remove from oven, loosen edges, and invert over a cake rack. Remove from pan about 1½ hours later, or when completely cold. Serve with either powdered sugar dusted over top, or spread with Butter Icing (see page 172), or spoon crushed strawberries over wedges in dessert dishes and top with whipped cream. *Serves 12 to 16.*

Old-Fashioned Gingerbread

Gingerbread and fresh cider heralded the coming of autumn in my childhood, and we continued to request this spicy dessert through the winter. It was a welcome addition to our school lunch boxes. Bites were taken alternately with crisp apple chunks.

⅓ cup butter
½ cup sugar
1 egg, beaten
⅔ cup molasses

2 cups flour
2 teaspoons ginger
1 teaspoon cinnamon
½ teaspoon salt
1 teaspoon baking powder
½ teaspoon soda
½ cup sour milk

Cream butter with sugar until fluffy, add egg and molasses, and continue beating until thoroughly mixed. Sift flour, spices, salt, and baking powder together twice and beat into batter. Dissolve soda in sour milk and add to batter, stirring until smooth. Turn into greased 8-by-11-inch pan and bake at 350° for about 40 minutes, or until top springs back when touched lightly with forefinger. Dust with powdered sugar, or serve with whipped cream or a generous dab of hard sauce. *Serves 10.*

Molasses Sweet Bread

A spicy gingerbread that may be served at any time, plain or topped with whipped or ice cream.

2 cups all-purpose flour
½ teaspoon salt
2 teaspoons baking powder
¼ teaspoon soda
1 teaspoon cinnamon
2 teaspoons ginger
1 egg
⅓ cup melted butter
1 cup molasses
¾ cup buttermilk

Sift dry ingredients together and set aside. Beat egg, add melted butter, molasses, and buttermilk in that order. Blend in dry ingredients, pour into 10-by-4-inch loaf pan and bake at 350° for 50 minutes, or until done. Turn out on rack to cool. Powdered sugar may be sprinkled over the top if desired. *Serves 8 to 10.*

Oatmeal Cake

An interesting textured cake, not too sweet, with lots of substance. It can also be served as a bread, sliced thin and spread with a sweet filling.

½ cup butter
1 cup oatmeal, uncooked
1½ cups boiling water
1 cup brown sugar
1 cup white sugar
2 eggs, lightly beaten
1½ cups all-purpose flour
1 teaspoon baking soda
1 teaspoon cinnamon
1 teaspoon nutmeg
¼ teaspoon salt
1 teaspoon vanilla

Slice butter into large mixing bowl, add oatmeal and cover with boiling water. Let stand for 20 minutes. Add sugar and eggs, mix well, and set aside. Sift flour, baking soda, spices, and salt together and stir into oatmeal mixture. Add vanilla and beat until thoroughly blended. Turn into well-greased 10-inch loaf pan and bake at 350° for about 50 minutes. Test for doneness by inserting a toothpick in center. If it comes out clean, cake is done. Let set in pan for 10 minutes, then turn out on wire rack to cool. *Makes a 10-inch loaf cake.*

Fresh Coconut Cake

As it was in great-grandmother's time, the true homemaker's crowning achievement is the excellence of her cakes. Each home had its own specialty, which appeared in all its glory at holiday gatherings. Fresh coconuts appeared in markets shortly before Christmas, and at least one beautiful, snowy fresh coconut cake would appear at the occasional holiday gatherings of our sizable "clan." This recipe is definitely Southern in origin.

¾ cup butter
¼ teaspoon almond extract
1½ teaspoons vanilla
1 teaspoon salt
2 cups sugar
3 teaspoons baking powder
3 cups sifted cake flour
½ cup milk or coconut milk
½ cup water
6 egg whites, stiffly beaten

Cream butter and add almond extract, vanilla, and salt. Add sugar gradually and continue creaming until fluffy and pale yellow. Sift flour with baking powder three times. Combine milk and water and add to creamed mixture alternately with flour, beating after each addition until smooth. Fold in stiffly beaten egg whites. Bake in 3 9-inch greased layer cake pans in moderate oven, 350°, about 25 minutes, or until cake springs back when pressed lightly with a fingertip. Turn out on wire racks to cool. When cold, spread fresh coconut frosting between layers and on top and sides of cake. To make fresh coconut frosting:

3 tablespoons butter
¼ cup hot milk or coconut milk
3 cups confectioners' sugar, sifted
¼ teaspoon salt
⅛ teaspoon almond extract
Meat of 2 coconuts, grated fine

Heat butter in hot milk until melted. Pour over combined sugar and salt and stir until sugar is dissolved. Add almond extract, and additional milk if needed. Spread frosting between layers and on top and sides of cake, sprinkling grated coconut liberally over layers and top, and patting onto sides. *Makes a 9-inch, 3-layer cake.*

Note: Packaged shredded coconut may be used if fresh coconuts are not available. For greatest eating enjoyment it is better to bake this cake two or three days before serving and store it in a tin box to allow the coconut flavor to permeate the entire cake.

Poppy Seed Cake

You won't find poppy seed cake around very much any more, and few cookbooks include it, which is too bad. Possibly poppy seeds fell into disfavor after the trauma of the drug scene in the 1960s. This cake looks interesting, and the custardy topping makes it a complete dessert.

⅔ cup poppy seeds
1 cup milk
1 cup butter
2 cups sugar
5 egg yolks
3 teaspoons baking powder
½ teaspoon salt
Grated rind of 1 lemon
2½ cups sifted cake flour

½ **cup milk**
1 **teaspoon vanilla**
5 **egg whites, beaten**

Soak the poppy seeds in 1 cup milk for an hour before starting to mix cake. Cream butter until lemon colored and fluffy, add sugar ¼ cup at a time, and beat until mixture resembles whipped cream. Beat in egg yolks, one at a time. Sift flour with baking powder and salt and add to batter in thirds, alternating with ½ cup milk. Stir in poppy seeds, lemon rind, and vanilla and blend thoroughly. Beat egg whites until stiff but not dry and fold into batter. Turn into 10-by-4-inch loaf pan or 10-inch round-form pan which has been lightly greased and dusted with flour. Bake at 350° for 45 minutes, or until cake springs back when touched lightly with fingertip. Turn out on wire rack to cool. Serve with cooked custard topping:

2 **cups milk**
1 **cup sugar**
4 **egg yolks, beaten**
3 **tablespoons cornstarch**
¼ **teaspoon salt**
1 **teaspoon vanilla**

Combine sugar, cornstarch, and salt in top of double boiler, add eggs yolks and beat until smooth. Add milk gradually and continue mixing until all lumps are removed. Set over boiling water and cook over medium heat until thick, stirring constantly. Stir in vanilla. Cool and pour over slices of poppy seed cake as served. *Makes a 10-inch loaf cake.*

Hickory Nut Cake

This cake is rich, without being icky, and has a pleasantly nutty flavor.

2 **cups sugar**
¾ **cup butter**
5 **egg yolks, well beaten**
3 **cups cake flour, sifted**
2 **teaspoons baking powder**
¼ **teaspoon salt**
½ **cup cream**
2 **cups hickory-nut meats, blanched and chopped**
½ **teaspoon almond extract**
5 **egg whites, beaten stiff**

Cream butter and sugar until fluffy, add egg yolks and beat well. Sift flour and baking powder together and beat into butter mixture in thirds, alternating with cream, to which salt has been added. Stir in nutmeats and almond extract. Fold in stiffly beaten egg whites and turn into greased and floured 10-inch tube cake pan. Bake 350° 1 hour and 25 minutes, or until top springs back when lightly touched with fingertip. Let set in pan 10 minutes, then invert over wire rack. When cold, remove from pan. No frosting is necessary; however, chocolate-flavored Butter Icing lends a real luxury finish (see page 172). *Makes a 10-inch cake.*

Spice Cake

Spice cake retains its popularity around this part of the country. It is good around pickling time when our supply of spices is fresh and plentiful. This cake is great for picnics, and the recipe has never failed—for me.

1½ cups sugar
¾ cup butter
3 egg yolks
2 cups cake flour, sifted before measuring
1 teaspoon baking powder
1 teaspoon soda
1 teaspoon cinnamon
1 teaspoon nutmeg
½ teaspoon ground cloves
½ teaspoon salt
⅞ cup buttermilk, or sour milk
3 egg whites, beaten stiff

Sift sugar. Cream butter until very soft and add sugar gradually, continuing to cream until light and fluffy. Beat in egg yolks. Resift cake flour twice with baking powder, soda, spices, and salt. Add dry ingredients to batter in 3 parts alternately with buttermilk, beating well after each addition. Whip egg whites until stiff but not dry and fold lightly into batter. Bake in a greased 9-inch tube pan at 350° for 1 hour or more. Test for doneness by inserting toothpick deep into cake. If it comes out clean, cake is done. Let cake stand for 10 minutes, loosen by running knife around outer edge. Invert over rack until cake falls from pan. Cool and ice with chocolate-flavored Butter Icing (see page 172). *Makes a 9-inch cake.*

Apple Cake

Launch the apple season with this easily mixed, moist cake, from a German housewife. It would keep well if you could put a lock on the cupboard.

2 cups chopped tart apples, unpeeled
1 cup sugar
½ cup butter
1 egg, beaten
1½ cups all-purpose flour, sifted
1 teaspoon baking soda
½ teaspoon salt
½ cup chopped nuts
½ cup grated coconut (optional)

Combine apples and sugar and set aside until juice forms, about 15 to 20 minutes. Cream butter, blend with egg, and add to apples. Sift flour, soda, and salt together and combine with apples. Fold in nuts and coconut. Turn into 8-inch square greased pan. Bake at 350° 40 to 45 minutes. Let set in pan for 10 minutes, then turn onto rack to cool. May be dusted with powdered sugar, or iced with your favorite butter icing. *Makes an 8-inch cake.*

Applesauce Cake

This cake keeps well, and our mom always had one on hand for our frequent family gatherings. As we had an ample supply of hickory nuts from our own trees, she always used them, and we dubbed it "Mom's Hickory Nut Cake."

½ cup butter
1 cup sugar
2 eggs, beaten
1 cup applesauce
1 teaspoon baking soda
2 cups all-purpose flour
¼ teaspoon ground cloves
¼ teaspoon nutmeg
¼ teaspoon allspice
1 teaspoon cinnamon
1 teaspoon vanilla
1 cup raisins, lightly floured
½ cup hickory nuts, chopped coarsely

Cream butter, add sugar, and continue creaming until fluffy. Beat in eggs, one at a time. Mix applesauce with soda and add to butter mixture. Sift flour and spices together and combine with butter mixture in thirds, beating well after each addition. Stir in vanilla. Fold in raisins and nuts and turn into greased and floured 9-by-13-inch loaf pan or 9-inch tube pan. Bake at 350° for 50 to 60 minutes, or until top springs back when touched lightly with fingertip. Let stand in pan for 10 minutes, then turn out on wire rack to cool. Dust with powdered sugar or frost with Butter Icing (see recipe page 172). *Serves 8 to 10.*

Note: The eggs may be omitted if they are scarce or too expensive. The cake will be slightly heavier, but still good. Pecans or walnuts may be substituted for hickory nuts.

Dundee Cake

A modernized treatment of a traditional Scottish sweet cake brought to southern Illinois by a Scotsman's lady.

2¼ cups cake flour, sifted
1 teaspoon baking powder
¼ teaspoon salt
½ teaspoon nutmeg
½ teaspoon cinnamon
¾ cup butter
1¼ cups powdered sugar, sifted
4 eggs
½ cup orange juice
1 cup raisins
1 cup currants
½ cup chopped mixed candied fruit
1 cup almonds, slivered
¼ cup almonds, chopped
2 tablespoons light corn syrup
2 tablespoons water

Sift together flour, baking powder, salt, and spices and set aside. Cream butter, add sugar gradually, and continue creaming until light and fluffy. Add eggs 1 at a time, beating well after each addition. Add flour alternately with orange juice, beginning and ending with flour. Beat well after each addition. Fold in fruits and 1 cup slivered almonds. Spread batter in a well-greased 9-inch tube pan. Bake 30 minutes at 350°. Sprinkle ¼ cup chopped almonds over top and continue baking 30 to 35 minutes longer, or until top of cake springs back when touched with a finger. Simmer syrup and water together for 1 minute. Using a pastry brush, spread syrup over top of cake to hold almonds in place and give a glossy finish. Cool cake 15 minutes in pan. Turn out on rack and let set until cold. Place in tin container or wrap in foil and let set in refrigerator for 24 hours before serving. *Makes a 9-inch cake.*

Grandmother's Fruit Cake

My husband's grandmother's favorite Christmas cake, originally from England. Usually baked at least a month before Christmas, wrapped in a brandy-soaked cloth and set in the pantry to "ripen." More brandy was poured over the cloth at intervals, to keep it moist.

1 cup butter
½ cup lard
1 cup brown sugar
2 cups molasses
Yolks of 4 eggs, beaten lightly
1 cup sour milk
1 teaspoon soda
2 cups cold coffee
4 cups all-purpose flour
1 teaspoon ground cloves
1 teaspoon cinnamon
1 teaspoon allspice
1 teaspoon nutmeg
2 pounds raisins
1½ pounds currants
1 pound citron, chopped
½ cup almonds, coarsely chopped
½ cup English walnuts, coarsely chopped

Cream butter and lard thoroughly. Mix sugar and molasses and stir until all lumps are dissolved. Beat egg yolks into butter mixture and combine with molasses mixture. Dissolve soda in sour milk. Sift spices with flour and add to batter alternately with milk, beating well after each addition. Stir in coffee and fold in raisins, currants, citron, and nuts. Turn batter into a large well-greased and floured tube pan, or 4 small loaf pans which have been greased, then lined with greased and floured paper. Bake large cake 3½ to 4 hours in 300° oven; the smaller cakes will require 2½ to 3 hours at 300°. Test for doneness by inserting a toothpick in cake. Will keep several weeks when stored in tightly covered tins. *Yield: About 10 pounds.*

Flat Cake

Very rich, fattening, and good-tasting. A variation of a flat cake which was very popular in the Philadelphia area during the first half of the nineteenth century. Excellent for nibbling with coffee, tea, or hot chocolate.

9 tablespoons butter
9 teaspoons sugar
9 egg yolks
4½ tablespoons water
¼ teaspoon salt
4½ tablespoons cream
1 tablespoon whiskey or brandy
4 cups all-purpose flour (approximately) sifted

Cream butter, add sugar and egg yolks, and beat until light and fluffy. Stir in remaining ingredients in order given. Add sufficient flour to make a fairly stiff dough. Let rest for a few minutes. Roll out on a lightly floured board, transfer to lightly greased cookie sheets and bake 8 to 10 minutes at 400°. Remove from oven when golden colored. Brush with melted butter and sprinkle lightly with sugar. Cut into 2-inch squares for serving. *Yield: About 24 to 30 squares.*

Lightning Cake

I'm not sure whether the name of this delectable cake (of German origin) comes from the speed with which it can be assembled, or the way it disappears from the plate. It melts in the mouth. Serve any time.

1⅓ cups all-purpose flour (sift before measuring)
½ teaspoon baking powder
½ teaspoon ground cloves
½ teaspoon baking soda
½ teaspoon salt
½ cup butter
1 whole egg, beaten well
1 egg yolk, beaten well
1 cup brown sugar, sifted
½ cup buttermilk
Topping:
1 egg white, beaten well
¼ cup brown sugar, sifted

Sift flour, baking powder, cloves, baking soda, and salt together and set aside. Cream butter, add beaten egg and extra yolk and sugar, and continue creaming until light and fluffy. Blend in flour mixture in thirds alternately with buttermilk and pour into greased and floured 9-by-8-by-2-inch cake pan. Beat egg white until stiff, add ¼ cup brown sugar, and continue beating until sugar has dissolved. Spread over cake. Bake at 350° for 35 minutes. Cool slightly and cut in squares. *Makes 12 servings.*

Pound Cake 1

My cousin Merta McNeill Sonner tells me this pound cake recipe is one hundred and fifty years old. Since she is ninety-five and has shared other very old recipes with me, I believe her.

8 egg whites
2⅔ cups sugar
2 cups sweet butter
8 egg yolks
3½ cups cake flour, sifted
⅔ cup coffee cream
1 teaspoon vanilla

Whip egg whites to a froth, and continue beating while you add 6 tablespoons of sugar, one at a time. When egg whites are quite stiff, set in refrigerator until needed. Cream butter to fluffy stage and add remaining sugar gradually, beating until light yellow. Add egg yolks two at a time, beating well after each addition. Add flour and cream alternately in thirds, beating well after each addition and ending with flour. Continue beating batter until very light. Fold in the egg whites very gently and add the vanilla last. Pour into a lightly greased 10-inch tube pan or a loaf cake pan and bake at 300° for 1 hour and 25 minutes, or until light brown. Merta says, "The cake will fall about one inch after removing it from the oven. Don't worry, this improves the texture. No icing is required; powdered sugar may be sprinkled over the top before baking if you wish." *Makes a 10-inch cake.*

Note: The absence of baking powder makes the extra beating necessary to force air into the batter. If this recipe seems to indicate too much work, follow the one directly below, or you may use your electric mixer, turning it to lowest speed for use.

Pound Cake 2

As everyone knows, the name of this cake originated from the fact that the original version called for one pound each of butter, sugar, and flour. This recipe has been adapted for today's efficient cooks.

2 cups butter
3 cups sugar
10 eggs (12 if small)
4 cups cake flour
2 teaspoons baking powder
¼ teaspoon salt
1 teaspoon vanilla
1 teaspoon anise extract

Cream butter and sugar until fluffy. Beat in eggs one at a time, until very well blended. Sift flour with baking powder and salt and add gradually to batter. Stir in vanilla and anise extract. Turn batter into a 10-inch tube pan which has been well greased and lined with waxed paper. Bake at 325° for 1 hour. Cool in pan for 10 minutes before turning onto wire rack. No frosting is necessary. *Makes a 10-inch cake.*

Note: Some recipes call for 2 tablespoonfuls brandy for flavoring, or you might use 4 tablespoons orange juice, or try your own ideas.

Marble Cake

A variation of Mom's old faithful two-egg family cake. On special occasions she added chocolate, which seemed to make it taste even better.

Melt 1 square chocolate in small pan over hot water and set aside to cool while mixing Butter Cake (see page 153). Divide batter in halves. Add melted, cooled chocolate to half of batter and pour into 10-by-10-by-2-inch greased baking pan alternately with yellow batter. Bake at 350° for 30 to 45 minutes. Test for doneness by touching center lightly with forefinger. *Serves 10 to 12.*

Note: After taking the extra time to make this variation, Mom often went all the way, grating another square of chocolate into the beaten egg and adding a little more sugar. This frosting was extremely well received.

Chocolate Potato Cake

A moist, rich, substantial cake which will keep well. It will maintain your reputation as a good cake baker, without too much work.

1 cup butter
2 cups sugar
1 cup hot mashed potatoes
¾ cup cocoa
4 eggs
2½ cups cake flour
2 teaspoons baking powder
½ teaspoon salt
½ teaspoon allspice
½ teaspoon nutmeg
½ cup milk
1 teaspoon vanilla
1 teaspoon lemon extract
1 cup small seedless raisins
1 cup chopped nutmeats

Cream butter and sugar together until light and fluffy. Combine mashed potatoes with cocoa and add butter mixture while potatoes are still warm. Beat in 4 eggs. Reserve ½ cup flour for mixing with raisins. Sift remaining 2 cups flour with salt, baking powder, and spices 3 times. Add to butter mixture alternately with milk, in 3 parts. Stir in vanilla and lemon extract. Mix reserved ½ cup flour with raisins and fold into batter, with chopped nuts. Turn batter into a 10-inch tube pan or a 9-by-5-by-4-inch loaf pan which has been greased and floured. Bake at 350° for about an hour, or until top springs back when touched with forefinger. Turn out onto rack and when cool, frost with Fluffy Icing (see page 173). *Makes a 10-inch cake.*

New England Raspberry Cake

Faintly reminiscent of England's world-famous Tipsy Cake or Trifle, except that the custard is omitted, as well as the wine. A tasty dessert nevertheless, brought to southern Illinois by one of the New Englanders.

½ cup butter
1 cup sugar
2 egg yolks
2 cups cake flour
1 teaspoon baking powder
¼ teaspoon salt
⅔ cup milk

Cream butter and sugar thoroughly. Beat egg yolks until foamy and combine with butter mixture. Sift flour with baking powder and salt and add to butter mixture in thirds, alternating with milk. Beat well after each addition. Turn into 2 10-by-14-inch greased and floured jelly-cake tins and bake for about 20 to 25 minutes at 350°, or until top of cake springs back when touched with forefinger. Remove from pans and cool. When quite cold, put together with the filling:

1 quart (4 cups) ripe red raspberries
2 egg whites
1 cup powdered sugar
1 teaspoon lemon juice

Crush raspberries slightly with wire potato masher. Beat egg whites which have been reserved from cake until stiff and add 1 cup powdered sugar gradually, continuing to beat vigorously. Fold in raspberries and lemon juice. Spread between layers and over top of cake. Chill several hours before serving. Top with whipped cream just before serving. *Serves 10 to 12.*

Butter Icing

This is very good and easily made. Let it stand over hot water for 15 minutes after mixing. Beat until cool and thick enough to spread well.

3 tablespoons butter
¼ cup hot water or cream
⅛ teaspoon salt
2 cups confectioners' sugar, sifted
1 teaspoon vanilla

Melt butter in saucepan over low heat; add water, or cream, and salt. Remove from fire and cool. Add vanilla and sugar gradually, stirring until all lumps are removed. Pour over cake when it reaches the right consistency for spreading and is not too runny. *Yield: Sufficient for 2 9-inch layers.*

Variations for Butter Icing:

Add 2 ounces melted chocolate to mixture.
Combine ¼ cup cocoa with melted butter and hot milk or water.
Add 2 tablespoons grated lemon or orange peel.
Substitute ¼ cup strong coffee for hot water.
Substitute orange juice for water or cream.

Fluffy Icing

A marshmallowlike icing for special cakes.

2 cups sugar
⅓ cup light corn syrup
⅓ cup water
2 egg whites
½ teaspoon salt
1 teaspoon vanilla

Cook sugar, syrup, and water over moderate heat, stirring until sugar is dissolved. Continue cooking slowly until mixture forms a soft ball when a spoonful is dropped into a cup of cold water. Beat egg whites until quite stiff, adding salt during beating. Pour hot syrup over egg whites, beating hard, and continue beating until icing holds its shape well. Add vanilla, blend, and spread on cake. *Yield: Sufficient for top and sides of a 9-inch, 2-layer cake.*

Boiled White Frosting

A glossy, fairly firm frosting. A word of caution: Don't overbeat.

2½ cups sugar
½ cup light corn syrup
½ cup water
2 egg whites
½ teaspoon salt
1½ teaspoons vanilla

Combine sugar, corn syrup, and water in a heavy saucepan. Stir gently over low heat until sugar is thoroughly dissolved. Bring to a boil, cover, and cook 5 minutes. Uncover and boil without stirring to the soft-ball stage. While syrup is cooking, beat egg whites until stiff. Pour syrup over whites in a fine stream, continuing to beat vigorously. Beat in vanilla and continue beating until frosting is stiff and almost cooled. *Yield: Sufficient for top and sides of a 2-layer cake.*

Cookies

Cookies

Hickory Nut Cookies

Hickory nut trees grew in abundance throughout southern Illinois when the first settlers came. The fine-textured hard wood was coveted for tool handles and farm machinery, with resulting scarcity of these sweet, delicately flavored nuts. When my father cleared land for his home he left 22 hickory trees standing near the house. We harvested all of the large shagbarks for use through the winter.

1 cup butter
1½ cups sugar
3 eggs, beaten until foamy
½ cup molasses
2 cups all-purpose flour, sifted
½ teaspoon cinnamon
¼ teaspoon cloves
¼ teaspoon allspice
⅛ teaspoon salt
1 teaspoon baking soda
1½ cups raisins, chopped coarsely
½ to ¾ cup hickory-nut meats, chopped coarsely

Cream butter and add sugar gradually, beating until the sugar dissolves and the mixture is fluffy. Beat in eggs and molasses. Sift flour, spices, salt, and soda together and stir into butter mixture. Blend thoroughly. Fold in raisins and nuts. If necessary, add a little more flour to make a firm dough. Roll to ¼ inch thickness on lightly floured board and cut into desired shapes with cookie cutter. Bake on greased cookie sheet at 350° for 10 minutes. Can be stored in airtight containers. *Yield: About 4 dozen cookies.*

Aunt Kate Dingman's Animal Cookies

From my husband's great-aunt, date mid-1800s. Children love these now as they did then.

2 cups sugar
1 cup butter or ¾ cup lard

2 eggs
1 cup sour milk
1 teaspoon soda
3 cups all-purpose flour (approximately)
2 teaspoons baking powder
1 teaspoon vanilla, almond, or lemon extract.

Cream sugar and shortening thoroughly. Beat in eggs one at a time. Dissolve soda in sour milk. Sift flour with baking powder. Add milk and flour to sugar-egg mixture in thirds, beating well after each addition. Stir in flavoring. Chill dough until it can be handled easily. Divide into 3 portions. Roll each portion out on lightly floured board to ⅛ inch thickness and cut into animal shapes with cookie cutter. Place carefully on greased sheet with spatula and bake at 375° for 8 to 10 minutes, or until delicately browned. Leave on cookie sheet for about 2 minutes to harden, then remove carefully with spatula. Cookies may be decorated with Butter Icing, if desired (see section, ''Cakes''). *Yield: 4 to 6 dozen, depending on size of cookie cutters used.*

Aunt Julia's Macaroons

I found this recipe among the collection of another aunt of my husband's. A memento of those pleasant days of long ago when ladies entertained at afternoon tea.

2 egg whites
2 tablespoons all-purpose flour
2 cups powdered sugar, sifted
Pinch of salt
1 teaspoon vanilla
1 cup grated coconut (approximately)

Beat egg whites until foamy. Sift sugar with flour and salt and add to egg whites gradually, beating constantly. Fold in vanilla and coconut. Drop by teaspoonfuls onto a lightly greased and well-floured cookie sheet. Bake in a slow oven, 300° for about 20 minutes. They should be firm but not browned. Let stand on baking sheet for a few minutes before removing carefully with a spatula. *Yield: About 3 dozen.*

Applesauce-Nut Cookies

These all-around cookies were to past generations what the chocolate chip cookies are to kids of today. They improve with age (if they last any length of time) and are great for the school lunch pail or basket, if there are such things any more.

2 cups all-purpose flour, sifted
½ teaspoon salt
½ teaspoon cinnamon
½ teaspoon nutmeg
½ teaspoon allspice
1 cup chopped hickory nuts or pecans
1 cup chopped raisins
½ cup lard or ½ cup plus 1 tablespoon butter
1 cup sugar
1 teaspoon baking soda
1 cup applesauce
1 egg, well beaten

Sift flour, salt, and spices together. Mix with nuts and raisins and set aside. Cream shortening until fluffy, add sugar gradually, and continue creaming until very light. Stir soda into apple sauce and combine with creamed mixture. Add beaten egg. Blend in flour-nut-raisin mixture. Drop by teaspoonfuls onto greased baking sheet. Bake 15 to 20 minutes at 350°. *Yield: 4 dozen.*

German Honey Cakes

A contribution of those good cooks, the German ladies who came with their families to southern Illinois during the early and mid-1800s. These are a bit tricky. (If noncommercially prepared honey is used, it should be well aged—at least 6 months to a year old. It is difficult to judge the acid content of new honey accurately enough to add the correct amount of soda to counteract it.) The cookies will keep for as long as 6 months.

2 pounds honey
1 pound sugar (2¼ cups)
2 tablespoons butter
1 tablespoon water
3 pounds all-purpose flour (10 to 12 cups)
2 teaspoons carbonate of powdered ammonia
8 egg yolks
½ pound citron, chopped fine
2 teaspoons potash (potassium bicarbonate)
¼ teaspoon cardamom
⅛ teaspoon ginger
2 teaspoons powdered cloves

⅛ **teaspoon cinnamon**
⅛ **teaspoon salt**
Grated peel of 1 orange
Grated peel of 1 lemon

Prepare honey mixture: Heat honey, sugar, butter, and water over low flame and stir constantly until it reaches boiling point and sugar is entirely dissolved. Sift flour with spices and salt into large bowl. Pour honey mixture over it slowly, stirring vigorously to prevent lumps. When thoroughly mixed, add 2 teaspoons carbonate of powdered ammonia (can be purchased from your pharmacist) which has been dissolved in ½ teaspoon of water. Cool. Beat egg yolks until lemon colored and add potash (can be purchased from your pharmacist) which has been dissolved in 1 tablespoon warm water. Beat well. Cover bowl and set in a cool place for 8 days to "ripen." When ready to bake, roll out ¼ inch thick on a lightly floured board, cut with cookie cutters and bake on cookie sheet in a slow oven, 325° for 10 to 12 minutes. Ice with lemon icing:

2 egg whites
⅛ **teaspoon salt**
Grated rind of 1 lemon
Juice of 1 lemon
Confectioners' sugar (enough to make a spreadable icing)

Whip egg whites until stiff. Add salt, lemon rind, and juice and beat in sugar until icing will spread easily without running. *Yield: About 10 to 12 dozen.*

Note: If preferred, bake in one sheet and decorate with icing made by mixing 3 tablespoons boiling water and 1 teaspoon vanilla with 2 cups confectioners' sugar. Beat icing until it is spreadable. Decorate with almonds. Cut while still hot.

Peppernuts

These spicy drop cookies are traditional Christmas favorites among German families. One finds them in many bakeries around the holidays and I used to wonder why more of them were not baked at home, until I learned they took considerable time to make, as the old recipes require that the dough be set aside to "ripen" for 2 weeks after mixing. This more modern version is quite satisfactory, and the ripening process can be carried out *after* baking.

¾ cup dark brown sugar, firmly packed
¾ cup white sugar
2 eggs
Rind of 1 lemon, grated
1 tablespoon citron, minced
1 tablespoon candied orange peel, minced
½ teaspoon ground cloves
½ teaspoon allspice
1 teaspoon cinnamon
¼ teaspoon cardamom
½ teaspoon freshly ground black pepper
3½ cups all-purpose flour
1 teaspoon soda
¼ cup grated unblanched almonds
1 cup powdered sugar
¼ cup brandy

Combine brown and white sugar, add eggs, and beat until mixture is very thick and light-colored. Add lemon rind, citron, orange peel, and spices and mix thoroughly. Sift flour with soda and stir into egg mixture. Add grated almonds. Turn onto a well-floured board and knead until smooth. Shape into long rolls 1 inch in diameter and cut into ½-to-¾-inch slices. Place on a buttered cookie sheet and let set overnight to dry at room temperature. Bake in preheated 300° oven, for about 20 minutes. Remove from cookie sheet with spatula and sprinkle with brandy before rolling in powdered sugar. These cookies will keep for several weeks if stored in a tin or other airtight container. *Yield: About 9 dozen.*

Cookies may be iced if desired:

⅓ cup confectioners' sugar
1½ tablespoons cornstarch
½ teaspoon vanilla
1 teaspoon brandy
Hot water

Combine sugar, cornstarch, vanilla, and brandy. Add hot water, 1 tablespoon at a time, until you have a smooth spreadable icing. Spread on cookies while warm. If icing thickens, add a little more hot water.

Hazlenut Cookies

Hazelnut bushes grew plentifully along the fence rows on and around our farm when I was a child. My dad used to take us on Sunday afternoon walks down the country lanes that bordered our farm and that of a great uncle. We would return home with pockets bulging with hazelnuts and more nature lore stuffed into our heads.

3 egg whites
1½ cups brown sugar, sifted
½ pound hazelnut meats, ground
½ teaspoon vanilla
Granulated sugar

Beat egg whites until frothy. Add sugar gradually, beating after each addition until quite stiff. Fold in ground hazelnuts and vanilla. Cut off pieces about ½ inch to ¾ inch in diameter with a teaspoon, roll in granulated sugar, and place carefully on lightly greased cookie sheets. Bake at 325° for 20 minutes. Handle gently; they are fragile. *Yield: About 30 cookies*

Note: 1 pound hazelnuts shelled will produce ½ pound hazelnut meats.

Ginger Cookies

This is another recipe which I found, written on old-fashioned lined tablet paper, in handwriting of days long gone by. My husband's mother evidently treasured it, for it bore the notation "Fine. Ida."

1 cup brown sugar
1 cup shortening (½ butter, ½ lard)
1 egg, well beaten
1 cup dark molasses
1 tablespoon vinegar
1 teaspoon soda
1 teaspoon ginger
2 tablespoons cinnamon
½ teaspoon salt
5 cups all-purpose flour, sifted

Cream sugar and shortening well and add beaten egg. Mix molasses and vinegar and dissolve soda in this mixture. Sift dry ingredients together and add to creamed mixture alternately with molasses. Beat thoroughly. Cover bowl and chill dough for an hour. Roll out a portion at a time on a well-floured board and cut in desired shapes with a floured cookie cutter. Bake at 375° for 8 to 10 minutes. *Yield: About 5 dozen 4-inch cookies.*

Note: This makes dandy gingerbread men. A little longer baking time is required. Yield depends on size of pattern. May be iced with Butter Icing (see section, "Cakes").

Ginger Snaps

Contributed by Alvin Over of Albion. Snappy, long-keeping cookies (provided there is a lock on the cookie jar).

**1½ cup molasses
⅔ cup butter
1 egg
4½ cups all-purpose flour
2 teaspoons ginger
1 teaspoon salt
1 teaspoon soda
1 teaspoon lemon extract**

Heat molasses to boiling point, remove from fire immediately, and add butter. Stir until butter is melted and set aside until almost cold. Beat egg slightly and add to molasses. Sift flour with ginger, salt, and soda and stir into molasses mixture. Add lemon extract. Dough should be stiff; if not, add a little more flour. Turn onto waxed paper and shape into 1 or more rolls. Chill several hours, or overnight. Slice in ⅛-inch-thick slices and bake at 350° for 8 to 10 minutes. Remove from cookie sheet with spatula and lift onto rack to cool. *Yield: About 100 cookies.*

Grandma's Sugar Cookies

These cookies have never lost their popularity through the years (since mid-1800s), and variations will be found in most popular cookbooks. Julia Etherton shares this one, handed down from Elizabeth Harrison of Herrin's Prairie.

**2½ cups sugar
1 cup lard
2 eggs
2 cups all-purpose flour (approximately)
1 teaspoon baking powder
¼ cup sour milk or cream
1 teaspoon salt
1 teaspoon soda
1 teaspoon vanilla extract**

Cream sugar and lard thoroughly. Add eggs and beat until fluffy. Sift flour with baking powder. Dissolve soda and salt in milk and add alternately with flour mixture. Add more sifted flour if necessary to make a soft dough. Chill for at least 1 hour. Roll out on lightly floured board and cut into desired shapes with cookie cutter. Bake at 375° on greased cookie sheet for 8 to 10 minutes. *Yield: About 4 dozen cookies*

Note: If using butter instead of lard, increase amount to 1 cup plus 2 tablespoons.

German Sugar Cookies

Good old-fashioned sugar cookies filled the cracks and crevices of the children's stomachs before the days of the Good Humor man and the pop machines.

2 cups sugar
1 cup butter
3 eggs
3 cups flour
1 teaspoon baking powder
½ teaspoon nutmeg (optional)
½ teaspoon cinnamon (optional)
2 teaspoons vanilla

Cream sugar and butter until fluffy, add eggs one at a time, and beat well. Sift flour with baking powder and spices and blend into creamed mixture. Add vanilla. Chill dough for several hours. When ready to bake, divide dough into 3 parts. Roll out each portion to ⅛ inch thickness on well-floured board, cut into desired shapes with cookie cutter and place on greased cookie sheet. Bake in moderate oven, 375°, for 10 to 15 minutes, until very pale golden colored. Remove pan from oven, set aside for a few minutes, then remove cookies with a spatula, placing each one on a rack to crisp. *Yield: About 80 cookies.*

Note: Sugar may be sprinkled over tops of cookies before baking, if desired.

Desserts and Confections

Desserts and Confections

Apples

Today's schoolkids are intrigued with the image of Johnny Apple-seed clomping through Pennsylvania, Ohio, and Indiana wearing a long-handled cooking pot on his head and planting apple seeds in clear spaces here and there. There is no doubt that at least a few of the apple orchards planted in southern Illinois in the first half of the nineteenth century were seedlings from Johnny Appleseed's (John Chapman) planting crusade. Apples were the hardiest of the early fruit plantings, which probably explains why so many apple recipes have been handed down. The early settlers would have fared poorly without cider, vinegar, apple butter, apple pies, puddings and cakes, dried apples for winter use, and applejack.

Apple Pudding 1

Puddings, baked or boiled, were the most popular desserts in the early days, possibly because they could be steamed on top of the stove or baked at variable temperatures without much damage being done. Cakes and pies required more even temperatures during cooking, for best results, to say nothing of closer attention needed to prevent overcooking.

5 apples, unpeeled and diced (2 cups) Jonathans or Winesaps best
½ cup butter
1 cup sugar
1 egg, unbeaten
1 cup all-purpose flour
1 teaspoon baking soda
1 teaspoon nutmeg
1 teaspoon cinnamon
½ teaspoon salt
Dash of cardamom, if desired
½ cup chopped pecans or hickory nuts (optional)

Prepare apples and set aside. Cream butter, add sugar gradually, and when fluffy and light, add egg, and mix well. Sift dry ingredients together and add to creamed mixture. Toss the apples into the batter, and if you wish a bit more texture, stir in ½ cup chopped pecans or hickory nuts. Turn into a greased 8-by-8-by-2-inch-pan. Bake at 350° for 45 minutes, or until done. May be served warm with hard sauce (see page 197) or cold with whipped cream. *Serves 6.*

Apple Pudding 2

It seemed that we were honored with unexpected guests on washdays, which were drudgery days at our house. When the crank-type washing machine was broken down, which happened frequently, our mother scrubbed out the clothing for her brood on the washboard, with a couple of us girls turning the wringer and smaller kids helping in various ways. During apple season this pudding was thrown together by our mother when these unexpected guests "stopped by," to top off an otherwise mediocre meal of perhaps beans and pork shank which had been simmering on the stove.

¼ cup butter
¾ cup sugar
1 egg, unbeaten
1 cup plus 2 tablespoons all-purpose flour
1 teaspoon soda
½ teaspoon cinnamon
¼ teaspoon nutmeg
1½ cups chopped tart apples
1 tablespoon cream (if needed)
¾ cup other fruit and/or nuts, if desired (may be apricots, plums,
    pecans, hickory nuts, walnuts)

Cream butter and sugar. Add unbeaten egg and beat well. Sift flour with soda, cinnamon, and nutmeg, and stir into butter mixture. Beat hard. Add apples and cream, and any additional fruit and/or nuts desired. Bake at 350° in lightly greased 8-by-8-by-2-inch pan for about 45 minutes. Serve with sauce. To make pudding sauce:

1 cup sugar
1½ teaspoons cornstarch
1 cup apple juice
¼ cup orange juice
1 tablespoon grated orange rind
2 tablespoons butter

Sift sugar with cornstarch. Combine apple and orange juice and stir into cornstarch slowly, continuing to stir until smooth. Add orange rind and butter, and cook over low heat until thick. Serve hot. *Serves 6 to 8.*

Note: This recipe can be extended by doubling the amount of apples used. For special occasions the pudding may be baked in individual greased molds. This recipe is enough for 6 molds; or 8, if more apple is added. Bake at 350° for 30 minutes.

Apple Pudding 3

A plain everyday dessert recipe from my family files. For one of those days when dinner time is at hand and there is no dessert for a dessert-loving family. It can bake while you're eating.

2 cups apples, unpeeled, chopped (Jonathans preferred)
1 cup sugar
1 cup all-purpose flour
⅛ teaspoon salt
1 teaspoon soda
½ teaspoon cinnamon
½ teaspoon nutmeg
¼ teaspoon ground cloves
1 egg, beaten
½ cup raisins (optional)
1 cup pecans, hickory nuts, or walnuts, chopped
1 tablespoon butter

Mix chopped apples with sugar and set aside while assembling remaining ingredients. Sift flour, salt, soda, and spices together. Beat egg and combine with flour mixture. Fold in apples and nuts. Turn into 8-by-8-inch greased baking dish, dot with butter, and bake at 350° for 30 to 35 minutes. Serve hot or cold. *Serves 4 to 6.*

Apple Crisp

An English friend of ours calls it "Apple Crumbly." It's a delicious moist dessert following a meal, or served to guests who drop in during an evening. Quick and easy.

3 pounds tart apples (Jonathans or Winesaps preferred) about 8
1 cup all-purpose flour
1 cup brown sugar
½ cup butter
½ teaspoon salt
Grated rind and juice of ½ lemon
¼ cup chopped nuts
1 teaspoon cinnamon (optional)

Peel, core, and slice apples thinly and place in 7-by-10-inch shallow baking dish. Sprinkle with lemon juice and rind. Mix flour, sugar, butter, salt, and cinnamon with a pastry blender or knife until the mixture resembles coarse meal. Spread evenly over apples. Sprinkle nuts over top. Bake at 375° for 30 minutes, or until apples are done. Serve hot with thick cream or cold with whipped cream. *Serves 6.*

Apple Dumplings

Merta McNeill Sonner wrote "I have dropped hundreds of these dumplings in the black iron kettle in boiling water. They were our favorite dessert at home. We served them with a dip of milk sweetened to taste."

8 tart apples
1 cup sugar
1 teaspoon cinnamon
Butter size of an egg (about 2 tablespoons)

Peel and halve the apples, removing cores. Fill depression with sugar, sprinkle with cinnamon, and dot with about ½ teaspoon butter. Rejoin halves. To make pastry:

4 cups all-purpose flour, sifted
¼ teaspoon salt
2 teaspoons baking powder
½ cup lard
¼ cup butter (or less)

Mix ingredients in order given, using just enough milk (or water) to make a stiff dough. Roll out to ¼-inch thickness on a floured board. Divide into 8 parts. Wrap each square around an apple, sealing edges by pinching together tightly. Drop dumplings into boiling water, cover tightly, and cook for 15 minutes. Remove from water with a slotted spoon and serve with sweetened milk or cream (about ¼ cup) to which a dash of nutmeg has been added. *Serves 8.*

Note: It is better to place the dumplings in a perforated pan and set it in the kettle of boiling water. Easier to handle.

Persimmon Pudding 1

Every farm family had its own persimmon tree, or trees, somewhere out in the pasture or along a fence row, which the kids watched as the fruit turned from green to deep orange. (No one bothered the green fruit after one trial.) The morning after the first hard frost, pickers would appear like magic to gather the fruit. This was the signal for mother to stir up a persimmon pudding. A variation of this recipe comes from my German-born grandmother, via my sister Lyla Graul.

½ gallon ripe persimmons, seeded and sieved, which should yield about 1 quart of puree
2 eggs
1 cup sugar
1 cup sweet milk
1 teaspoon butter, melted
1 teaspoon cinnamon
1 teaspoon baking powder
½ teaspoon salt
½ teaspoon vanilla

Beat eggs until pale yellow, add sugar, and continue beating until sugar dissolves. Stir in milk. Mix remaining ingredients with persimmon puree and combine with egg mixture. Beat hard for a few minutes and pour into a 6-cup greased casserole. Bake at 325° for 45 minutes to an hour, or until top is golden brown and a knife inserted in the center comes out clean. Serve warm or cold, with fresh, heavy whipped cream. *Serves 6.*

Persimmon Pudding 2

Merta McNeill Sonner's own recipe: "Made by Nina Mitchell for over 60 years. This is a very old receipt." This one probably used during the hens' molting season. (A minor crisis arose when molting season arrived, for the hens did not lay while shedding their feathers, and while this season usually occurred in late summer, the hens might occasionally quit producing eggs for other reasons.)

1 quart persimmons (remove seeds by squeezing in hands and run through a colander)
1½ cups sugar
1 rounded tablespoon butter, melted
1 cup all-purpose flour
1 teaspoon soda
2 cups sweet milk
Salt to taste, about ½ teaspoon

Sift sugar with flour, soda, and salt. Blend with butter and add milk. Beat until smooth. Add persimmon pulp and blend well. Grease and dust a baking pan with flour as for a cake. Pour batter into a 12-by-8-by-2-inch pan and bake at 325° for about 1 hour. "It will fluff up beautifully, then when done it will fall. It is a soft pudding. Take up with spoon." *Serves 4 to 6.*

Indian Pudding

Maize became known as Indian corn, to distinguish it from the white corn developed by the Americans, which was regarded at the time as finer and more desirable for certain dishes. This pudding loses some of its character if white cornmeal is used.

½ **cup yellow or Indian cornmeal**
4 **cups cold milk**
⅔ **cup dark molasses**
1 **large egg, well beaten**
¼ **teaspoon nutmeg**
¼ **teaspoon cinnamon**
½ **teaspoon salt**
½ **cup raisins**
½ **cup cold water**

Mix cornmeal and ¼ cup cold milk to a smooth paste. Heat 3¼ cups milk in a double boiler and add the meal mixture gradually, stirring constantly, to prevent lumps from forming. Cook for 10 minutes longer, or until mixture thickens slightly, continuing to stir. Add 2 tablespoons of the meal mixture to the beaten egg, mix well, and pour into the cooked mixture very slowly, beating meanwhile. Remove from heat, stir in remainder of egg mixture, spices, salt, and raisins. Blend well, and pour into a well-buttered, 6-cup baking dish. Bake at 350° for 30 minutes. Remove from oven and stir in ¼ cup cold water. Bake 30 minutes longer. Add remaining ¼ cup cold water and bake 1 hour longer. Remove from oven and set aside for 30 minutes before serving. Garnish with thick cream. *Serves 6.*

Old English Plum Pudding

Handed down to Mrs. Etta Over of Albion, Illinois, from her husband's grandmother Over's recipe collection. Evokes memories of Dickens's *Christmas Carol.*

⅔ **cup butter**
1½ **cups sugar**
4 **eggs**

⅓ cup molasses
2 cups all-purpose flour
1 teaspoon baking powder
2 teaspoons salt
1 teaspoon cinnamon
½ teaspoon ground cloves
½ teaspoon nutmeg
1 teaspoon soda
1 cup buttermilk
1 pound raisins
1 pound currants
¼ cup all-purpose flour
1 cup chopped nuts (optional)
½ cup citron, chopped (optional)
½ cup candied pineapple (optional)
½ cup candied cherries, chopped (optional)
½ cup coconut (optional)

Cream butter and sugar. Add eggs and molasses and beat thoroughly. Sift flour, baking powder, soda, salt, and spices together and add to batter in thirds, alternately with buttermilk. Combine raisins and currants with ¼ cup flour and fold into batter. Add any or all of the optional ingredients. The batter should be stiff enough to hold a spoon upright. If not, add enough flour to obtain this consistency. Wet heavy muslin pudding cloth with hot water and flour and place in a bowl to give a good shape. Spoon batter into center of the cloth and tie securely, leaving a couple inches of space to allow pudding to rise. Adequate space can be assured if, after twisting the top of the cloth, one person holds the twisted ends while another person ties the cloth at the top of the fist. Place pudding in sufficient boiling water to cover; add boiling water as needed to keep pudding covered during cooking process. Simmer for 2 hours. Turn pudding over and boil 2 hours longer, until top of cloth dries quickly when the lid is removed. Lift from boiling bath and remove cloth, to avoid pudding sticking to the cloth. Reserve some of the water for the sauce:

1 cup sugar
⅓ cup brown sugar
2 teaspoons flour
¼ cup butter
¼ teaspoon nutmeg

Mix above ingredients well and gradually stir in 2 cups water in which pudding was cooked. Add butter and serve hot. (This was called "dip" in original recipe.) *Serves 10 to 12.*

Suet Pudding

Another pudding recipe from my husband's mother's collection, inherited from her Irish mother. Handwritten on yellowed, crumbling paper, possibly brought over from the Ould Country.

2 cups suet
1 cup sugar
2 cups molasses
2 eggs, beaten
1 cup bread crumbs
2 cups sweet milk
1 teaspoon soda
2 cups flour (approximately)
1 teaspoon salt
1 teaspoon cinnamon
1 teaspoon nutmeg
1 teaspoon ground cloves
1 teaspoon allspice
1 cup currants
1 cup raisins
1 cup sliced citron

Chop suet fine. Add sugar and molasses and stir until thoroughly blended. Add beaten eggs and bread crumbs. Stir until crumbs are dissolved into batter. Combine soda and milk. Sift 1 cup of flour with salt and spices and beat into mixture alternately with milk. Add sufficient flour to make a stiff batter. Fold in currants, raisins, and citron. Turn into greased mold, cover tightly, and steam or boil for 3½ hours. Serve with hard sauce, whipped cream, or your favorite sauce. Before serving, pour ½ cup brandy over top and flame. *Serves 8 or more.*

English Pudding

Brought from England by one of my husband's great-aunts, a couple generations ago and given to me by his mother.

½ pound suet
¾ pound dark brown sugar (2¼ cups)
5 eggs, beaten
¾ pound bread crumbs (2 cups)
½ pound all-purpose flour (approximately 2 cups)
1 teaspoon cinnamon
½ teaspoon nutmeg
1 teaspoon salt
½ cup sour milk

1 teaspoon soda
1 pound peeled, chopped apples (3 cups)
Juice and grated rind of 2 lemons
1 pound raisins
1 pound sultanas (large yellow raisins)
1 pound currants
½ pound mixed peel
2 ounces blanched almonds, chopped
1 cup red wine

Chop suet fine. Add sugar and eggs and mix thoroughly. Stir in bread crumbs and let stand while sifting flour with spices and salt. Dissolve soda in sour milk and add to egg mixture alternately with flour-spice mixture. Fold in apples, raisins, currants, peel, almonds, lemon juice, and rind. Add wine and a bit more flour, if necessary. The batter should be quite stiff. Pour batter into 8 small greased pudding molds. Cover closely and steam for about an hour.

If preferred, the pudding may be steamed in one large mold, in which case it should be cooked for at least 2 hours. Serve hot with wine sauce (see below). *Serves 8 to 10.*

English Pudding Cake

Contributed by Mrs. Etta Over of Albion, a southern Illinois town which cherishes its English traditions.

½ cup butter
1 cup sugar
2 eggs
1½ cups all-purpose flour, unsifted
½ teaspoon baking soda
½ teaspoon salt
½ teaspoon baking powder
½ teaspoon cinnamon
½ teaspoon nutmeg
½ teaspoon allspice
⅔ cup buttermilk (or sour milk)
⅔ cup currants or chopped raisins
½ cup chopped nuts

Cream butter until soft, add sugar and eggs, and beat well. Sift flour, soda, salt, baking powder, and spices together. Add alternately with buttermilk to butter mixture, beating well after each addition. Fold in currants and nuts. Turn into greased and floured pudding mold and steam for 2 hours. Serve hot or cold, with favorite sauce or topping, or with hard sauce (see below).

Note: During the holiday season, a dramatic effect can be created by pouring ¼ cup brandy over the pudding immediately before serving, and igniting it.

Sweet Potato Pudding 1

A hurry-up dessert—really a souffle, as the eggs puff it up high and mighty.

1½ pounds sweet potatoes (2 large ones) boiled until very tender
½ pound butter (1 cup)
½ cup sugar
1 cup milk
6 eggs, beaten lightly
1 teaspoon salt
⅛ teaspoon nutmeg
Juice and grated rind of 1 lemon

Peel boiled sweet potatoes and mash. Add butter and stir until it is melted. Rub both together through a sieve. Add eggs and milk and beat together until thoroughly mixed. Stir in salt, nutmeg, lemon juice, and rind and blend. Turn into a 2-quart greased casserole and bake at 350° 20 to 25 minutes, or until it rises and is lightly browned on top. Serve with whipped cream or hard sauce (see below). *Serves 6.*

Note: This may also be baked in a crust as a pie. Irish potatoes may be used instead of sweet potatoes.

Sweet Potato Pudding 2

Lack of quick-mixes or close proximity to a supermarket did not prevent the old-time homemaker from providing her family with satisfying desserts. My cousin Merta McNeill Sonner shared this recipe, which she obtained from a friend's church-circle cookbook. She vouches for its Southern origin.

3 cups sweet potatoes (ground or grated raw)
½ cup butter
1 cup sugar
2 eggs
1 cup milk
1 teaspoon cinnamon or nutmeg
½ teaspoon salt, or to taste
½ cup walnut or pecan meats

Grate sweet potatoes and set aside. Cream butter and sugar until light and fluffy. Beat in eggs and add milk, continuing to beat until well blended. Add potatoes, spice, salt, and nuts. Pour into a greased baking dish and bake at 350° for 1 to 1½ hours. Serve with any tart jam whipped with cream, or hard sauce. If a richer pudding is desired, molasses may be substituted for part of the sugar and ¼ cup of raisins added. *Serves 6 to 8.*

Note: The sweet potatoes may turn dark shortly after being ground or grated. This does not harm them in any way, but if it bothers you, pour the milk over them and add both together.

Hard Sauce

The proof of the pudding may be in the eating, but it's the sauce that takes it out of the good stage to a memorable experience. This sauce may be used with other puddings, and other flavorings of your choice may be used—orange juice, lemon extract or lemon jucie, etc.

1 cup sugar
1 tablespoon butter
1 tablespoon cream
3 egg whites
⅛ teaspoon salt
2 tablespoons cream
1 tablespoon brandy, sherry, or vanilla

Beat butter until soft. Sift sugar and work into butter a little at a time and beat until the mixture is quite fluffy. Add 1 tablespoon cream. Whip egg whites with salt until stiff. Fold into sugar mixture. Add 2 additional tablespoons cream, and brandy or other flavoring of your choice. Beat well. Chill before serving. *Yield: About 1½ cupfuls.*

Hot Wine Sauce

A delightful pudding sauce.

1 cup sugar
½ cup butter
1 egg, beaten
¾ cup sour red wine
¼ teaspoon nutmeg (optional)
1 teaspoon grated lemon rind

Cream sugar and butter and add beaten egg. Blend in wine, nutmeg, and lemon rind. When ready to serve, heat over hot water, beating until foamy. *Yield: About 1½ cupfuls.*

Strawberry Shortcake

Southern Illinoisans are very fortunate to have access to an abundant supply of strawberries. Strawberry shortcake is served to top off meals and in between meals during the season. The good cooks differ in their choice of the shortcake however. Piecrust and sponge cake vied for top honors in our household; others preferred a rich biscuit. Here are directions for making all three. Take your pick.

Biscuit Dough for Shortcake

2 cups all-purpose flour
½ teaspoon salt
3 teaspoons baking powder
3 tablespoons butter
2 tablespoons sugar
¼ to ⅓ cup sweet milk

Sift dry ingredients into large bowl. Cut butter into them with a fork, 2 knives, a pastry blender, or work with your fingers. Add milk until a soft dough is formed. Roll or pat out on well-floured board to ¼ inch thickness. Cut rounds with large biscuit cutter. Brush lightly with melted butter. Top with a second round of dough. Bake in lightly greased pan for 12 to 15 minutes at 425°, or until golden brown. To serve: Remove top biscuit, heap crushed, sugared berries on bottom biscuit placed in a good-sized dessert dish, lay second biscuit on top, crust side down. Heap on another good stack of berries. Top with whipped or thick cream. Best served warm. *Yield: 12 biscuits.*

Sponge Cake for Shortcake

For those who prefer real cake as the base for their strawberry shortcake, this is a good one.

1 cup cake flour, sifted
1 teaspoon baking powder
¼ teaspoon salt
⅞ cup sugar

3 eggs, lightly beaten
1½ tablespoons water
1 teaspoon vanilla

Resift flour with remaining dry ingredients into a large bowl. Make a well in center. Drop in 3 eggs, lightly beaten, 1½ tablespoons water, and 1 teaspoon vanilla. Beat until batter is smooth. Turn into 8-by-8-inch ungreased pan and bake at 350° for about 20 minutes. Cut into squares for serving. Place in good-sized dessert dish, spoon plenty of crushed strawberries on top, garnish with whipped cream, and serve immediately. *Serves 12.*

Piecrust for Shortcake

Piecrust made with lard seems to produce excellent crust for fruit or cream pies; however, our family has always used butter when making crust for strawberry shortcake.

2 cups all-purpose flour (sifted before measuring)
1 teaspoon salt
⅔ cup butter
¼ cup ice water (or a bit more if needed)

Resift flour with salt. Measure ⅓ cup of this mixture into a cup and stir into it ¼ cup ice water to form a smooth paste. Cut butter into remainder of flour until it is the size of peas, using 2 knives or a pastry blender. Stir the flour paste into the dough and work it quickly into a ball. Chill for at least ½ hour, well wrapped in waxed paper. When ready to use, roll out on floured board to ⅛ inch thickness. You should have enough dough for 3 10-inch discs. Prick lightly with fork tines and place on cookie sheets. Bake 10 to 12 minutes at 425°, or until pale golden colored. Cool slightly. Put together immediately before serving. Layer in a large shallow bowl with crushed sweetened strawberries, until crust is used up, making sure you heap strawberries on top. Spoon into individual dessert dishes, and top with whipped cream. *Serves 10.*

Strawberries for Shortcake

Hull 2 quarts strawberries and wash quickly. Slice, or crush lightly with wire potato masher. Sweeten to taste. Stir lightly and chill about 2 hours.

German Cheesecake

Cheesecake is so delicious, and oh so fattening. But this old recipe from the German ladies is so easy to make that we can't resist including it.

2 cups smooth cottage cheese
1 cup sugar
2 eggs
2 teaspoons all-purpose flour
Juice and grated rind of 1 lemon

Press cottage cheese through sieve. Blend with sugar, add eggs and flour, and beat hard until well blended. Stir in lemon juice and rind. Spoon into a 9-inch cake pan and bake at 400° for 15 minutes. Reduce heat and continue baking at 350° for 1 hour. Turn off heat and let cake set in oven until cold. *Makes a 9-inch cake.*

Ice Cream

One of the winter chores of bygone days was harvesting ice for the icehouse, to be used during the following summer. The blocks, each weighing 25 to 50 pounds, were hauled from the nearest river, lake, or stream and stacked between thick layers of straw and/or sawdust in a heavily insulated outbuilding. On special summer evenings Dad would remove a block of ice from that cool icehouse, place it in a burlap bag (tow sack), and with the side of an ax, pound it into small pieces for packing the ice cream which Mom would have ready.

All nine of us grew up, as kids do, and left the old place to find our own places in the world. Our family gatherings continued. On the Fourth of July weekends we all tried to get home. The old icehouse was long gone, but brother Vern's first utterance after he greeted us was "let's make ice cream." Dad would haul the old beat-up freezer out of the shed, a committee would head for town to buy a block of ice, and Mom made, or supervised the making of, the custard for freezing. To make ice cream custard:

2 cups sugar
4 tablespoons cornstarch
¼ teaspoon salt
4 cups rich milk
4 cups cream (half and half)
4 eggs, beaten
2 tablespoons vanilla

Mix sugar, cornstarch, and salt in top of a double boiler, or a heavy saucepan. Gradually add milk, while stirring so the cornstarch will not get lumpy. Cook over low heat, or over boiling water if using double boiler, stirring occasionally, until thickened. Beat eggs until foamy and stir several spoonfuls of the hot mixture into eggs, then blend them into the hot mixture. Cook about 5 minutes longer, stirring constantly. Remove from fire and cool slightly. Stir in cream and vanilla. Chill in refrigerator for 2 hours. If in a hurry, set custard in a pan of chipped ice and stir frequently. Pour into 4-quart freezer, filling it about ¾ full (it expands during freezing). If any of the custard is left over, pour it into a container and freeze for another time.

Insert dasher in cream container and set lid in place. Pack freezer container about ⅓ full of chipped ice, then alternate remaining layers with coarse salt, allowing about three measures of ice to one measure of salt. When container is well filled, attach crank to top of dasher in ice cream container and fasten securely. Turn slowly at first, then as a slight pull is felt, turn faster until crank will no longer turn.

Pour off the salt water in the outer container. Wipe lid carefully, remove it, remove dasher, scrape off ice cream clinging to it and pass to the nearest kid to "lick"; or set it in a pan of water. Pack ice cream down with a heavy spoon, replace lid, insert a cork in hole left when dasher is removed, and cover with a piece of heavy waxed paper or clean cloth. Repack ice cream in additional ice and salt, cover freezer with a piece of heavy material—burlap, an old rug, etc. If possible, let the ice cream set for an hour before serving. *Yield: 1 gallon or 16 to 20 servings.*

Snow Ice Cream

One of the best times for us kids after a winter snow was enjoying a large dish of snow ice cream while sitting around the hearth.

Our dad would fill a large china bowl with clean freshly fallen snow, pour syrup or warmed honey over it and set the bowl outside again, in a snowy nest, for a while. After what seemed like hours to us kids he would bring it in to the dining room and serve us. It melted rapidly, of course, but while it lasted we enjoyed it to the hilt.

Marshmallows

This one turned up in an old cookbook, offering evidence that earlier generations were not deprived of all the goodies we take for granted today.

1 ounce gum arabic
3½ ounces confectioners' extra-fine sugar
½ teaspoon vanilla
Cornstarch

Cover gum arabic (can be obtained from your pharmacy) with 4 tablespoons water and let stand for an hour. Heat in a double boiler until dissolved. Strain through cheesecloth and whip in about 3½ ounces confectioners' extra-fine sugar. Set over a fairly low fire and beat constantly for 45 minutes, until mixture fluffs up to a stiff froth. Remove from fire, beat 2 to 3 minutes while cooling, and stir in ½ teaspoon vanilla. Sift sufficient cornstarch into an 8-by-8-inch pan to cover bottom, pour in the marshmallow mixture, smooth surface with the back of a spoon, and sift cornstarch lightly over the top. When cold, cut into squares with a sharp knife dipped in cornstarch, roll squares in the starch, and pack in tin or other containers which can be tightly covered. *Yield: 64 1-inch pieces.*

Molasses Taffy

Young ladies of dating age often entertained their friends with a taffy pull, back in the olden days before TV, the radio, automobiles, and other modern conveniences. The kitchen was preempted by the giddy group and the youthful hostess would have assembled the following ingredients for the festivities.

1 cup molasses
2 teaspoons vinegar
⅛ teaspoon salt
¾ cup sugar (optional)
1 tablespoon butter
⅛ teaspoon baking soda

Boil molasses, sugar (if used), and vinegar to hard-ball stage, when a little bit poured in a glass of cold water becomes brittle. Remove from fire; add baking soda, butter, and salt. Stir until blended well. Pour into well-buttered pan. Set aside to cool and adjourn to the parlor to gather around the pump organ and sing "Annie Laurie," "My Bonnie Lies over the Ocean," "Old Black Joe," or whatever suits your mood. When the candy is cool enough to handle, butter hands, pick up a handful, and pull until light and porous, or appears to be full of air bubbles. Lay on marble slab or hardwood cutting board and cut into 1-inch pieces. *Yield: About 1 pound.*

Aunt Ett's Ball Chocolate Candy

My dearly beloved late great-aunt Ett (all 4 feet 9 inches of her) had an enviable reputation in our little village. No one ever left her home without a cookie, a bouquet, a rose cutting, a recipe, or some kind of remembrance. She had lost her only child in its infancy, and she loved all children. I am happy to share her recipe for chocolate candy, as she wrote it for her niece (my cousin) Weltha McNeill Toland, who in turn shared it with me.

1 box powdered sugar
3 tablespoons butter, melted
3 tablespoons cream
1 teaspoon vanilla or almond extract
½ cake paraffin, melted
1 cake bitter chocolate, melted

Mix sugar, butter, and cream well, to make a stiff batter. Add flavoring to batter. Mold this batter in small round balls. Melt ½ cake of paraffin; melt 1 cake of bitter chocolate. Dip the balls in chocolate and paraffin. *Yield: About 40 pieces.*

Popcorn Balls

Ridgeway, Illinois claims the title Popcorn Capitol of the U.S.A., so it is easy to understand that popcorn balls are a popular confection of southern Illinois. The following directions were followed in the early days, long before electric corn poppers were heard of: "It will be found a great aid in popping corn to swing a wire from a hook in the ceiling having a loop at the right height above the stove through which the handle of the popper can be passed. Thus the popper may be held over an open coal fire with less labor."

After the corn is popped by the above or your own chosen method (most of us plug in the electric corn popper these days) select only those kernels which are fully open, discarding any unpopped, burned, or partially opened kernels. (The birds will love them.) To make syrup:

1 cup sorghum
2 tablespoons butter
½ teaspoon lemon extract

Boil sorghum about 12 minutes, to the soft-ball stage. Test by pouring a few drops from a teaspoon into a half cup of cold water. If it hardens into a soft ball, the syrup is ready for use. Remove from fire immediately, add butter and lemon extract. Place 2 quarts of popcorn in a wet earthenware bowl, pour the boiling syrup over it, mix with wooden paddles, and roll with wet hands into balls of the desired size. If there isn't any sorghum handy, here's another syrup recipe:

2 cups sugar
½ teaspoon butter
1 tablespoon vinegar
¼ cup water

Boil sugar, butter, vinegar, and water until large bubbles form on surface. Test by lifting a spoonful of the syrup about a foot above the pan. If it forms a thin thread which snaps, the syrup is ready for use. Remove from fire. Work up as directed in foregoing recipe. *This syrup is sufficient for working 8 quarts of popped corn into balls.*

Popcorn Cakes

Prepare syrup by one of above methods. Crush popped corn with a rolling pin. Stir the corn into the kettle when the syrup is at the hard-snap stage and pour into buttered tins. Lay over the top a piece of buttered or waxed paper and cover with a heavy board. When cold and hard cut into squares or wedges with a thin, sharp knife.

Crystallized Rose Petals

This will fill your party guests with envy. Gather 1 quart freshly opened roses early in the morning before the dew has evaporated. Wild roses are especially desirable, but any roses may be used which have not been sprayed with insecticides. Deep-red ones, or dark rose-colored ones will be most attractive. If cultivated roses are used, snip off the white base of each petal, which is often bitter. Dip each petal in egg white, then in sugar, making sure to coat all surfaces. Place carefully on ungresed cookie sheets and dry in the sun or in a very slow oven (250°) until firm and crystallized. Store in a tin container between layers of waxed paper, sealed tightly. Keep in a cool, dry place until ready to use. Served as after-dinner confections these are sure to invite compliments. They also make very pretty garnishes for cakes, puddings, or ice cream desserts. *Yield: About 1 cup petals.*

Peach Leather

This positively delicious sun-cured fruit candy is so easy to make and so addictive, that a plateful of it disappears like snow in June.

4 pounds ripe freestone peaches
1 cup sugar

Peel ripe, soft peaches and mash to a puree. Measure. Add ¼ cup granulated or brown sugar to each cup of puree. Mix well, set over low heat, and cook until it comes to a good boil. Boil 1 or 2 minutes, covered (it sputters wildly). Remove from fire. Pour into shallow pans to a depth of about ¼ inch or less. (I use two cookie tins.) Cover with mosquito netting or cheesecloth and set in the sun for 3 to 5 days. Bring in each night. Repeat until the mixture attains the consistency of good pliable leather. Length of time required depends on heat of the sun. Make sure the covering is fastened securely and tucked in well under the pan, as ants, flies, and other bugs love this stuff. When the leather is firm enough, cut in squares in pan, and roll in granulated sugar. Lay on waxed paper for an hour or so. Sprinkle with powdered sugar and stack between layers of waxed paper. Store in tin containers with tightly fitted lids. *Yield: About 1 pound.*

Candied Sweet Flag Root

The medicinal uses of sweet flag, or calamus, were well known to the Indians, who used it for a great many ills. The English were well acquainted with its medicinal qualities; they also used it for aesthetic purposes: the floors of their cathedrals were often strewn with it, a custom carried across the Atlantic by the New Englanders. They also knew about converting it to sweetmeats, and were delighted to find it growing in the New World. They were somewhat surprised to find that the Indians also knew how to candy the roots. Gather sweet flag roots from marshy places, clean well, cut into good-sized pieces, and toss into the old iron pot or other heavy kettle. Simmer off and on for two or three days, until the roots are soft. Cut into small pieces and boil in a sugar syrup. Remove from syrup, drain, and cool. Roll in sugar, set aside to dry, and then store in tightly covered jars for nibbling and serving to "company."

Pickling, Preserving, Jams and Jellies

Pickling, Preserving, Jams and Jellies

To Pickle Asparagus

Not strictly from southern Illinois, but quite possibly shared with, or by southern Illinois relatives, since asparagus was grown extensively around Makanda and Grand Tower and shipped to St. Louis for market. From a handwritten "memory book," ca. 1845, written by Jane Magill, daughter of Dr. Samuel and Eleanor Sullivan Magill, early settlers of Florissant, Missouri. Sent to me by John S. McCormick of Banning, California, who inherited the book. The following is an exact copy of the handwritten recipe:

Take the largest asparagus you can get; cut off the white ends. Wash the green ends in spring-water, then put them in another clean water and let them lie for two or three hours. Then have a large broad stew-pan full of spring-water, with a good large hand-full of salt. Set it on the fire, and when it boils put in the grass, not tied up but loose, and not too many at a time for fear you break the heads. Just scald them and no more. Take them out with a broad skimmer and lay them on a cloth to cool. Then take a gallon or more, according to your quantity of asparagus, of white-wine vinegar and one ounce of bay-salt, boil it, and put your asparagus in your jar, to a gallon of pickle, two nutmegs and a quarter of an ounce of mace, the same of whole white-pepper and pour the pickle hot over them, cover with a white linen cloth, three or four times double, let them stand a week and boil the pickle. Let them stand a week longer, boil the pickle again and pour it hot on as before. When they are cold, cover them with a bladder and leather.

Note: Bay-salt, a coarse common salt originally obtained from sea water, may be purchased at your supermarket.

To Make Piccalitto or Indian Pickle

Another entry from Miss Jane Magill's "memory book," courtesy of Mr. John S. McCormick, Banning, California:

209

Take a pound of race-ginger [ginger root], and lay it in water one night, then scrape it, and let it stand in the sun to dry; take long pepper, two ounces, and do it as the ginger. Take a pound of garlic, and cut it in thin slices and salt it and let it stand three days; then wash it well and drain it and put it in the sun to dry. Take a quarter of a pound of mustard-seed bruised, and half a quarter of an ounce of tumeric [old-time spelling of turmeric]. Put these ingredients, when prepared, into a large stone or glass jar with a gallon of very good white-wine vinegar, and stir it, very often for a fortnight, and tie it up close. In this pickle you may put white-cabbage, cut in quarters and put in a brine of salt and water for three days, and then boil fresh salt and water, and just put in the cabbage to scald, and press out the water and put it in the sun to dry in the same manner as you do cauliflowers, cucumbers, melons, apples, French beans, plums, or any sort of fruit. Take care they are well dried before you put them into the pickle; you need never empty the jar, but as the things come in season, put them in and supply it with vinegar as often as there is occasion. If you would have your pickle look green, leave out the tumeric and put them green into the pickle cold.

My Best Pickles

This is one of those "so-good" recipes. Somewhere along the way they were served to me and I found them so irresistible that I asked my hostess how to make them. Regrettably her name has been lost. If she reads this, she has my heartfelt thanks.

7 pounds 3-inch long, fresh-picked cucumbers
2 cups lime

Wash cucumbers, and place in a large crock in which 2 cups of lime have been dissolved in 2 gallons of water. Let stand 24 hours. Remove, rinse well, and return to crock. Cover with cold water and let stand for 3 hours. Mix:

2 quarts vinegar
4 pounds sugar
1 tablespoon pickling spice
1 tablespoon whole cloves
1 2-inch long cinnamon stick
1 tablespoon salt
1 teaspoon celery seed

Stir until sugar is dissolved, and heat to boiling point. Drain pickles, cover with pickling solution, cover crock, and let stand overnight.

Heat to boiling point (*do not boil*) and place in hot, sterilized jars. Cover with pickling syrup. Seal immediately. *Yield: About 4 quarts.*

14-Day Pickles

This is an old standard, which assures crisp, crunchy pickles with a flavor that calls for more.

1 peck strictly fresh assorted cucumbers, bell peppers, and green tomatoes

Wash and cut cucumbers into 6-to-8-inch strips, the peppers into quarters or eighths if quite large, and the tomatoes into quarters if large; small ones may be left whole. Place the mixed pickles in a large stoneware crock and fill to the top with water. Add ½ cup coarse salt, mix well, and let stand in a cool place for 9 days. At the end of the ninth day pour off the brine, wash pickles well, and return them to the crock. Add 3 tablespoons powdered alum and fill to top with boiling water. Cover and let stand 24 hours. Drain liquid, wash pickles, and return them to the crock. To make syrup:

2 quarts vinegar
9 cups sugar
4 or 5 pieces ginger
1 tablespoon pickling spice
1 tablespoon celery seed

Heat syrup to boiling point, pour over pickles, and let stand for 24 hours. Drain liquid into kettle, bring to boiling point, and pour over pickles. Repeat this for four days in a row. Place in hot sterilized jars, fill jars with liquid, and seal. *Yield: About 6 quarts.*

Sweet-Sour Yellow Pickles

Not everyone discards those ripe cucumbers which have ballooned to oversize proportions beneath the vines. They can be preserved for serving with hot dogs or hamburgers during the fall and winter months.

4 large ripe cucumbers

Peel cucumbers and remove seeds. Cut each cucumber into 8 strips. Place in a good-sized crock containing a brine made of 1 part salt to 9 parts water. Let set for 12 hours. Drain well. Prepare pickling solution:

½ cup vinegar
½ cup sugar
1½ teaspoons mustard seed
1½ teaspoons celery seed
½ teaspoon turmeric

Mix in a large graniteware kettle and boil for 10 minutes. Dump cucumber sticks into syrup, bring to a boil, and simmer for 10 minutes, or until cucumbers can be easily pierced with a fork. Pack in hot sterilized jars, cover with syrup, and seal. *Yield: About 2 pints.*

Pickled Peaches

The high point of a winter Sunday supper at our house was a half-gallon jar of Mom's pickled peaches, with cake. To make these peachy goodies took a bit of time, but we judged it worth the effort and hope our mother found our pleasure sufficient reward for her hours of work in the heat of summer.

1 peck clingstone peaches
7 cups sugar
4 cups mild vinegar
3 whole cloves in each peach
6 2-inch cinnamon sticks

Pour boiling water over peaches, drain, and peel. Stick 3 whole cloves in each peach. (This is optional: Our mother simply dumped a handful of cloves into the syrup. Some of them wound up in each jar and were served with the fruit. No harm was done and a lot of time was saved. Most of us enjoyed biting through the cloves for the tingling sensation on our tongues.) Make a syrup by mixing the sugar and vinegar in a large kettle and stirring until sugar is dissolved. Place over medium heat, bring to a boil, and boil for 10 minutes. Tie cinnamon sticks and whole cloves in a cheesecloth bag. Fasten tightly and add to syrup. Have hot sterilized jars ready for action. Drop about a gallon of the peaches into the syrup, bring to a boil and allow to boil until peaches are heated through. Lift peaches from syrup with long-handled ladle and place gently in jars. Cover jars to keep them hot, but *do not seal.* Repeat this cooking process until all peaches are in jars. Boil syrup again for 10 minutes, remove spice bag, and pour syrup over peaches, making sure all jars are filled to the top. Seal jars immediately. *Yield: About 4 quarts.*

Mushrooms

For those who can identify the edible ones, wild mushrooms are a treat, whether fried, served as garnish for meat or vegetable dishes, pickled, or raw. The Indians acquainted the uninitiated with those which were edible.

Pickled Mushrooms

1 pound mushrooms

Wash mushrooms carefully. Steam for 15 minutes. Set aside to cool while pickling liquid:

1 bay leaf
10 whole cloves
1 teaspoon dry mustard
10 peppercorns
1 quart vinegar

Mix spices and bay leaf with vinegar, in a granite saucepan and bring to a boil. Remove bay leaf. Place cooled mushrooms in hot, sterilized glass jars, cover with pickling liquid, and seal. *Yield: About 4 pints.*

Mixed Vegetable Relish

A fine way to utilize the odds and ends of vegetables at the end of the summer. The following is merely a guide. Use whatever you have at hand. It requires a little time each day for 5 or 6 days.

First day: Slice very thin ½ gallon green tomatoes, mix with ½ cup salt, and let stand overnight.

Second day: Slice very thin 1 pint green peppers, or mix with red and yellow ones for color, and 1 pint onions. Sprinkle with 2 teaspoons salt. Set aside.

Shred ½ gallon cabbage (1 large head). Cover with 2 teaspoons salt. Set aside for about an hour. Peel and slice thin 4 or 5 carrots and cook until tender. Drain all vegetables well, mix together, and stir in:

2 teaspoons celery seed
1 teaspoon yellow mustard seed
2 bay leaves
10 or 12 peppercorns

Boil 1 ½ cups sugar with 1 ½ pints cider vinegar for about 10 minutes. Remove from fire and cool slightly. Combine all vegetables with syrup and turn into a crock. Cover tightly and set in a cool place for 3 or 4 days. Place in hot sterilized jars, seal, and keep in cool place until ready to use. *Yield: About 6 or 7 pints.*

Holiday Pepper Relish

This will look attractive on a tray of sandwiches; it also adds a lift to slaw and potato salad.

12 green sweet peppers
12 red peppers
12 large onions
2 cups sugar
1 quart cider vinegar
3 tablespoons salt
1 tablespoon celery seed

Mince peppers, or run through food grinder, using coarse blade. Cover with boiling water, then drain. Place in large graniteware kettle, cover with cold water, set over heat, and bring to boiling point. Drain off liquid. Add sugar, vinegar, salt, and celery seed. Stir until sugar dissolves and cook for 10 minutes over medium heat. Add more sugar and salt if desired. Fill hot sterilized jars and seal immediately. *Yield: 6 to 7 pints.*

Pear Relish

After the choicest pears were pickled, and the seconds converted to pear preserves, we ground up the "culls" and made this pear relish. It's a good accompaniment for pork or ham dishes.

8 quarts firm but ripe pears, unpeeled
6 medium-sized onions
2 pounds sugar
5 cups vinegar
1 tablespoon allspice

Cut pears in quarters and remove core. Grind with onions in food grinder, using coarse blade. Add vinegar and sugar, mix thoroughly, and cook over low heat for 30 minutes. Pour into hot sterilized jars and seal immediately. *Yield: About 6 pints.*

Green Tomato Mincemeat

As a cousin of mine says, the best mincemeat contains *meat,* but there are cooks who prefer to omit it. Here is a recipe which fills the bill, and tastes good too.

3 quarts firm green tomatoes
3 quarts tart apples, unpeeled
4 cups suet
7 cups sugar
1 cup vinegar
4 teaspoons salt
2 teaspoons cloves
2 teaspoons allspice

Grind tomatoes, apples and suet together, using medium-fine blade. Mix with remaining ingredients, pour into a large graniteware kettle and bring to a boil, stirring occasionally. Reduce heat and simmer until quite thick. Pour into hot, sterilized jars and seal. *Yield: About 4 quarts.*

Grape Leaves

Cooks who wish to prepare dishes calling for grape leaves may purchase the leaves in jars from a well-stocked supermarket. Back in the olden days it was necessary to gather them in the proper season and preserve them. Those who have access to a grapevine may still do so.

Select perfect leaves more or less uniform in size. Wash and drain. Pack loosely in jars with a liberal amount of table salt on each leaf. (Salting tenderizes the leaves.) Seal and store in a cool place for use during the winter. When ready to use, wash leaves well and soak overnight in water. If preferred, the leaves may be dried. Tie selected leaves in clusters and hang in a well-ventilated room. When ready to use, soak until pliable and drain. Fill with choice of meat mixture. Fresh grape leaves are at their best in June and are ready for use by rinsing well. Pat dry and fill as directed.

Hominy

Another of the fall chores on our farm was hominy-making day. Our dad's method corresponded rather closely to the directions published by *Country Gentleman* magazine in the 1860s:

"For a nice batch of hominy shell a dozen ears of ripe, dry corn. Place in a large iron kettle and cover with cold water. Tie two cups of fresh wood ashes in a bag made of flour-sacking. Boil until the corn looks yellow and tastes strongly of alkali. Remove the bag and continue boiling the corn in the lye solution for at least an hour. Pour off lye-water, add fresh water and simmer until the corn swells, stirring frequently. If the hulls do not rise to the top while stirring, drain off the water and rub the grains with a coarse towel. Add cold water to cover, and simmer for three or four hours, stirring frequently to prevent the corn from burning. When the grains swell and become soft and white, add salt to taste and let the water simmer away."

Our old iron kettle was hauled out of the shed, scrubbed thoroughly, and set over the open fire built at a safe distance from the house, sheltered from the chilly, late-fall winds. The kettle was filled with about 15 gallons of water, the wood ashes added, and two or three gallons of corn poured in. The corn had been shelled the previous evening, and all imperfect grains discarded. Dad built the fire but detailed one or two of the boys to keep it going during the day, just enough to keep the corn simmering. When a kid yelled that the corn grains were turning yellow, Dad yanked the lye bag out of the kettle.

Along in the afternoon Dad removed a spoonful of the grains and rubbed them between his fingers. If the hulls loosened, the first cooking period was finished. The kettle was lifted from the fire, the lye water drained off and replaced with fresh water. Frequent stirrings were required after the pot started simmering again, and hulls began to float to the surface, this development being gleefully reported by the kid who was doing the stirring.

Dad made another inspection, to determine whether the water should be replaced with fresh water and the corn boiled another hour or so, or whether several rinsings with cold water would remove the loose hulls. If the latter, Dad worked with his hands, rubbing the corn hard, draining the water, replacing with fresh water, more rubbing, until at last the hulls were washed away, along with the "black eyes."

The cleaned corn was then covered with more fresh water, seasoned with salt, and simmered for several more hours until the grains were soft and white. At this stage our mother took over the operation and the hominy was canned, with us girl-children taking our turn as helpers.

For those who are interested, smaller quantities of hominy can be made in the kitchen. Shell about 15 ears of white grainfield corn by hand so that all imperfect grains can be discarded. Fill canning kettle about ⅔ full of fresh, cold water. Add 2½ tablespoons commercial lye and stir until it is dissolved. Dump corn into kettle and cook over low heat for 5 to 6 hours. When the corn looks yellow and a few husks float to the top, spoon out a few grains, and rub between your fingers. If the husks slip off easily, remove kettle from fire. Cool. Drain. Wash corn in cold water, rubbing grains briskly between your hands to loosen the black eyes and hulls. A colander with holes large enough to permit the eyes to drain through will hasten the process considerably. Repeat scrubbing and draining until all eyes and hulls have been washed away, working with a handful at a time if necessary. Don't be discouraged. Each batch of corn is different. Sometimes a dozen washings are necessary. Wash kettle well, to remove all traces of lye, refill with sufficient water to cover corn, add cleansed corn, and cook for about 4 to 5 hours longer, or until corn is tender but not mushy. You now have hominy.

The hominy is now ready to freeze or can. If canning is your preference, pack it in hot sterilized jars to ½ inch of top of jar. Add ½ teaspoon salt to pints; 1 teaspoon to quarts. Fill with boiling water, seal, and process: 60 minutes in hot water bath for pints; 70 minutes for quarts. If using pressure cooker, follow directions for cooking. It freezes well; use either plastic containers or plastic bags. Cover with clear water or the water in which the hominy was cooked. (According to instructions given by freezer manufacturers, this preserves the hominy better.)

I have been asked during these past several months if hominy flakes will be included. Two ladies recall eating these flakes as breakfast food with milk, as cornflakes are eaten today, but they do not recall how they were made. I regret that I have been unable to find anyone who can give me directions for making them. No information was found in the old cookbooks available to me.

Sauerkraut

Making sauerkraut was one of those late summer chores which we didn't look forward to with eager anticipation, even though we enjoyed eating it on a cold winter day, boiled with a fresh or home-cured ham hock and mealy Irish potatoes. We grumbled, but took the well-worn kraut-cutter from its place on the storehouse wall, washed it, set it in its place over a 5-gallon earthen crock out in the yard, and went to work, taking turns every hour or so.

Dad had provided us with a bushel basket full of firm cabbage heads, washed and inspected to make sure they were free of cabbage worms. The tattered and heavier outer leaves had been removed, the more perfect ones put aside for later use.

The cabbage was shredded by pushing the head back and forth across the cutting blade, turning the head around so the core remained. This core was discarded. As we filled the crock our mom appeared, with a neat sense of timing, and packed it down with a beetle, or wooden pestle, and sprinkled salt over the shredded cabbage, using about ½ cup for each gallon.

When the crock was filled, the reserved cabbage leaves were spread over the top. A heavy flat rock was laid over the leaves, to hold the cabbage beneath the brine which formed as the salt dissolved. The crock was set in the storehouse to ferment. The scum which rose to the top was skimmed off as it appeared, and the cabbage leaves replaced with fresh ones, or a clean cloth, at intervals. If the kraut seemed dry, a little salt water was added. After about 10 days the mass began to assume the flavor of kraut.

When Mom decided to serve kraut on a certain winter day, one of us girls was sent to the storehouse with a granite cooking pot and the admonition to "bring in plenty." It was no great treat to plunge one's hand into the icy cold mass and scoop out "plenty." But it was worth the momentary discomfort.

Canning kraut is easy and is a satisfactory method of storing the finished product when no storage place is available. Fill canning jars with kraut which has been heated to the boiling point, making sure kraut is well covered with brine, and seal. Or, pack in canning jars, place jars in canning kettle, bring to a boil, remove, and seal tightly.

Tomato Catsup

This is worth making, if only for that good aroma which permeates the house. If you feel sentimental about St. Valentine's Day and want to make a heart-shaped meat loaf for your beloved, you can cover it lavishly with this fruit of your labors and be as sentimental as you wish.

1 peck ripe tomatoes (8 quarts)
6 large or 8 medium-sized onions
½ cup white sugar, or ¾ cup brown sugar, closely packed
1 clove garlic
2 bay leaves
2 long red peppers, seeded

Combine in a cloth bag:

1 tablespoon whole allspice
1 tablespoon whole cloves
1 tablespoon celery seed
1 tablespoon peppercorns
2-inch cinnamon stick

Peel and cut into pieces the tomatoes, onions, garlic, and peppers. Combine in a large granite kettle with bay leaves and boil until they are very soft. Remove bay leaves and strain. Stir the sugar into the strained liquid, add cloth bag of spices. Set over high flame until the liquid is reduced to half the original volume. Remove spice bag. Add:

2 cups vinegar
Salt to taste
A couple of dashes of cayenne pepper

Boil catsup for 10 minutes longer. Pour into sterilized bottles and seal immediately. *Yield: 5 to 6 pints.*

Mushroom Catsup

Try this on your not-so-easily-impressed friends.

4 cups mushroom pulp (about ½ gallon mushrooms)

Rinse mushrooms lightly and slice thin. Place them in layers in a stone crock, alternating with a liberal sprinkling of fine table salt. Let stand overnight. Rub mushroom slices through a sieve and add any liquor left in the crock. To make pickling liquid:

2 cups vinegar
2 tablespoons cloves
2 tablespoons mustard
2 tablespoons allspice
2 tablespoons mace

Mix above ingredients in granite kettle, add mushroom puree, and cook over low flame until quite thick. Pour into small, wide-mouthed bottles which have been sterilized, and seal immediately. *Yield: About 2 pints.*

Homemade Vinegar

Making your own vinegar is as easy as falling off a log, if you follow directions and exercise patience. Be sure you have the proper equipment to start with: large stoneware or glass containers. *Do not use copper, zinc, iron, or galvanized ware.* The zinc coating will dissolve and render the vinegar poisonous.

You can accumulate a whole shelf of herb vinegars if you work at it. A couple of suggestions are included at the end of this section, to give you the idea.

A powerful vinegar was made in the very early 1800s by simply mixing 1 pound of honey with 1 gallon of cider. This was made during cider-making time, in the autumn, and the mixture allowed to stand for several months, until it reached a stage of considerable authority. It was then poured off into glass or stoneware jugs for storage.

Apple cider is most generally used for making vinegar. The thrifty housewife also used pears, peaches, grapes, berries, clover blossoms, barley, corn, beets, sugar, and molasses—whatever was at hand when the vinegar jug was empty. To make apple, pear or peach vinegar:

Wash and peel fruit, discarding rotten spots. Core the apples. Discard peach stones. Grind fruit in food grinder, using fine blade. Boil fruit pulp in enamel kettle until soft. Press pulp through double thickness of cheesecloth into stone crock or glass jar. Boil peelings separately if you wish to use them, and strain separately, adding pulpy juice to fruit juice. Measure juice. Add ¼ pound sugar to each quart of juice. Mix well in stone or glass jar and cool to lukewarm. Measure again. Add 1 yeast cake to each gallon of juice. Dissolve yeast in ½ cup of the juice, then stir into larger container of juice. Cover crock or jar with cloth and allow to ferment for about 2 weeks. When fermentation ceases, pour off juice into a separate crock or jar, leaving sediment in container. Measure juice again. Add 2 cups of good unpasteurized vinegar to each quart of fermented juice. Cover crock or jar with cloth and let stand until vinegar reaches desired strength. Separate from "mother of vinegar" (that white slippery mass of bacteria that forms in vinegar) by straining into glass jars, bottles, or jugs, and cork. It is now ready to use as is, or for making your herb vinegar. Yield depends on amount of fruit used.

Spearmint Vinegar

Gather clean, fresh spearmint or peppermint leaves and pack loosely into a widemouthed glass or stone jar. Fill with vinegar, cork, and let set for 21 days. Pour liquid off into another bottle and cork tightly. This vinegar is excellent for serving with cold meat and roasts and for flavoring soup or stew.

Clover Bloom Vinegar

Gather ½ bushel fresh, clean white clover blossoms. Place in 10-gallon stone crock. Add:

8 pounds brown sugar
1 gallon molasses
9 gallons boiling water

Stir well and cool. Add 3 pints hop yeast (may be obtained from a health food store). Cover with cloth and set in a corner somewhere for about 2 weeks, until fermentation ceases. Pour fermented liquid into another stone crock or glass jar, leaving sediment in first container. Measure. Add ½ pint good unpasteurized vinegar to each quart of liquid. Cover crock with cloth and set aside until vinegar is strong enough to use. Test in a couple weeks or so. Pour carefully into bottles, leaving any sediment and "mother of vinegar" behind. Cork tightly. Now, you have an exceptional vinegar that can be sold or given to your friends as gifts. *Yield: 10 gallons.*

Cottage Cheese

Cottage cheese is a very nutritious food and is easily obtainable at all markets today. Somehow it doesn't taste as good as that made by my German grandmother, and my own mother. Mom served it fairly frequently.

1 gallon sour unpasteurized milk
1 teaspoon salt
1 tablespoon butter
Sweet milk (about 2 tablespoons)
2 tablespoons chopped parsley or chives (optional)

Set a pan of sour, unpasteurized milk on stove over a very low flame, or over pilot light, and allow it to remain until the whey rises to the top. (We used to set it well back on the old woodburning cookstove.) Do not let it boil, as this will cause the cheese to become hard and tough. Pour into a cloth bag, or strain through a clean cloth placed over a sieve, and let it drain for two or three hours. Remove from bag and chop fine with a spoon. Add 1 teaspoon salt, 1 tablespoon softened butter, and sufficient sweet milk to soften. Refrigerate or set in a cool place until ready to serve. Add chopped parsley or chives just before serving. *Yield: About ¼ to ½ pound.*

Hand Cheese

Longer-lasting than the everyday cottage cheese. Will keep for several weeks when stored in a cool place.

1 gallon clabbered skim milk (see note below)
1 tablespoon caraway seed

Pour clabbered milk into a large flat pan and heat to lukewarm. Pour into a bag made of 4 thicknesses of cheesecloth and hang over a bowl for at least 24 hours so that all of the whey drips out. Remove curd from bag, place in a pan, and salt to taste. Add 1 tablespoon caraway seed. Mix thoroughly with hands and form into flat cakes about 2 inches thick. Set cakes on a board and place in a dry spot in the pantry to cure. After 4 weeks, wash cheese cakes in warm water, wrap in clean white cloths about 6 inches square. Pack in a crock and cover tightly. Set in a fairly warm spot in the pantry for 7 days and then remove to coolest spot in house, basement, or cellar until ready to eat. *Yield: 2 cheeses about ¼ pound each.*

Note: At a certain stage soured milk separates into soft lumps or curds. When heated, the lumps become more solid curds floating on almost clear liquid or whey.

Toasted Pumpkin Seeds

The early settlers learned from the Indians how tasty these were.

2 cups seeds
1 tablespoon melted butter
1 ½ teaspoons salt

Separate seeds from pulp and spread in shallow pan. Combine salt and melted butter and pour over seeds. Bake in slow oven, 250°, until lightly browned, stirring occasionally. Cool. Store in tightly covered jar. Will keep for a month. *Yield: 2 cups.*

Note: Sunflower and squash seeds may be treated this same way.

Rose Hip Jam 1

As has been mentioned previously, everything that grew around the home in pioneer days was utilized in some way or other. If there were no fruit trees in the vicinity, or the bears ate up all the berries, one could depend on wild rose hips for something sweet for the table.

Pick bright red, thoroughly ripe rose hips after the first frost. Cut off crown and stem ends with a sharp knife, wash carefully, and drain. Use a stainless steel knife, wooden spoon, earthenware, china or glass bowls, and enamel saucepans while working with hips. Copper or aluminum utensils and pans will lower vitamin C content and may poison you.

2 pounds hips
2 cups white wine vinegar
1½ pounds sugar (approximately)

Place hips in a crock or granite kettle and pour white wine vinegar over them, allowing 1 pint to each 2 pounds of hips. Let stand for 3 days, stirring twice a day. On the fourth day, rub through a fine wire sieve. To every pound of puree allow 12 ounces of sugar. Measure correct amount of sugar and add enough water to dissolve it, stirring constantly. Set over low heat and cook until thickened. When little beads form on the back of the spoon, add rose hip puree. Stir well and continue stirring occasionally until jam is cool. Pour into hot sterilized jars and cover with paraffin immediately. When quite cold, set lids on jars and store in dark, cool place. *Yield: About 2 pints.*

Rose Hip Jam 2

Here's another recipe, utilizing apples for an extender.

2 pounds red or orange rose hips
2½ pounds (5 cups) sugar
2 cups water
4 apples

Trim crown and stem ends of hips and place in granite saucepan with 2 cups water. Boil 20 minutes, or until tender. Rub through a sieve. This should yield 2 pints of puree. Wash and peel apples, cut into quarters, and core. Cook until tender, with just enough water to cover. Combine apples, rose hip puree, and 5 cups sugar. Stir over low heat until sugar is dissolved. Then boil until skin forms on surface of a test sample poured onto a cold plate. Pour jam into hot sterilized jars and cover with paraffin immediately. When cold, set lids on jars and store in dark, cool place. *Yield: About 3 pints.*

Note: Be sure jam is thoroughly cooked to evaporate excess moisture. For best results, cook fruit well before adding sugar, and cook shortest possible time after sugar is added.

Rose Extract

An old-time, *different* flavoring for soups, stews, pot roasts, meat loaf, and other dishes.

1 cup cleaned rose hips
1½ cups boiling water
1 tablespoon lemon juice

Prepare hips as directed in recipe for Rose Hip Jam 1 (see above). Cover with 1½ cups boiling water and simmer for 15 minutes. Pour into crock and let stand 24 hours. Strain into an enamelware pan, set over fire, and bring to a rolling boil. Add 1 tablespoon lemon juice, pour into sterilized jar, and seal. *Yield: 1 small jar.*

Apple Butter

The Pennsylvania Dutch are generally credited with the introduction of apple butter to this country, and those who settled here in southern Illinois introduced it to us, bless their souls. One of the more pleasant autumn scenes is that of a group of assorted ages gathered around an enormous copper kettle set over an open fire in a sheltered spot some distance from the house. The tantalizing aroma emanating from this kettle is that of apple butter, one of the fringe benefits of farm life. Church and social organizations have revived this custom with enthusiasm, making batches of 60 to 100 quarts or more for sale.

My own family shared a 20-gallon copper kettle, which was handed down from my great-grandfather's day and used by the brothers, sisters, and cousins. It could tell some interesting stories if it could speak. The shrinkage of families and elimination of storage pantries make home production of apple butter in any quantity rather impractical nowadays; however, for those who yearn for a taste of the real thing, here is a recipe, scaled down to household proportions.

12 pounds well-flavored red apples, cut in quarters
1½ quarts sweet cider
3 cups brown sugar
2 teaspoons ground cloves
2 teaspoons cinnamon
1 teaspoon allspice
½ teaspoon salt
Juice and grated rind of 1 lemon
1 cup bourbon or port wine

Pour cider into large, deep enamel kettle and boil hard for about 30 minutes, or until it is reduced to about half. Add apples and simmer until very soft, stirring often. Press through sieve and return puree to kettle. Add sugar, spices, lemon juice, and rind and salt. Simmer, stirring almost constantly, until mixture is quite thick (about 2½ to 3 hours). Stir in wine or bourbon and continue cooking. Test for doneness by dipping a spoonful from kettle. Cool it slightly. Tilt the spoon over the kettle and if the apple sauce falls in a single "sheet," the time for action has arrived. Remove from fire immediately, pour into sterilized pint jars, and seal. *Yield: About 5 to 6 pints.*

Watermelon Preserves or Pickle

Regarded as somewhat exotic in my childhood, for it lent an aura of distinction to the supper table and was not served to just *anybody* who came to our house.

Watermelon rind

Remove all green peel and the last vestige of red meat from watermelon rind and cut into any desired shape—strips, balls, heart shapes, or whatever. Weigh the rind and start with 5 pounds. Place in earthenware, glass, or granite kettle and cover with brine made by adding 1 cup salt to each 4 quarts cold water. Soak at least 12 hours. Drain well. Turn into kettle of boiling water to cover and cook until it is barely tender—not soft. Drain well. To make syrup:

5 cups water
5 cups vinegar
10 cups sugar
6 3-inch cinnamon sticks
¼ cup cloves with heads removed
6 tablespoons preserved ginger (optional)

Tie the cinnamon and cloves in a cloth bag and drop into kettle. Boil syrup until it is thick and heavy. Add rind and cook until it reaches the boiling point. Remove spice bag. Lift pickle from syrup and place in hot, sterilized pint jars. Cover with syrup and seal. *Yield: 5 to 6 pints.*

Tomato Preserves

As mentioned elsewhere in this book, we were fortunate that our mother was an adventurous cook, and a thrifty one. Our pantry was the repository for quite a variety of jellies, pickles, jams, and preserves. One of the prettier ones was tomato preserves, made with the small, pear-shaped yellow tomatoes. In order to test this recipe I grew a yellow pear tomato plant this past summer, and made preserves like Mom did.

5 pounds yellow tomatoes (weigh after seeds are removed)
5 pounds sugar
2 lemons
1-inch piece of ginger root, or 1 teaspoon powdered ginger

Skin tomatoes, remove seeds, and cut in quarters. Add sugar and lemons sliced thin, drop into granite kettle, and simmer until thick, stirring frequently to prevent pulp from sticking to bottom of pan. If using ginger root, remove it. Pour preserves into hot, sterilized jars and seal immediately. *Yield: About 5 pints.*

Crab Apples

In early spring the fragrant, pink blossoming wild crab apple trees resemble huge bouquets. In late autumn the ripe red fruits may be gathered for jelly, preserves, and pickles. The Indians were very fond of crab apples and taught the early settlers to bury them before cooking them the following spring, to allow the winter snows to leach out their overacidity.

Pickled crab apples provide a garnish for many meat dishes which not only lends to their attractiveness but provides edible accompaniment. Crab apple jelly is a lovely deep pink, accenting bountiful tables.

Crab Apple Jelly

1 peck crab apples

Wash and remove stems and blossom ends from crab apples. Pour them into a large kettle and add water until it is visible through top layer of fruit. Cover kettle and cook apples until they are quite soft. Drain through a coarse sieve. Put juice through a jelly bag (*do not squeeze bag*). Cook juice 4 cups at a time. Allow ¾ to 1 cup of sugar for each cup of juice. Follow rule for making jelly under Wild Plum Jelly (see below). *Yield: About 6 cups jelly.*

Pickled Crab Apples

8 pounds crab apples

Wash fruit, cut off blossom ends. Leave stems on. To prepare pickling syrup:

6 cups vinegar
8 cups brown sugar
2 teaspoons cloves, with heads removed
1 3-inch stick cinnamon

Boil fruit until tender. Pack in hot, sterilized jars and cover with syrup. Seal jars immediately. *Yield: 4 to 5 quarts.*

Wild Plum Jelly

Wild plums grew in profusion around here a long time ago, and they may still be found if one knows where to hunt for them. Our mother made beautiful clear red wild plum jelly. Their ample supply of pectin guaranteed success for the most inexperienced cook.

1 peck not-too-ripe plums

Wash plums and pour into large granite kettle. Add just enough water to be visible beneath top layer. Cook until quite soft. Strain, then put through a jelly bag. Do not squeeze the bag if you want clear, sparkling jelly. Boil only 4 cupfuls of juice at a time. Allow to each cupful ¾ to 1 cup sugar. Boil juice very rapidly for five minutes. Skim any froth from top. Add sugar, stir until it is dissolved, and continue to boil juice very rapidly without stirring. Begin testing 5 minutes after adding juice by spooning up 1 teaspoonful of the juice, cooling slightly, and dropping it back into the pan from the side of the spoon. When two large drops form along the edge of the spoon and come together, the jelly is ready to be removed from the fire. Cooking time should require about 10 minutes, but no longer than 20 minutes. Have sterilized glasses ready. Fill each glass to within ¼ inch of the top. Cover and let jelly cool. Coat with a very thin coating of paraffin. On the following day, cover jelly with another thin coating of paraffin, tilting glasses to make sure paraffin covers entire surface. The two coatings should not be more than ⅛ inch thick. Cover the glasses with lids and store in a cool, dark place. *Yield: 4 cups juice should make about 6 cups jelly.*

Violet Jelly

Wild violets grow almost everywhere in southern Illinois. One of my fondly remembered childhood joys was slipping away from Mom's watchful eye in early spring, heading for a carpet of blue not far from home, shedding shoes and stockings, and wading barefoot through the beautiful blue blossoms. Feeling guilty afterward, I would put shoes and stockings back on, pick a big bouquet of these lovely little flowers, and take them home to her. Pioneer housewives put the blooms to more practical use by making violet jelly.

Pick a couple gallons of violets with very short stems. Add a very small amount of water, mash the blossoms to pulp, and simmer them gently for a while, covered. Strain through a linen cloth. You should net 2 cups of violet juice. Add:

1 package unflavored gelatin
4 cups sugar
Juice of 1 lemon

Bring juice, gelatin, sugar, and lemon juice to a boil, stirring constantly to dissolve sugar. Boil hard for 1 minute, skim any scum from top, pour into hot sterilized jars, and seal. *Yield: About 4 small glasses.*

Drying, Butchering, and Curing Meats

Drying, Butchering, and Curing Meats

Jerky

Jerky was the Indians' practical method of preserving meat for use in their nomadic life-style. Venison replaced the buffalo as a meat source when the latter began retreating westward in the vanguard of "civilization." The Indians passed their method on to the white man, who used it to his advantage. Campers and hikers swear by it. In fact, the commercial meat-packers have caught on to its efficiency and value, and jerked beef can be purchased in supermarkets today.

It was a mainstay of westwardbound pioneers, mountain men, and even the cowboys when riding the line. The more forethoughted of our early white ancestors in southern Illinois—those who didn't exactly hanker after wading hip-deep in snow during cold winters to bring in fresh meat for the wife and kids—found that it helped to have a few hundred pounds of jerky hanging from the rafters.

The meat was cut into thin strips, about ¼ inch thick, hung over a line stretched between two stakes, and dried in the sun. If the weather wasn't cooperating, he stretched his line over a green wood fire which was sheltered under a tree or the animal's hide. The fire was kept low and wood was added as needed to produce plenty of smoke. If the meat wasn't dry and hard by the end of that day, it was taken inside and the process repeated the following day.

The Indians pounded bear fat, wild fruits and berries, pits and all, into their dried meat. They called the finished product pemmican. Fortified with several hundred pounds of this all-in-one, ready-to-eat meal, they could survive quite well without bothering to cook.

A word of caution: Readers should be aware that a few cases of botulism have been noted in dried and/or smoked fish, beef jerky, smoked beef, and sausage products made at home. It is recommended that anyone who plans to dry meat obtain complete, detailed instructions.

Summer Sausage

A row of these sausages hanging in the basement or cellar will give assurance of quick snacks for unexpected guests, impromptu picnics, and always-hungry kids.

1 gallon lean pork
½ gallon lean beef
¾ cup salt
½ cup yellow mustard seed
1 teaspoon pepper

Grind pork and beef through food grinder, using fine blade. Combine with salt, mustard seed, and pepper. Mix thoroughly with hands. Stuff into casings and hang over slow-burning hickory wood fire to cure. Will keep indefinitely. *Yield: About 2 to 3 pounds.*

Note: Commercial casings for sausage can be obtained either by ordering from a packing house, if you need a large quantity, or by ordering from your local butcher or meat market. However, if you are doing your own butchering, you can do as my family did—clean the intestines from the slaughtered hog and use them for casings. All you need is a large washtub and a strong stomach.

Pork Sausage

What better way to start a winter day than a breakfast of homemade pork sausage, scrambled eggs, coffee and fruit.

4 cups raw ground pork
2 tablespoons salt (or to taste)
3 tablespoons yellow mustard seed
4 tablespoons black pepper
2 tablespoons coriander, powdered

Mix all above ingredients thoroughly, adding more seasoning if desired. Press into casings (to obtain, see note above), using sausage stuffer or funnel, and store in cool place. Or, treat as our forefathers did: Pinch off round balls the size of walnuts, cook in a large pan in the oven so they will brown evenly, and pack in earthen crocks or glass jars. Fill with melted lard, and seal. Meat will keep indefinitely if stored in a dark cool place. *Yield: About 1 pound.*

Braunschweiger

This is a bit more subtly seasoned than liver sausage, and utilizes beef liver rather than the all-pork ingredients in liver sausage. It's another German sausage.

1 ½ **pounds beef liver**
¾ **pound fat pork**
4 **teaspoons salt**
1 **teaspoon pepper**
½ **teaspoon cloves**
3 **tablespoons onion**
⅛ **teaspoon marjoram**
¼ **teaspoon thyme**

Cook liver and pork until tender. Cool. Put through food chopper, using fine blade. Add seasonings and knead with hands until thoroughly blended. Press into casings (to obtain, see note above) with sausage stuffer or funnel. Place in a large kettle, cover with water, and simmer for 15 minutes. Chill thoroughly before serving. *Yield: About 1 pound.*

Oatmeal Sausage

A southern Illinois variation of the famous Philadelphia scrapple, using oatmeal instead of corn meal. Erma Brunkhorst of Grand Tower, one of those superb German cooks who have added their hearty traditional dishes to the area, brought a loaf of this to me as a small holiday remembrance. It was so tasty that I asked her how it was made.

4 **cups oatmeal (approximately)**
4 **cups cooked pork shoulder from which fat has been trimmed**
Salt to taste
3 **tablespoons pepper**
1 **teaspoon dried marjoram or sage (optional)**
½ **teaspoon summer savory, dried (optional)**
½ **teaspoon cayenne pepper (optional)**

Pour oatmeal into large bowl and add sufficient warm meat broth to cover. Stir until oatmeal is moistened and let set for 15 minutes or so. Shred cooked pork and season with salt, pepper, and any or all of the herbs. Combine with oatmeal, mix thoroughly with wooden spoon, and pat into flat trays. Chill until firm. When ready to eat, cut into ½ inch thick slices and sauté until golden brown. *Yield: About 2 pounds.*

Smoking Fish

Another food-preserving technique which friendly Indians taught their white-skinned brothers was that of smoking fish.

Clean fish as soon as caught. Wash thoroughly, rub liberally with coarse salt, and let stand for 24 hours. Wipe salt off, and if the fish is large, cut into 1-pound chunks. A 2- or 3-pound fish can be split up the back and a stick inserted so it will remain open. Build a fire of hardwood. Lay the fish on a large piece of pierced metal or hang on hooks suspended from a tripod hung over the fire. Protect the fish by building a roofed enclosure around it if you do not have a smokehouse. Smoke for at least 12 hours. The longer it is smoked, the longer it will keep. Store in a cool, dry place.

Head Cheese

We usually killed more than one hog at a time, and my dad saved one head for his good head cheese.

1 hog's head
1 hog's tongue
2 to 4 hogs' ears
Sage
Salt and pepper
Cayenne pepper

Clean and scrape hog's head. Wash thoroughly. Wash and trim tongue and ears. Place them in a deep kettle, cover with cold water, add 1 tablespoon salt, and simmer until meat falls from bones. Clean hog's stomach thoroughly, inside and outside. Place in a pan and cover with cold water. Drain cooked meat. Skin tongue. Remove all bones. Grind in food chopper, using coarse blade. Season with salt, pepper, dried sage, and cayenne pepper. Mix thoroughly. Press into cleaned stomach of hog, using sausage stuffer or funnel. Close stomach opening by tying with stout string. Place in large kettle, cover with water and simmer for about an hour. Test by pricking stomach with a fork. If clear grease comes out, sausage is done. This is good sliced thin, with mustard, horseradish, or catsup on the side. *Yield: About 1 gallon.*

Blood Sausage

People are likely to react rather violently when blood sausage is mentioned. They either like it with fanatical fervor, or loathe it. For those who like to experiment, the following directions will serve as a guide. (Reserve ½ gallon of blood when butchering hog.)

Hog jowls
Hog's heart
Hog's kidneys
Hog's lungs
Sections of pork fat

Cook hog parts until very well done. Cool. Grind in sausage mill, using fine blade. Add blood saved from butchering and mix thoroughly. Season with:

3 to 4 tablespoons salt
Crushed marjoram to taste (about 1 tablespoon)

Mix well and stuff sausage into casings (to obtain, see note above) with a sausage stuffer or funnel. Place in large kettle, add water to cover, and cook for about 1½ hours. While cooking, prick casing with a fork at intervals, to release excess blood. When liquid runs clear, the sausage is cooked. Drain. Cool sausage for at least 2 days. Cut into portions, wrap well, and freeze. Serve cold or fried. *Yield: 2 to 3 pounds.*

Liver Sausage

The German colonists acquainted their new friends and neighbors with their excellent sausages and popularized a new way of utilizing the organs, which some people had thrown away.

1 hog's head
½ hog's heart
1 pork kidney
1 hog's liver
½ pound skin sections (approximately)
6 tablespoons pepper
Salt to taste
Broth

Cook meat from hog's head and a few small sections of skin. Cook heart, kidney, and liver separately. Combine all meat and grind in food chopper, using fine blade. Add salt to taste, 6 tablespoons pepper, and mix thoroughly, adding several tablespoons of the broth from cooking head. Stuff into casings (to obtain, see note above) with sausage stuffer or funnel, place in large kettle, and cook for 30 to 45 minutes. Cool for 2 days. Wrap in portions and freeze. Serve cold, or sliced and fried. *Yield: About 5 to 6 pounds.*

Sugar-Curing Hams

Each family which has an abiding interest in food preparation has its own favorite method of curing hams (sometimes secret). My father left this world with his own secret in his head and none of us can recall all of the various steps. I turned to my true and faithful friends Dot and Bob Farnsworth, who prepare at least one of their sugar-cured hams each year which they serve at their New Year's Day open house. Bob has very generously shared his sure-fire method:

Hams have been cured in this way for several generations in our family in Missouri, and I have never heard a complaint. No smokehouse or special gear required.

14-to-16-pound ham, fresh, unfrozen (be sure all animal heat is out of ham)
1 quart coarse salt
1 pint brown sugar
2 tablespoons red pepper
2 tablespoons black pepper

Mix salt, sugar, and pepper well. Work mixture into ham with your hands until its juice forms a paste. Continue rubbing until paste covers ham to a depth of ¼ inch to ⅜ inch. Lay ham skin side down on a wooden block if available, and let drip for 12 hours. Wrap well in heavy brown paper and tie closely with a lot of string, to hold paste close to ham. Fit heavy muslin around ham to form a bag and sew in place with a darning needle and stout string. Hang, small end down, for 5 to 6 weeks in cool area where temperature will not get high enough to cause the ham to spoil but not cold enough to freeze it (between 45° and 32°). (*Caution:* If the ham freezes, the salt-sugar mixture can't pull the moisture out so the ham will cure. Be sure to set a pan under ham to catch the mixture as it drips.)

After the initial cure, you can bring the ham inside and hang it in the kitchen, and enjoy watching it age. I prefer to keep mine 1 to 2 years, but Gen. Hap Arnold, who is an expert, says a sugar-cured ham isn't worth its salt until it is 7 years old. He has said that he cures about six a year so that he has an old backlog at all times. To prepare to eat:

Unwrap and pound off salt-sugar mix. Lay ham in a large container. Scrub with stiff brush and Ivory soap until all ham is thoroughly cleaned. Rinse well, cover with fresh water, and let set for 24 hours. Bake or boil as you would any fresh ham. Sugar cured ham is salty and spicy. If not to taste, slice ½ inch thick and simmer in covered pan for a while. After this it can be browned, if preferred, for breakfast.

Drying Fruits and Vegetables

Drying Fruits and Vegetables

In the dim, dark ages before glass jars for canning were available in quantity, and home freezers were undreamed of, pioneer families depended on Old Sol to assist in preserving Mother Nature's bountiful gifts of fruit and vegetables for the long winter months ahead. Long strings of drying apples, peaches, and other fruits festooned along kitchen walls were a familiar sight in certain relatives' homes as recently as my own childhood.

Sun-drying had certain drawbacks: These fruits and vegetables had to be brought indoors when rain threatened and when the nights were drenched with dew. Air-drying in a sheltered place such as the attic or loft, took longer. Stringing the long rows above the kitchen range was another method used; and Grandmother also used the oven of her wood cookstove for late-autumn fruits and vegetables.

There are tricks to all of these home-processing procedures, and it is impossible to foresee every contingency that might arise to puzzle the novice. On these pages are given general rules followed by our early forebears, for those who are willing to experiment. More complete directions may be obtained from your County Extension Office, particularly if you plan to buy the produce instead of experimenting with that grown in your own garden.

It is essential that the produce be completely dry before storing; otherwise it will mold.

The material should not be sliced too thick, or too thin. If a cutting device such as a meat grinder with special slicing disks, a kraut slicer, or other slicing machine, is not available, use a large sharp kitchen knife.

It goes without saying that cleanliness in preparing the material is essential.

Cheap 4-foot-square trays can be made by joining ¾-by-2-inch strips of lumber to form ends, with laths nailed on to form the bottom; or galvanized-wire screen with ⅛-to-¼ inch mesh can be fitted to a 4-foot square frame.

Since this book deals chiefly with very old-time cookery and food preservation, general directions for sun-drying are chosen. Material may be oven-dried and a few suggestions for this procedure are included.

Some housewives prefer blanching material with steam or treating it with sulphur to prevent discoloration. The directions which follow suggest the old-time method of dipping the cut fruits and vegetables in a weak salt solution as this seems to have been the most-used predrying preparation. With the above cautionary preliminaries, let us start the drying procedure.

Drying Fruits

Apples

Apples are probably the easiest fruits to work with. Select fruit which is perfect and fully ripe. Peel, core, trim, and slice winter apples ¼-inch thick. Dip in weak salt solution containing 8 teaspoons of salt to each gallon of water, to prevent discoloration. Spread out on trays to dry in the sun. The apple slices should be stirred several times during the drying period in order to insure uniform exposure. It is only necessary to dry apples long enough for them to become somewhat leathery but still pliable. It is not advisable to leave them outside overnight. After removing the fruit from the trays, it should be placed in boxes and poured from one box to another once a day for 3 or 4 days, in order to mix it thoroughly and give an even degree of moisture to the entire mass. If the slices seem too moist they should be replaced on the drying trays for more drying. The well-dried apples can be stored in glass jars, cardboard boxes with tight covers, heavy paper bags, or moisture-tight containers. They keep best in a cool, dry, well-ventilated place.

Another method: Peel, core, and cut apples into eighths, or core and slice in rings with a fruit slicer. Dip for 1 minute in a salt bath made by adding 1 ounce of salt to 1 gallon of water. Spread on trays and dry in sun for 4 to 6 hours, or longer if necessary. If you wish to try oven-drying, set trays at 110°, raising temperature gradually to 150°. Drying time: 4 to 6 hours. Beware of scorching fruit.

Cherries

Remove stems of cherries, and if the fruit is large, the pits also. Follow directions given above for apples, for drying in the sun. If drying in oven, wash, remove surface moisture, and spread cherries in thin layer on trays. If they are seeded, there will be a loss of juice. Dry from 2 to 4 hours at 110° to 150°, increasing temperature gradually during drying process. Pour into box and transfer to another box, repeating this process once a day for 3 or 4 days until fruit is thoroughly dry.

Peaches

Although peaches may be dried unpeeled, it is better to peel them before drying. Remove stones, cut fruit in halves, or into smaller pieces if preferred. Spread on trays to dry in the sun. Because of the larger pieces they will need longer to dry than apples. If oven-drying, follow same procedure as that given for apples.

Pears

Treat pears in the same way as apples. Steaming them for 10 minutes before drying will hasten the drying process.

Plums and Apricots

Select medium-ripe plums. Remove pits but do not peel. Cut fruit into halves and spread on trays to dry from 4 to 6 hours in the sun. Follow directions given for apples and peaches.

Raspberries

Sort out imperfect berries, discard green ones, and spread selected berries on trays. After 3 hours check by squeezing a berry between the fingers. If it does not stain the hand, remove the fruit to boxes and handle the same way as apples.

Blackberries, dewberries, and huckleberries may be dried the same way as raspberries.

Rhubarb

Select young, succulent stalks and prepare as for cooking, skinning the leafstalks and cutting into pieces about ¼ inch to ½ inch in length. *Do not use any part of the leaf.* Spread in sun and dry. Condition same as beets (see below).

Drying Vegetables

Beets

Select young, tender beets. Wash, peel, slice about ⅛ inch thick, and dry. Condition by placing beets in boxes and pouring from one box to another for 3 or 4 days, to give all pieces an even degree of moisture.

Cabbage

Select well-developed heads of cabbage and remove all loose outside leaves. Split cabbage, remove hard, woody core, slice remainder of head with a kraut cutter, and dry. Condition same as beets.

Carrots

Wash, peel, slice lengthwise into pieces about ⅛-inch thick, and dry. Discard carrots having a large woody core. Condition same way as beets.

Celeriac

Treat same way as carrots.

Celery

Treat same as carrots.

Irish Potatoes

Select good, sound, well-matured potatoes. Wash and boil, or steam, until nearly done. Peel and run through a potato ricer or meat grinder. Spread potatoes in layers on a tray and dry until brittle. Stir once or twice during drying process. The flavor will be improved if the riced potatoes are toasted slightly in an oven after drying.

Kohlrabi

Treat same as carrots.

Leeks

Select well-matured leeks and remove outside papery covering. Cut off tops and roots. Slice into ¼-inch strips and dry quickly. Condition same as beets. Store in a light-proof container to avoid discoloration.

Lima Beans

Gather young, tender beans which have not yet reached maturity. Wash, shell, and blanch for 5 to 10 minutes. Set in the sun to dry. Condition same as beets.

Onions

Select well-matured onions and remove outside papery covering. Cut off tops and roots. Slice into ⅛-inch pieces and dry quickly. Condition and store same as leeks.

Parsley

Select greens in prime condition. Remove leaves from roots and wash thoroughly. Spread the leaves on trays to dry thoroughly. Slicing the bunches will facilitate drying. Condition same as beets.

Parsnips

Treat same way as carrots.

Peas

Shell barely mature peas, spread on trays, and dry in the sun. Pack in boxes and transfer from box to box once a day for 3 or 4 days, or until perfectly dry.

When drying very young and tender sugar peas, the pods may also be used also. Wash and cut in ¼-inch pieces, blanch in boiling water for 6 minutes. Handle same as beets.

Peppers

Small varieties of red peppers may be spread on screens in the sun until dried completely. Or, the whole plant may be hung up in an airy place until the pods are dry. String on stout string and hang in easily accessible place. Large peppers may be handled the same as smaller varieties.

Pumpkins

Select sound, well-grown specimens. Cut into strips and peel. Remove all seeds and soft flesh surrounding them. Cut strips into smaller pieces about ¼-inch thick and 2-inches long. Spread on screen and dry. Condition by placing dried pieces in boxes and transferring from one box to another one a day for 3 days.

Salsify, or Oyster Plant

Treat same way as carrots.

Spinach

Select greens in prime condition. Remove leaves from roots and wash thoroughly. Spread the leaves on trays to dry thoroughly. Slicing the bunches will facilitate drying. Condition same as beets.

Squash

Treat same way as pumpkins.

String Beans

Select young, perfect, tender beans. Wash; remove tip, stem, and any strings. Cut or break beans into pieces ½ inch to 1-inch long, place on trays, set in the sun and dry. Condition same as beets.

Or, follow the very old way by preparing as above, stringing the beans on coarse strong thread like long necklaces, hanging them above the stove or outdoors to dry. They may be boiled until almost done before stringing. This is optional.

Sweet Corn

Select young, tender ears and process immediately after picking. Cook in boiling water 2 to 5 minutes, or long enough to set the milk. Cut kernels from cobs with a sharp knife, being sure not to cut off pieces of the cob. Spread in very thin layers on trays and place in sun to dry. Stir occasionally. The process will be shortened if the corn is set in a warm oven for 10 to 15 minutes before transferring it outside to the sun. Pack in boxes for a few days, transferring from one box to another once a day for 3 to 4 days, to insure completion of the process and prevent spoilage.

Sweet Potatoes

Select sound, mature potatoes. Wash, boil until almost done, peel, and run through a ricer. Spread on trays and dry until brittle.

Alternative 1: Treat as above, but slice potatoes instead of ricing them.

Alternative 2: Wash, peel, slice, spread on trays, and dry. The dried potatoes will be brighter if the slices are dipped in salted water just before spreading on drying trays.

Swiss Chard

Select perfect, young greens. Wash carefully, cut into sections about ¼-inch long, spread on screens, and dry. Condition same as carrots.

Turnips

Treat same as beets.

Drying Herbs

Celery tops, mint, sage, and other herbs should be washed, spread on screens, and dried in the sun. They may then be crushed and placed in jars or bags. (See section, "Herbs, Spices, Roots and Weeds.")

Herbs, Spices, Roots, and Weeds

Herbs, Spices, Roots, and Weeds

Seasoning with Herbs and Spices

All good cooks know that food flavors are enhanced by the addition of herbs and spices. Our forefathers who came to the New World from Europe brought seeds of their favorite seasonings across the ocean with them. Wild plants used by the Indians were quickly adopted. Our great-grandmothers' gardens had a section set aside for herbs, many of which were also used for medicinal purposes as well as for adding zest to soups, stews, meats, fruits, and vegetables.

For the benefit of those who regard themselves as "salt and pepper cooks," the homegrown or easily obtainable herbs and spices will heighten the natural flavor of foods and transform ordinary dishes from the ho-hum into the gourmet. Herbs are from the leafy parts of the plants; spices are the dried seeds, buds, fruit or flower parts, bark or roots of plants, most generally grown in the tropics or of tropical origin. The leaves of herbs may be used in fresh form throughout their growing season; at the end of summer the perfect leaves may be gathered, placed in a mesh bag, and hung in a dry, airy place to dry. They will last through the winter. Spices are sold in whole or ground form; they gradually lose flavor and color, and should not be purchased in quantity.

The French colonists in the "American Bottoms," particularly the ruling class and the clergy, made efforts to maintain their sophisticated eating habits in their new land. Their cookery was lighter and more imaginative than that of the Americans who came later. Their rich sauces and subtle seasonings followed the traditional cookery of their home country. As they were very religious and observed the rather numerous Catholic fast days faithfully, egg dishes and vegetarian meals were required, testing the ingenuity of the cooks.

Therefore the kitchen herb garden was essential to their life-style. According to the records, their herb gardens included angelica, balm, basil, chervil, chives, dill, lavender, leeks, mustard, parsley, peppermint, sage, spearmint, summer savory, sweet marjoram, thyme, and bitter wormwood. Their favorite spices seemed to be allspice, anise, caraway, cardamom, cayenne pepper, cinnamon, cloves, ginger, mace, mustard, nutmeg, paprika, pepper, poppy seeds, saffron, tumeric, and vanilla. A reproduction of such a French herb garden will be found at Old Fort Kaskaskia, near Chester, where visitors may look and smell and acquaint themselves with these herbs if their acquaintance has been limited to those purchased in dried form.

As of this writing, no similar German garden has been located. Old German cookbooks and conversations with traditional German cooks indicate that they were familiar with, and their home gardens included, basil, chives, dill, garlic, lavender, mustard, parsley, sage, summer and winter savory, sweet marjoram, and thyme. They also used caraway seeds, anise, horseradish, and bay leaf. The Southerners who came North followed their own traditions, which overlapped with those of the Germans and French in some respects, and included sorrel, tarragon, tumeric, and watercress.

The following list of herbs and spices with which our forefathers were familiar may be helpful to readers who wish to try some of the old-time recipes.

Angelica. Decoction of oil from the leaves was added to liquors to enhance their flavor. Leafstalks candied and used as a confection and for garnishing cakes.

Anise. Used in candy, cookies, and liquer. Seed for flavoring; leaves used as garnish.

Basil. Used in sauces, gravies, stews, sausage, soups, cheese dishes, fruit drinks. Use fresh or dried.

Bay leaf. Grows as a tree. Dried leaves used in soups, gravies, meat dishes.

Caraway. Seeds used in cookies, rye bread, cake, sauerkraut. Leaves in salads and garnishes.

Chervil. Flavor similar to that of parsley, slightly more peppery.

Chives. Leaves used in soups, salads, omelets, and in cheese.

Dill. Used mainly in pickling cucumbers. Fresh dill also used to add zest to soups, sauces, salads, fresh tomatoes.

Fennel. Leaves used as fish garnish. Seed used mainly with fish cookery.

Lavender. Leaves used in flavoring homemade candies. Also used to perfume stored clothing and bed linens and for rose jars.

Leeks. Milder than onions, but in onion family. Stems and roots used in stews, soups.

Marjoram. Used fresh or dried in soups, stews, egg dishes, salads, roasts, and poultry.

Mint. Spearmint, peppermint, and other kinds. Tender young leaves used in iced tea and other cooling drinks. French used mint sauce for meat dishes and for making teas.

Mustard. Seeds used by French and local Indians in salads and sauces. Mustard used on salted meats.

Parsley. Generally used in fresh form as garnish and seasoning for salads, meat dishes, vegetable dishes.

Rosemary. Used fresh or dried in stews, soups, meat dishes, sweet sauces, or as garnish.

Sage. Used fresh or dried in poultry dressing, pork sausage making, green beans, stewed tomatoes, and many cheese dishes.

Savory. A relative of sage; a bit milder in flavor. Used same as sage. Winter savory darker in color and not as delicately flavored as summer savory.

Sorrel. Fresh or dried leaves used for flavoring soups, salads, omelets. Fresh raw leaves used in making soups, or in sorrel pie, or cooked like spinach.

Tarragon. Used by the French for flavoring pickles and making tarragon vinegar.

Thyme. Used fresh or dried in soups, or fowl and meat sauces. Slightly lemon-scented.

Watercress. Used as garnish for cold meats or in salads.

Wormwood. Used by French when roasting goose, to cut grease; also used for medicinal purposes.

There are no hard and fast rules governing the correct amount of herbs and spices to be used in cooking. It goes without saying that certain ones are more compatible with certain foods. Trial and error is recommended, for what delights one person might not be liked at all by another. The use of these herbs and spices will not automatically elevate you to Julia Child's or Graham Kerr's class of cooking savvy. One word of caution: don't overdo it. It's always easier to add a bit more than it is to take it out.

Whole spices may be added to slow-cooking dishes at the beginning of the cooking period, tied in a cheesecloth bag to be discarded when the cooking is done. Ground spices are to be added about 15 minutes before the end of the cooking period. Leaf herbs should be crumbled, to release their flavor.

Edible Roots

So much has been published in recent years about the art of living off the land that it seems pointless to add to the literature on the subject. I have found no written records indicating that the early settlers made a practice of eating the roots of nut grass, water lilies, wild sweet potatoes, Solomon's seal, brake fern, arrowhead, wild potato, cattail or burdock, which were used by the Indians. Perhaps the tender cattail roots were roasted when potatoes were scarce.

The Jerusalem artichoke was well known to both the Indians and whites. It fell into disuse, but has made a spectacular comeback and may be found in the supermarkets.

Dandelion roots were dried, roasted, and ground to be used as "coffee" by the early settlers. The flowers made an acceptable tea when dried.

The roots of the brake fern were eaten raw or roasted, and the starch chewed out of the root.

The roots of the chicory were roasted and used as a coffee substitute, during hard times, or combined with coffee as an extender.

Among the edible roots, the wild onion ranked high. Experiments with this plant have been quite rewarding in our household. Used as an alternative to garden onions, it imparts a unique flavor to roasts and soups—so much so that a clump from a field has been transplanted in our garden.

It is not suggested that readers grab a shovel and rush out looking for edible roots. Give Mother Nature a chance to continue their existence.

Edible Weeds

Wild greens were used extensively by early settlers who had not cleared a garden space. Since they sent up their tender green leaves and shoots before planted gardens, they made welcome additions to the starchy diet.

Novices are cautioned to use only the young, early growth of leaves and stems. They should be washed and cleaned thoroughly before placing in salted water. If various kinds are combined, it is suggested that they be parboiled at least once, and perhaps twice, to eliminate the bitter taste. After parboiling and draining thoroughly, the greens may be cooked with ½-inch cubes of salt pork or bacon and seasoned with salt.

The edible weeds include sorrel, pigweed, lamb's quarters, winter cress, blue violet leaves, wild lettuce, dandelions, broadleaf plantain, and very young pokeweed shoots.

Helpful Household Hints

Helpful Household Hints

When spreading butter on sandwiches or toast, use a silver knife which has been heated in boiling water. This is easier and quicker than softening the butter.

On making cake when fresh milk, buttermilk, molasses, and sour milk are lacking, use a cup of applesauce into which a teaspoon of baking soda has been stirred. The sauce makes a delicious spice cake, and no eggs are required.

The rather flat taste of prune pies can be improved by adding 1 teaspoon of vinegar to each pie.

For nicely flavored butter, with the buttermilk well worked out, mix 1 teaspoon of clear honey to about 3 pounds of butter. You will not taste the honey and it improves the butter.

Heat a coconut in a 300° oven for 10 minutes before breaking the shell. A slight blow will crack it and it will come off easily.

When making a small quantity of peanut butter, mix the ground peanuts with cream or milk instead of olive oil. It is delicious, although it will not keep longer than a few days.

To hasten the baking of potatoes, scrub well, immerse in very hot water for 15 minutes, then wipe dry, rub with bacon drippings and place in 350° oven.

Instead of discarding tops when preparing celery for the relish dish, dry them and store in a glass jar. Toss a cluster or two into the soup pot, then remove when the soup is cooked. You will find the flavor is better than that of the celery stalk.

If your omelets burn because you have no omelet pan, sprinkle a tablespoon of table salt in the skillet. Heat very hot. Discard salt and wipe pan clean with a paper towel. Use a very small amount of butter when cooking the omelet and it will not burn easily.

The juice of half a lemon with 1 teaspoon each of water and sugar added to grated or sliced pineapple will enhance its flavor.

Pare potatoes in cold water to prevent staining your fingers.

If a kitchen window is kept open two inches at the top while frying foods, boiling cabbage, or other odorous vegetables, the unpleasant odor will go out the window instead of spreading through the house.

After boiling tongue or beets, remove from fire, and plunge immediately into cold water. The skins will peel off very easily.

To improve flavor of applesauce, add a sprig of mint when cooking.

Odor from cooked cabbage can be somewhat reduced if a little vinegar is kept boiling on the back of the stove.

To prevent fish odor, rub both the fish and cooking pan with lemon juice before cooking.

Vinegar will stay clear if one teaspoon of salt is added to each quart bottle.

Milk will not scorch or stick if one half teaspoon of sugar is added to each quart before boiling.

To keep onions whole while cooking, remove the skin and scrape or shave the ends clean without cutting.

When making jams or jellies or pickled fruits, add a bit of butter the size of a navy bean to the juice after sugar has been added. No scum will form on the juice.

Sweet peas will last much longer, after they are cut, if they are arranged in a vase half filled with moistened sand.

To measure a fraction of a spoonful of dry ingredients, level the spoonful, then cut lengthwise of the spoon for half and crosswise for a quarter.

To soften brown sugar, place in an airtight container and cover with slices of fresh bread. Leave for about 30 minutes.

Sweet milk can be soured by the addition of a few drops of lemon juice or vinegar.

When beating eggs separately, beat the whites first, then "steal" a little bit of it to start the yolks. The yolks will not stick to the beater and will whip up twice as quickly.

Make individual molds of tart lemon jelly and add a few nutmeats, for serving as a garnish with chicken salad or other chicken dishes. They may be tinted to carry out any desired color scheme and are very attractive as well as pleasing to the taste.

Popcorn will pop faster and make fluffier flakes if kept in the refrigerator. If this has not been done, soak the popcorn in a bowl of water for 10 minutes then drain thoroughly before popping.

Substitute slices of orange for the usual lemon when serving tea. This is especially delicious when combined with green tea.

Fresh sliced cucumbers also give an agreeable flavor to hot tea if a dash of rum is added to the beverage.

Sometimes it is impossible to obtain sour milk for a favorite dish. A good method is to dilute condensed milk until it has the consistency of skimmed milk. Add a little sugar and keep in a warm place until it sours.

When using the skins of navel oranges or lemons, pare thin, so as not to include any of the bitter white inner skin. Chop or grind coarsely and place in a quart glass jar with 1 pint of granulated sugar. After the sugar has absorbed enough of the citrus oil, it is ready to use for flavoring cakes, cookies, and puddings. The bits of rind may be used for flavoring sauces.

To keep cheese fresh, cut in long strips and place in a glass jar. Cover tightly. It will keep for several weeks without losing its flavor or harming other foods.

To prevent citron, raisins, or currants from sinking to the bottom of cakes, warm them in the oven before adding to the batter.

When you have accumulated celery leaves from 3 or 4 bunches, chop them and cook as you would spinach or other greens. They are flavorful and attractive.

Before cooking wild mushrooms, sprinkle salt on the spongy part, or gills. If they turn yellow, they are poisonous. *Throw them away.* If they turn black, they are edible.

Cook parsnips and oyster plant (salsify) with the thin skins on, then peel when cold. Your hands will not be stained and the flavor will be preserved.

When poaching eggs, add a tablespoon of vinegar to the water along with the salt. This sets the eggs and preserves their shape.

Brush the bottom of pie pastry with white of egg to prevent crust from being soaked.

Oil green peppers before stuffing them and they will not turn brown in the oven.

Uses for Baking Soda

A pinch of soda added to the water in which green beans, peas, or cabbage is to be boiled will preserve their fresh color and enhance their flavor. It is especially helpful if the vegetables have passed their prime.

If you have the misfortune to burn food in your favorite saucepan, don't panic: Pour about 3 tablespoons soda onto the burned area (after removing as much of the food as you can), add enough water to moisten, and boil for a few minutes. Set aside to cool. If all of the burned food cannot be removed easily, sprinkle a little more soda over burned spots and rub with a damp sponge.

Soak fish or game in a gallon of cold water to which 2 teaspoons each of soda and salt have been added. Rinse well in cold water and drain thoroughly before cooking. This will enhance the flavor.

Uses for Table Salt

A pinch of salt added to egg whites will enable you to beat them more quickly.

This also applies to whipping cream.

Salt sprinkled on the pantry shelves will drive away ants.

Always add salt when chocolate is used in cooking.

Homemade Lye Soap

The judicious handling of grease and lye leached from wood ashes provided all-purpose soap used by pioneer families, and in some cases as recently as earlier in this century, within my memory. Methods of making this brownish-grayish cleaning agent differed rather widely; some housewives claimed that boiling the grease and lye produced a superior soap; others maintained that boiling was unnecessary, and that their soap was as good as the boiled kind.

There are still old-timers around who complain that commerical lye does not serve as well as that leached from wood ashes. In view of increased population and decreased use of wood as fuel, there seems to be no alternative to the use of modern detergents for laundry and cleaning purposes.

For those who are so inclined, the following recipe for cold-water soap is offered as the most effective of the several found from various sources. This one, of German "descent," dates from the mid-1800s.

1 can lye
9 cups melted (not hot) clean grease
11 cups lukewarm water (rain water is best; soft water is essential)
2 tablespoons borax
½ cup household ammonia

Mix lye into water in large enamelware kettle until dissolved and let stand 10 to 12 hours. Stir in warm grease, borax, and ammonia and stir for 30 minutes, or longer, until the mixture drops heavily from a wooden spoon. The longer the mixture is stirred, the whiter the soap. Pour mixture into a tight-fitting wooden box approximately 12-by-24-by-4 inches, and let set at least 24 hours. Cut into bars with sharp knife. Let stand for another 24 hours or more. Wrap each bar well in waxed paper and store in cool place to cure.

Note: Be sure only clean grease is used. This may be bacon drippings, fat trimmed from meat, etc. Clarify grease by heating and dropping in a sliced raw potato. Leave potato slices in grease until it is cold. Pour off grease carefully, leaving in pan the sediment which has settled in bottom. Talcum powder or cologne may be added to perfume the soap, if desired.

Rose Jar

Preparing one of these potpourris will provide a pleasant summer pastime for those who have rose gardens. Its fragrance when used during the long winter months will be a reminder of warm, sunny, rose-scented gardens.

Gather fresh unbruised petals of several varieties of roses, both pale and dark, after the dew has dried but before the roses have lost their fragrance. Separate petals carefully; spread on clean cloth or screen to dry in the shade for 3 or 4 days. You will need 4 cups dried petals. While petals are drying, assemble the following:

6 oz. dried lavender flowers, or
4 tablespoons lemon verbena leaves
¼ ounce crushed orris root
1 pound coarse table salt
2 ounces crushed cloves
1 small stick cinnamon, crushed
¼ ounce crushed allspice
¼ ounce nutmeg
5 drops oil of jasmine (optional)

After petals are thoroughly dried, pack into rose jar in layers; sprinkle each layer lightly with salt. When jar is filled, cork tightly and allow to stand for 3 weeks. Remove petals from jar and place in a large mixing bowl. Blend orris root (may be purchased from your pharmacy) and spices well. Add to the rose petals, using a wooden spoon for mixing. Add dried lavender, return to jar, and cork tightly for 6 weeks longer. When jar is ready to use, shake gently. Remove cork and add oil of jasmine (may be purchased from your pharmacy) drop by drop. Keep jar closely covered except when perfume is desired. On those occasions, remove lid and moisten contents slightly.

Reducing Tips

From an 1880 cookbook:

A strong decoction of sassafras, drunk frequently, will reduce the flesh as rapidly as any remedy known. A strong infusion is made at the rate of an ounce of sassafrass to a quart of water. Boil it 30 minutes very slowly, and let it stand until cold, heating again if desired. Keep it from the air.

From *Godey's Lady's Book,* 1868:

Sixty-six-year old Mr. Banting reduced from 202 to 156 pounds in 20 days by following this regimen. For breakfast: 4 or 5 ounces of beef, mutton, kidney, bacon, or cold meat of any kind except fresh pork; a large cup of tea without sugar or milk; a small biscuit or 1 ounce of toast without butter. For dinner: 5 or 6 ounces of fish (no salmon) or meat except fresh pork; all kinds of vegetables except potatoes; 1 ounce of toast; the fruit of a tart but not the crust; poultry, game; two or three glasses of good claret, sherry, or Madeira but no champagne, port wine, or beer. For tea: 2 or 3 ounces of fruit; about 1 ounce of toast; and a cup of tea without sugar or milk. For supper: 3 or 4 ounces of such meat or fish as at dinner, with one or two glasses of claret or sherry. Before going to bed: A glass of claret or sherry.

This plan of Banting's has been tried again and again with advantage and without the least unfavorable accident. The wine, we presume is not necessary, only that Banting liked a little tipple.

Home Remedies

The wealth of home remedies concocted and decocted by the early settlers who had no physicians nearby would provide sufficient volume to fill another book. In some cases the cure was almost as bad as the illness. When one of my sisters felt a sore throat coming on she ran crying for our mother, asking for "doot-dreet" or goose grease to be rubbed on throat and chest.

Grandma Walker would concoct a remedy for sore throats which was worse than awful, but as I recall, effective. At the first sign of a hacking cough and runny nose she would slice an onion into a pie pan, add honey and lemon juice, and simmer it on top of the heating stove in the dining-sitting room. After it had simmered for an hour or so, the liquid would be strained and bottled and administered at intervals. Here are two remedies for the common cold which are not as distasteful as the honey-onion concoction.

Red Clover Cough Remedy

An old-time remedy. It is said that a teaspoonful morning and evening will alleviate throat irritation and prevent coughing.

1 pint red clover blossom heads

Gather fresh, clean blossom heads in the morning. Boil and strain. To each ounce of liquid add:

1 pint honey

Mix well and bottle.

Horehound Candy

The aromatic, bitter-tasting herb was brought from England by early colonists, as the dried leaves and seeds were highly regarded for making cough syrup. My parents kept horehound candy on hand during the winter. Its beautiful amber color appealed to the eye, but the rather puckery taste assured my mother that it wouldn't be nipped away at by us kids.

2 ounces dried horehound
3½ pounds brown sugar
Water (1½ pints)

Add horehound to 1½ pints water and boil for 30 minutes. Strain and add 3½ pounds brown sugar. Stir until sugar is dissolved, then boil rapidly until mixture spins a thread when a teaspoonful is lifted in the air above the saucepan. Pour into a flat, well-greased tin pan and mark into small squares or strips. Use as lozenges, to alleviate the never-ending series of sore throats and colds which afflict children during the winter. This is not a cure-all, merely a means of easing the distress.

Invalid Cookery

Home nursing was the order of the day in Grandmother's time. Sometimes the family member who served nobly as nurse was faced with the challenge of providing nourishment for the patient who could not, or would not eat. Here are a few old standbys for such cases:

Beef Tea

1 pound lean beef, cut into tiny pieces or ground coarsely in food chopper
1 cup cold water

Put meat into quart glass fruit jar, add water, and let stand 15 to 20 minutes. Place on rack in pan of cold water. Simmer (*do not boil*) for 2 hours. Season with ¼ teaspoon salt, strain, cool, and remove all fat. Serve hot or cold.

Egg-Orange Drink

1 egg white
Juice of 1 orange
Sugar

Squeeze orange juice, add to egg white, and beat to a froth. Chill and serve cold.

Spanish Cream

2 cups scalded milk
4 egg yolks
¼ cup sugar
2 tablespoons powdered gelatin
¼ cup cold water
1 teaspoon vanilla
1 pint cream, whipped

Scald milk over very low heat or in top of double boiler and set aside to cool. Beat egg yolks and sugar together until pale yellow. Pour cooled milk slowly over egg mixture. Pour into top of double boiler and cook until thick and smooth. Pour over soaked gelatin and mix well. Add vanilla and beat with wire whisk until thick. Add whipped cream and chill in molds.

Chicken Broth

When Grandma started making chicken broth, everyone knew someone was really sick. When beef was not available, it was easy to send a kid out to chase down an old chicken for this purpose.

1 stewing hen

Clean hen and cut into pieces. Simmer until tender. Set aside all portions except back, rib cage, and wings, for serving to other family members. Remove skin from back, rib cage, wings and cut into small pieces. Remove bones. Return to broth in which chicken was cooked, add an onion slice, 1 blade of mace or ½ teaspoon powdered mace, and ten white peppercorns. Simmer for about an hour. Add salt. Beat in ¼ ounce of sweet almonds mixed with water; simmer for 10 minutes longer. Strain and cool. Remove all fat. Serve hot or cold.

Kumiss

Genghis Khan and his Mongolian hordes throve on a liquor distilled from camel's or mare's milk. The Germans had a knack of borrowing appealing food and beverage ideas from their neighboring countries. This recipe for kumiss probably came to southern Illinois via the German settlers, who had learned about it from the Russians.

The following recipe for kumiss made from cow's milk does not pack as powerful a wallop as the original, but it combines the nourishing qualities of sweet milk with the healthful action of buttermilk. It is well liked by young and old who have difficulty in assimilating milk in its natural state.

2 quarts sweet milk
½ cake of yeast or ½ package powdered yeast
2 tablespoons sugar

Heat milk to 100° and while warm add yeast and sugar which have been dissolved in two or three tablespoons of lukewarm water. Set aside for 2 hours. Bottle and let stand for six hours in a moderately warm room. Chill. Will keep four or five days when kept cold. Enough for a 4-day supply.

Kumiss is especially beneficial to the patient suffering from diarrhea or who is dehydrated. It often produces sleep for the insomniac, so it is said.

Glossary
Index

Glossary

of Cooking Terms

Baste	To moisten meat, fowl, or other dish while baking, with juices from pan or other liquids.
Beat	To mix thoroughly by rapid rotary motion.
Blend	To mix two or more ingredients until well combined.
Bouquet garni	A bunch of parsley, onions, bay leaf, and thyme, tied together and used in soups.
Braise	To cook meat by searing, then simmering in covered pan in small amount of liquid.
Chop	To cut into pieces.
Cobbler	A deep layer of fruit covered with biscuit dough or pastry.
Combine	To mix two or more ingredients.
Cracklings	The well-browned, crisp rind of roasted pork.
Cream	To work shortening until it attains the consistency of heavy cream.
Croutons	Small cubes of bread toasted or fried; used for garnishing dishes or in soup.
Curds	The coagulated or thickened part of milk, as distinguished from whey, or watery part.
Dice	To cut into tiny cubes.
Dip	A liquid, as a sauce or gravy, served at table with a ladle or spoon—such as sweetened cream, served with puddings, etc.
Dot	To place small pieces of butter, cheese, etc., over the surface of food, usually to be baked.
Draw	To extract the bowels of, eviscerate—as, to draw a fowl.
Dredge	To coat with flour or sugar.
Dress	To prepare for cooking—as, to dress a fowl.
Drippings	Liquid and small particles of meat remaining in pan in which meat or poultry has been cooked.

267

Fillet	Cut portions of boneless or boned fish or meat.
Fold in	To add beaten egg or whipped cream to another mixture and blend in lightly with an over-and-over motion.
Giblets	The liver, gizzard, and heart of poultry and wild birds.
Glaze	To coat with diluted fruit jelly or a sugar syrup that has been cooked to candy stage.
Grind	To reduce meat or vegetables to tiny pieces by putting through food chopper.
Infuse	To extract liquid from herbs, coffee, tea, etc.
Knead	To work dough by stretching, pressing with hands, and folding it over and over on itself.
Lard	To place strips of fat bacon or salt pork on top of lean meat.
Marinade	A mixture of vinegar, spices, oil, and herbs in which meat or other food is allowed to stand to attain tenderness and flavor.
Marinate	To soak meat or other food in vinegar, lemon juice, spices, etc.
Mince	To chop very fine with a knife.
Mix	To combine by stirring or beating.
Panbroil	To cook meat in a skillet without grease, pouring off fat as it accumulates.
Parboil	To boil food until partially cooked.
Pepper vinegar	A mixture of tiny red hot peppers, vinegar, salt, and spices, used as a condiment.
Press	To squeeze so as to extract juice or contents of fruit, grapes, etc.
Puree	To press fruit or vegetables through a sieve, ricer, etc.; a soup made with the pulp to which cream or stock has been added; also the pulp of fruit or vegetables.
Render	To separate fat from connective tissue by heating slowly so that the fat melts and can be drained off.
Roux	A cooked mixture of flour and butter used to thicken soups and sauces.
Samp	An Indian term for coarse hominy.
Saute	To cook on top of stove in a very small amount of fat.
Scald	To heat liquid to just below the boiling point. Or, to immerse fowls to be plucked in boiling water, for a short time, to loosen feathers.

Shred	To cut into very fine strips or slices.
Simmer	To cook in liquid just below the boiling point.
Skewer	To fasten meat, fowl, fish, with pins of wood or metal to hold it in shape while cooking.
Sliver	To cut into lengths.
Sponge	Dough after it has been raised or converted into a light, porous mass by yeast or leaven.
Steam	To cook with heat of boiling water in a steamer or double boiler.
Stew	To cook very gently and slowly in liquid.
Stir	To blend ingredients with a spoon or other utensil, using a circular motion.
Stock	The liquid from cooking meat, fish, or vegetables.
Truss	To fasten with a skewer—as, a fowl's wings to its body.
Try out	To heat meat slowly until fat is liquid. Used most often in connection with making lard.
Whey	The liquid separated from the solid part of milk after it sours.
Whip	To beat rapidly with a cooking utensil to increase volume by incorporating air into the ingredient.

Index

Helen Walker Linsenmeyer was
a native southern Illinois writer and
a homemaker from Grand Tower,
an historic Mississippi River town.